湖北省博物館
HUBEI PROVINCIAL MUSEUM

辉煌時代
罗 马 帝 国 文 物

A SPLENDID TIME
The Heritage of Imperial Rome

湖北省博物馆　编
Edited by Hubei Provincial Museum

文物出版社
Cultural Relics Press

展览主办 Hosted by	湖北省博物馆 Hubei Provincial Museum 馆长　包东波 Bao Dongbo　Director 吉林省博物院 Jilin Provincial Museum 院长　赵瑞军 Zhao Ruijun　Director 秦始皇帝陵博物院 Emperor Qinshihuang's Mausoleum Site Museum 院长　曹玮 Cao Wei　Director
展览支持 Mainly Supported by	佛罗伦萨国家考古博物馆 Museo Archeologico Nazionale di Firenze
特别支持 Endorsed by	意大利文化遗产部 Ministero per I Beni e le Attività Cuturali 托斯卡纳考古文化遗产局 Soprintendenza per i Beni Archeologici della Toscana 佛罗伦萨国家考古博物馆 Museo Archeologico Nazionale di Firenze (Logo) 意大利驻北京文化处 Istituto Italiano di Cultura Pechino
策展人 Curated by	Giuseppina Carlotta Cianferoni（朱塞平娜·卡洛塔·钱菲诺尼） 与（With） Eugenio Martera（尤金尼奥·马特那） Patrizia Pietrogrande（帕特里齐亚·皮特格兰德） Linda Carioni（琳达·卡瑞奥尼）
展出时间 Exhibition Date	湖北　2012年9月28日至2013年1月5日 Hubei, September 28, 2012 - June 5, 2013 吉林　2013年1月19日至4月21日 Jilin, January 19, 2013 - April 21, 2013 陕西　2014年9月1日至11月30日 Shaanxi, September1, 2014-November 30, 2014
参展方 Lenders	佛罗伦萨国家考古博物馆 Museo Archeologico Nazionale di Firenze 锡耶纳的国家考古博物馆 Museo Archeologico Nazionale di Siena 基安奇安诺泰尔梅德拉水域公民考古博物馆 Museo Civico Archeologico delle Acque, Chianciano Terme
图录编辑 Catalogue Editor	湖北省博物馆 Hubei Provincial Museum
图录主编 Chief Editor	包东波　赵瑞军　曹玮 Bao Dongbo, Zhao Ruijun and Cao Wei
图录副主编 Deputy Editor	万全文　吴辉　郭向东 Wan Quanwen, Wu Hui and Guo Xiangdong
图录执行编辑 Managing Editor	王纪潮 Wang Jichao

展览组织与制作（中方） Organization and Production(China)	湖北省博物馆 Hubei Provincial Museum 吉林省博物院 Jilin Provincial Museum 秦始皇帝陵博物院 Emperor Qinshihuang's Mausoleum Site Museum
展览组织与制作（意方） Organization and Production(Italy)	意大利CP公司 Contemporanea Progetti, Florence, Italy (CP) 意中桥(上海)会议展览有限公司 Triumph Asia Co., Limited (TA)
项目执行及协调（中方） Executive Coordination(China)	王纪潮　苏雷　郭向东 Wang Jichao, Su Lei and Guo Xiangdong
展览协调（中方） Coordinators(China)	湖北：余文扬　张翔　程陶　伍莹　姚嫄　曾攀 Hubei: Yu Wenyang, Zhang Xiang, Chen Tao, Wu Ying, Yao Yuan and Zeng Pan 吉林：范胜丽　翟威 Jilin: Fan Shengli and Zhai Wei 陕西：彭文　叶晔　张升 Shaanxi: Peng Wen, Ye Ye and Zhang Sheng
项目执行及协调（意方） Executive Coordination(Italy)	Eugenio Martera（尤金尼奥·马特那），CP Patrizia Pietrogrande（帕特里齐亚·皮特格兰德），CP Linda Carioni（琳达·卡瑞奥尼），CP Raimondo Gissara（纪松澜），TA
展场策划 Exhibition Management	Silvia Iannelli（西尔维娅·杨内利），CP Luciano Vanni（露西亚诺·万妮），CP Pilar Ramirez de Arellano（艾雅诺），TA 邵陈（Sheila Shao），TA Tommaso Vallini（李托马），TA
艺术顾问 Art Consultant	尹荣(Yin Rong)，TA
展览设计 Exhibition Design	Eugenio Martera（尤金尼奥·马特那），CP Manuela Montacci（曼努埃拉·蒙塔齐），CP Andrea Del Genio（安德里亚·戴尔吉尼奥），CP
平面设计（意方） Graphic Design(Italy)	Benedetta Marchi（本内塔·马齐），CP Pier Francesco Martini（皮尔·弗朗切斯科·马提尼），CP
平面设计（中方） Graphic Design(China)	伍莹（Wu Ying）
展品管理 Conservator	Giuseppe Venturini（朱塞佩·文托瑞尼） 托斯卡纳考古遗产监管局 Soprintendenza per i Beni Archeologici della Toscana
摄影 Photos	Niccolò Orsi Battaglini（尼科洛·奥尔西·巴塔格林尼） 托斯卡纳考古遗产监管局摄影办公室（© Gabinetto Fotografico della Soprintendenza per i Beni Archeologici della Toscana） 意大利CP公司 Contemporanea Progetti, Florence, Italy (CP)
技术团队 Technical Team	湖北省博物馆陈列部 Exhibition Department of Hubei Provincial Museum
翻译 Translations	优言优格 EUROLOGOS
鸣谢 Acknowledgement	上海对外文化交流协会 Shanghai International Cultural Exchange Association
运输 Transportation and Handling Arteria	上海华协国际珍品货运代理有限公司 Shanghai Huaxie Fine Art Freight INT'L Forwarding Co., Ltd

目 录
CONTENTS

祝　辞
COMMENDATORY
MESSAGE

古希腊和古罗马文明是现代西方文明的基础。相传拉丁人罗慕洛于公元前753年，在罗马的台伯河畔建城，由此开启了古罗马的文明。罗马在历经了王政时代（公元前753年~公元前509年）、共和时代（公元前509年~公元前27年）之后，于公元前1世纪进入帝国时代。经过数个世纪的征服和扩张，罗马从一个小城邦发展成横跨欧、亚、非三大洲的强大帝国，在公元3世纪达到鼎盛，其经济繁荣，军力强盛，政治体制稳定，疆域范围西起不列颠，东至小亚细亚，北达多瑙河、莱茵河，南抵埃及，整个地中海成为罗马帝国的内海。公元3世纪后期，帝国发生深刻变革，战争频仍，帝位更迭频繁。公元395年罗马帝国分裂为东西两个帝国。随着经济衰落和蛮族的入侵，西罗马帝国于公元476年灭亡。东罗马帝国则绵延千年之久，直到1453年才沦陷于奥斯曼帝国。

罗马统一了古代两河流域、埃及和希腊文明的发源地，其统一的帝国对后世的国际政治产生了深远的影响。罗马文化深受古希腊文化的影响，它全面吸收并改造了古希腊的哲学、文学和艺术。东罗马帝国更是保存了大量古希腊时期的文化遗产，直接促发了近代文艺复兴运动。基督教诞生之后在帝国内得到广泛传播，最终成为罗马帝国的官方宗教，也由此奠定了基督教在西方文明中的核心地位。罗马法是罗马人精神的体现，它奠定了近代西方法律体系的基础，对世界的影响超过了任何的罗马文化遗产。

在罗马帝国称霸西方的同时，秦汉帝国正雄踞东方。西汉时期，张骞凿空，出使西域，拉开了东西方文化交流的序幕。汉唐至元明，中国历代王朝与罗马帝国交往不绝于书。湖北省博物馆与意大利博物馆界一直保持友好往来。2006年，本馆与西安博物院联袂在罗马举办"中国秦汉文物精品展"，2009年又与中华世纪坛等文博单位在意大利举办"秦汉—罗马文明展"。本馆一直想有机会在内地举办反映罗马帝国文化的展览。在国家文物局、意大利文化遗产部、托斯卡纳大区文化遗产局的支持下，此次本馆、秦始皇兵马俑博物院和吉林博物院联合举办的"辉煌时代——罗马帝国文物特展"终于能在武汉首展。该展由意大利佛罗伦萨国家考古博物馆、锡耶纳考古博物馆，以及佛罗伦萨国家考古博物馆馆长Carlotta Cianferoni策划，在意中桥（上海）会议展览有限公司、意大利CP公司等单位的配合下得以顺利实施。展览包括了雕塑、钱币、首饰、生活用品等近300件文物，展现了罗马帝国的政治、经济、文化、军事以及宗教生活，为内地观众展现了一幅辉煌壮阔的罗马帝国的历史画卷，使之能领略西方古典文明的源头和魅力。在此，我谨向为展览成功举办的各界人士表示衷心的感谢，并祝展览取得圆满成功！

湖北省博物馆馆长

2012年8月

The ancient Greek and Roman civilizations provided the foundation of modern Western civilization. Legend has it that the Latin Romulus founded Rome on the banks of the river Tiber in 753 BCE. Following experiences with monarchy (753-509 BCE) and Republican rule (509-27 BCE), Rome became an imperial power in the 1st century BCE. Centuries of conquests and expansion created a Roman empire that reached far beyond its city walls, an empire that stretched over Europe, Asia and Africa. In the 3rd century CE the Roman Empire reached its apogee, with a prosperous economy, strong military and stable government, stretching from Britain in the west to Asia Minor in the East, and from the Danube and the Rhine in the north to Egypt in the south. The entire Mediterranean Sea was under the control of Rome. In the later part of the 3rd century CE, the Empire experienced profound changes, frequent wars and a quick succession of Emperors. In the year 395 CE, the Roman Empire split into two, into the Eastern and Western halves. Economic decline and barbarian invasions brought the Western Roman Empire to an end in the year 476 CE. The Eastern Roman Empire managed to last for another thousand years before succumbing to the Ottoman Empire in 1453.

The Roman Empire united two great civilizations, the Egyptian and the Greek under its umbrella, and the Empire has had a profound influence on international politics later on in history. Roman culture was deeply inspired by ancient Greek culture, and the Romans completely absorbed and remade Greek philosophy, literature and arts. The Eastern Roman Empire retained a large proportion of ancient Greek culture and played a direct role in the modern Renaissance. Christianity found widespread dissemination within the Empire and eventually became the official religion of the Empire and sealing its central position in Western civilization and culture. Roman law was the expression of the Romans' spirit and also provided the basis for modern Western legal systems, exerting an influence on the world that far surpassed any Roman artistic legacy.

At the same time as the Roman Empire was reigning supreme in the West, the Qin and Han Dynasties constituted the major power in the East. During the Western Han Dynasty, Zhang Qian set out on his western expeditions which sparked off a series of East-West cultural interactions. Beginning with the Han era all through to the Yuan and Ming dynasties the Roman and Chinese empires were in constant contact. The Hubei Provincial Museum has always had a positive working relationship with Italian museums. In 2006, the Museum collaborated with the Xi'an Museum to organize the "Exhibition of Qin and Han Antiquities" in Rome, and in 2009 partnered cultural organizations such as the China Millennium Monument to hold the Qin/Han – Roman Civilizations exhibition in Italy. It has always been the intention of the Museum to hold an exhibition on the culture of the Roman Empire in China. With the support of the State Administration of Cultural Heritage, Italy's Ministry of Cultural Heritage and Activities and the Tuscany Cultural and Heritage Bureau, the Museum has joined hands with the Museum of Qin Shihuang Terracotta Warriors and Horses and the Jilin Museum to finally open *Days of Glory: an exhibition of Roman Empire Antiquities* in Wuhan. The exhibition the Museo Archeologico Nazionale di Firenze and the Museo Archeologico Nazionale di Siena curated by Carlotta Cianferoni Director of the Museo Archeologico Nazionale di Firenze and realized with the joint effort of Triumph Asia Co., Ltd and Contemporanea Progetti. The nearly 300 antiquities on show at the exhibition include sculptures, coins, jewelry and articles for daily use, offering visitors a glimpse of political, military and religious life in the grand tapestry and the fountain of Western civilization that was the Roman Empire. I would like to take this opportunity to offer my sincere gratitude to all who have helped to make this exhibition possible, and I wish the exhibition every success!

Bao Dongbo
Director of Hubei Provincial Museum
August 2012

众所周知，地中海地区是人类文明孕育和发展的重要地区。人类历史上的四大文明中就有两个诞生在地中海沿岸。而亚平宁半岛处在地中海北岸，海的南岸是早期文明高度发达的北非地区，东方与西方文明另一发祥地希腊隔爱琴海相望。正是在这独一无二的地理条件之下，诞生了是人类文明史上高度发达的代表——罗马帝国。

罗马帝国以其自身的高度发达的文化、政治、经济、军事，在相当长的历史时期里影响和辐射着周边地区。其起步于城邦，最终将版图连接欧、亚、非三个大洲。可以想象，在两千多年以前人类的生产力尚不发达的时代，从不列颠岛到尼罗河畔都曾是这一帝国的疆域，整个地中海成为罗马的内湖，可见当时罗马国力之强大。

罗马帝国的兴起、繁荣、鼎盛、衰落、灭亡，每一阶段，无不伴随着整个欧洲人类历史的重大事件。罗马城邦的诞生，是人类文明发展的结果；罗马的帝国化，是欧洲生产力进步的体现；罗马的覆灭，是人类社会进步的必然趋势。在某一角度上看，罗马帝国已经不再是一个城邦的简单发展史，而是人类文明演进的一本鲜活的教科书。

两千年后的今天，我们与佛罗伦萨国家考古博物馆、锡耶纳国家考古博物馆、意中桥（上海）会议展览有限公司、意大利CP公司合作，将他们珍藏的300余件罗马文物精品引进到中国，引进到吉林省，其意义是不可言表的。

这次联合举办展览的目的，就是为亚欧大陆东岸曾经的一个伟大帝国的后裔们，提供一个与其祖先同时代的大陆西岸另一个伟大文明相识和了解的机会。也希望籍这次展览开启中意历史文化交流的新领域。

现在，我们联合将这次展出的文物图片资料整理成册，编辑出版，以留下这一珍贵的历史瞬间。出版在即，是为序。

吉林博物院院长　赵瑞军

2012年8月

The Mediterranean is well known as an important region in the birth and emergence of human civilization. Two of the four major historic civilizations in human history originated on the Mediterranean coast, with the Italian Peninsula situated on the north shore of the Mediterranean, and the early advanced civilizations of North Africa on the south shore. Another birthplace of both Eastern and Western civilization, Greece, is across the Aegean Sea. Under these unique geographical conditions, a highly developed civilization was born - The Roman Empire.

The highly developed culture, government, economy and army of the Roman Empire influenced and radiated to many surrounding areas over a relatively long period of time. Starting as a city state, it eventually flourished to connect territories from the continents of Europe, Asia, and Africa. Two thousand years ago, in a period of low human productivity, the dominance of the Romans was such that they commanded an empire stretching from Britain to the banks of the Nile, encapsulating the entire Mediterranean region.

Every step in the rise of the Roman Empire, through its prosperity and peak, to its decline and eventual disintegration, accompanied major historical events on the European continent. The birth of the Roman city state was the result of human cultural development; the spread of its Empire an exemplification of progress in productivity on the European continent; and its collapse an inevitable result of human civilization trends. On one level, the Roman Empire is no longer simply the simple history of a city-state's development, but is a vivid textbook of the evolution of human civilization.

Today, two thousand years on, we are working with the Museo Archeologico Nazionale di Firenze, the Museo Archeologico Nazionale di Siena, Carlotta Cianferoni Director of the Museo Archeologico Nazionale di Firenze, Triumph Asia Co., Ltd and Contemporanea Progetti to bring a collection of nearly 300 Roman artifacts to China and to Jilin Province, an event of great significance.

The object of this jointly organized exhibition is to give the Eastern descendants of this once great Eurasian empire an opportunity to meet and understand their ancestors and get acquainted with another great civilization. We hope this exhibition will open up new areas of Sino-Italian history and cultural exchange.

We are currently working together to compile images and information about these cultural artifacts from this exhibition into a book – which will be published very soon – in order to commemorate this precious historical event.

Zhao Ruijun
Director of Jilin Provincial Museum
August 2012

2012年9月，由湖北省博物馆、吉林省博物院、秦始皇帝陵博物院接力承办的"辉煌时代——罗马帝国文物特展"，将正式拉开在中国大陆三地巡展的序幕。值此展览武汉首展开幕之际，我谨代表秦始皇帝陵博物院，向为展览做了大量前期准备工作的湖北省博物馆、佛罗伦萨国家考古博物馆馆长Carlotta Cianferoni和鼎力协助此次展览的意中桥（上海）会议展览有限公司及意大利CP公司表示衷心的感谢！

罗马帝国的文化既具有鲜明的传统特征，又具有开放性的特点。"辉煌时代——罗马帝国文物特展"，汇聚了近300件罗马帝国时期的文物，主要包括陶器、肖像、浮雕、青铜和大理石雕像等，这些富有罗马文化特色的物品，将全面展示罗马帝国的宗教、艺术和生活等诸多方面，使中国观众不出国门，就能领略古罗马人创造的高度发达的文明，和曾在世界历史上产生过重大影响的异域文化风采。

罗马古代文明和中国古代文明，是人类在不同地域发展出的两朵文明奇葩，是东西方文化的基石。我们相信，两国人民也有着彼此了解和沟通的良好意愿。多年来，秦陵博物院探索并践行"走出去"与"请进来"相结合的双向对外交流模式，致力于促进和加深中西方文化的彼此交流和了解。一方面，以秦兵马俑为代表的秦代艺术文化，屡屡走出国门，充当文化交流的使者。一方面，我们也积极引入了一批国外优秀的文化精品展览。这次，由我们三家博物馆合作引入的"辉煌时代——罗马帝国文物特展"，既是文博界创新探索的新举措，也是博物馆推进文化惠民、推动社会主义文化大发展大繁荣的新实践，更是文博界文化自觉和文化自信的展现。

最后，让我们一同品鉴这场古罗马的文明盛宴，让我们共同预祝"辉煌时代——罗马帝国文物特展"圆满、精彩！同时，也期待与各位在秦陵博物院再次相见！

秦始皇帝陵博物院院长　曹玮

2012年8月

In September 2012, the Hubei Provincial Museum, the Jilin Provincial Museum, and the Museum of Qin Shihuang Terracotta Warriors and Horses are taking turns to host "A Splendid Time – The Heritage of Imperial Rome", as the exhibition embarks on a three stop tour of China. On this occasion of the Wuhan exhibition opening, on behalf of the Qin Shihuang Museum I would like to express my sincere gratitude to the Hubei Provincial Museum for their work in the exhibition's preparation, Carlotta Cianferoni Director of the Museo Archeologico Nazionale di Firenze, Triumph Asia Co., Ltd and Contemporanea Progetti for their enthusiastic assistance. Thank you!

The culture of the Roman Empire was marked by its openness as well as an adherence to tradition. "A Splendid Time – The Heritage of Imperial Rome" brings together nearly 300 pieces of Roman cultural artifacts, including ceramics, portraits, sculptures, and bronze and marble statues. These distinctly Roman cultural artifacts comprehensively showcase the religion, arts, and lifestyle of the Romans, allowing a Chinese audience to appreciate an advanced culture which had a significant impact in human history, all without leaving the country.

Ancient Rome and ancient China are two human treasures from different parts of the world, cornerstones of both Western and Eastern cultures. We believe that citizens of both countries are interested in learning more about each other. Over the years, the Museum of Qin Shihuang Terracotta Warriors and Horses has explored and practiced an international exchange model that combines "Going Out" and "Inviting In", a model which is dedicated to advancing and deepening Sino-Western cultural communications and mutual understanding. On the one hand, the Terracotta Warriors represent the Qin Dynasty's artistic culture, exhibited time and time again to audiences outside China to serve as a messenger of cultural exchange. At the same time, we have also actively sought to introduce world-class exhibitions of foreign cultural artifacts. Now, in working together to bring "A Splendid Time – The Heritage of Imperial Rome" to China, our three museums have broken new ground in this realm. This collaboration also represents our efforts as part of the government's "culture to the people" campaign, promoting new practices for the prosperous development of socialist culture, and demonstrates the awareness and self confidence of our circle.

Finally, let us all enjoy this grand Roman banquet. Let us join together in wishing the exhibition success! I look forward too to seeing everybody again at the Qin Shihuang Museum!

Cao Wei (Handwritten)
Director of Emperor Qinshihuang's Mausoleum
Site Museum
August 2012

专 文
ESSAYS

遥远的参照：秦汉与罗马帝国

台湾中研院史语所院士　邢义田

图1　陈介祺旧藏皇帝信玺封泥
Imperial Letter Seal from the Chen
Jieqi Collection

图2　石门颂石刻拓本局部"高
祖受命"
"By Order of [Han] Gaozu",
partial rubbing of the *Shimensong
stone inscription*

一　秦汉与罗马帝国的统治形式

俗话说："罗马不是一天造成的。"
秦汉王朝，同样的，也不是突然冒出来。

秦在一统中原以前，华夏大地早已
经历商、周，甚至更早的夏代的统治，
累积了上千年的政治文化传统。从周
人行封建到春秋战国封建崩溃，诸国争
霸，秦也从封建诸侯一变而为争霸的列
国之一。秦一统后的统治体制，有些是
战国时秦制的延续和扩大，有些是秦始皇
的创新，更有些部分继承了周制。例如
秦在征服过程中，划分新征服的土地为
郡县，不再分封诸侯，一统天下后，进
一步将郡县制扩大到了全帝国。这可以
说是战国秦制的延续和扩大。不过，很
显然秦始皇觉得自己的成就超越了三皇
五帝，周天子的"天子"名号不足以彰
显自己的伟大，因而创造了"皇帝"这
一新头衔(图1)。这是创新。此外，他承
用某些周以来的传统。比如没有放弃自
周以来的天命观，也没有放弃周以来天
子的称号。他相信自己像周人一样拥有
天命(图2)，是靠老天爷的支持得到天
下，因而并不觉得自己统治的正当性是
来自被统治的齐民百姓。这种天命观，
从此主宰了中国最根本的意识形态和政
治格局达两千年。

正因为如此，古代中国就出现不
了罗马帝国那样的统治形式。罗马帝国
继承的是一个地中海世界存在已久的城
邦传统。这个传统主要是由希腊城邦建
立起来的。他们基本上相信，城邦的公
民就是城邦的主人，管理城邦的正当性
来自于所有公民的同意和承认。城邦的
管理者应由公民推选，管理规则或法律
须由富于管理经验者组成的长老会议提
出，并经全体公民组成的公民大会同
意。这种对统治正当性或权力来源的看
法和政治体制，造成了古代地中海城邦
世界和古代中国的根本性不同。

罗马人后来统一了地中海世界，
由小小的城邦化为庞大的帝国，但保守
的罗马人仍顽强地维持着共和城邦的传
统。罗马在共和时代已经有公民大会和
元老院。组成元老院的元老们是罗马公
民中的上层阶级，实际控制着对内和对
外的政治。共和时代罗马所有的法律和
政策都必须由元老院提出和同意(图3)。

奥古斯都以后，皇帝的身份仍须经
元老院认可，才具合法正当性，皇帝的
权力也由元老院制定的法律来规范。在
古代中国，完全看不到这样的情况。秦
汉帝国和罗马帝国看起来都是大一统帝
国，但背后的政治文化传统和对权力正
当或合法性的认识可以说南辕北辙。

二　人治对比法治：权力运作的特色

秦自商鞅变法后，号称以"法"治国，实际上秦王或皇帝说了算。所谓以法治国，是指用严刑峻法治理官员和百姓，皇帝和太子却在法律之上。所谓"太子犯法，与民同罪"，只是有此一说，不曾真正实现过。人治才是秦汉，甚至秦汉以降中国政治的特色，和讲究法律的罗马帝国形成强烈的对比。

在秦汉中国压根就没不可改变的制度或法律。皇帝说的就是法律。汉武帝时，管司法的廷尉杜周曾说过这样的话："三尺安出哉？前主所是着为律，后主所是疏为令。"律令书写在三尺长的竹木简上，官吏办事必得尊之奉之，皇帝自己高高站在律令之上。皇帝如此，其他握权的层层官僚有样学样，也往往制造一些自己可以不遵，他人必须遵守的条条框框。法律不是源出社会成员的主体，没有一体适用性，也没有真正的超越性，可以说是传统中国"法"的特色。这个特色从秦汉一直保持到今天。

此外，司马迁清楚告诉我们，秦始皇每天从早到晚，要看完一定量的公文才肯休息，国家大小事经他核定才算数，丞相不过是"备员"或摆饰而已。秦汉一统天下，为人类历史建立起第一个空前庞大的官僚体系；这个体系的一大特色即在没有任何制度性的设计或个人能够制约皇帝的权力。平心而论，这是中国传统政治设计上的一个弱点。传统中国虽有"天命有德"、"灾异示警"和"祖宗之法"等等道德劝谏或警告性的论说，却不曾建立起足以制约皇权的制度。理论上，皇帝有自天而来至高无上和无限的权力。他要如何施展，

就看他要怎么做。如果他礼贤下士，决策时愿意和丞相或周边大臣商量，就像余英时先生说的宋神宗愿意跟王安石"共商国是"，这时丞相和大臣们才能说得上话；如果像秦皇、汉武这样的人，一个人说了算，其他人都只能成为司马迁所说的"备员"罢了。尽管有人认为丞相和大臣们可以用种种方法削弱或制衡皇帝的专制，例如某官有权批驳皇帝的诏书，或以御史、州刺史之制等等达成统治集团内部的监督和制衡，但这些制度通常不够坚强，或者说缺乏真正超越人事的制度性保障。

制度和法律在中国社会中始终没有真正超越性的地位，事随人转或因人设事是较为通常的现象。人治和法治之别，可以说是秦汉和罗马帝国一个重要的不同。最少3世纪初以前，罗马的法学家还认定"法律超越皇帝"（leges super principem），而皇帝享有的权力须由元老院以法律的形式一条条明订并颁授给皇帝。由元老院通过"皇帝权力法"，是罗马帝制中一项顽强的制度，至今还有一块1世纪刻在铜牌上的"韦帕芗皇帝权力法"残件传世(图4)。

即使到三、四世纪以后，帝国重心东移，康士坦丁大帝仍然要在新都康士坦丁堡另立一个橡皮图章式的元老院，象征一个古老传统的延续，也象征着统治者对制度的尊重。制度和法律的超越性由此得以彰显。

三　统一对比宽容：文化政策

秦汉和罗马帝国在处理异民族和异文化的态度上有同有异。就其同者而言，秦建立郡县制，由中央任命郡县的太守

图3　罗马铜币上有代表罗马公民和元老院主权的"SPQR"和代表元老院诏令的"S(enatus) C(onsultum)"缩写字母
Roman copper coin bearing the letters "SPQR", which represent the sovereignty of the Roman citizenry and the Senate, and the letters "SC", an abbreviation of Senatus Consultum or "decree of the Senate"

图4　韦帕芗皇帝权力法铜牌残件
Part of a Vespasian bronze medallion granting the bearer Imperial powers

和县令以外，还有另外一种制度，凡是地方上杂居有蛮夷的，就不设郡，而设置"道"。凡道中蛮夷可以保留原来的治理方式和风俗习惯，他们甚至不用像郡县的百姓那样缴纳租税，象征性进贡一些方物特产即可。此外还有所谓的属邦，凡臣属于秦的国家，为属邦，只要顺服，因其故俗而治，秦对其内部不加干涉。这种"道"和"属邦"的设置，意味着程度不同的宽容，不要求百分之百的同化，这跟罗马帝国有相似的地方。

虽说罗马帝国征服了地中海世界，实际上罗马人采取相当宽容的统治政策。地中海各地本来有很多城邦或城市，罗马人对他们的统治很大程度上是象征性的。罗马把除了意大利之外的地方都划分为行省，派元老去各省当总督。总督基本上只负责收税、治安和司法秩序。其他方面各省城市都有市议会，由市议会选出的官员管理各自的城市。这些城市只要如数纳税，敬拜皇帝，其原来的习俗和信仰等等都不会受到干扰。因为统治不涉地方内部，罗马帝国在3世纪以前从没有建立，也没必要建立像秦汉帝国那么庞大，由中央到地方层层节制的官僚体系。

就其异而言之，罗马人不曾像秦始皇一样统一文字。罗马人自己用拉丁文，行政命令用拉丁文发到各地，但没有要求帝国百姓都用拉丁文。这就是为什么罗马帝国建立几百年，西半边多用拉丁文，东半边的希腊化王国旧地仍以用希腊文为主。此外，应该一提，罗马的贵族自知没有太多文化，不像中国的统治者有非常强烈的文化优越感。罗马人因此不认为自己是文化上的教化者，而是接受别人教化的。他们自始至终卖力地学习希腊文和希腊文化。罗马诗人

贺拉斯（Horace）曾说过一句有名的话："野蛮人（即罗马人）征服了希腊，却又成了希腊的俘虏。"这点跟中国正相反。

四　严密对比松散：官僚机器和人力物力控制

罗马帝国的统治机器相对于秦汉中国来说比较松散，罗马没有像中国那么庞大的官僚体系。根据《汉书·百官公卿表》的记载，西汉末期有官吏十二万多人，可是罗马帝国一直到公元3世纪，在日耳曼蛮族入侵和军队需索不断增加等等的压力下，才建立起比较庞大的官僚体系。在此之前基本上是城市自治。罗马中央除了担任皇帝秘书的奴隶，没有三公九卿，没有分工明确的六部，连最基本的全国性财税和人口数字都没有具体统一的记录。各城市或自有统计，但无需上报中央，各城只要按时向省督缴纳一定的税额就可以。所以到今天没人能说清楚罗马帝国一年能收多少税，有多少人口或多少土地。

罗马早期有恶名昭彰的包税制。共和末期，化征服的土地为行省，各个行省要收多少税，采用拍卖的方式决定。参加拍卖的主要是罗马骑士阶级的人。他们可以承包某个行省的税收。比如马其顿省的上缴税收底线是六百万，拍卖时有意承包者竞相出价，他出八百万，你出一千万，没人比你高，这个省就包给你收税。承包人拼命搜刮，最好能收到一千五百万，除了上缴一千万，多出米的五百万可以进自己的腰包。没有公民权的行省老百姓因此受尽剥削。罗马政府利用剥削来的钱建设罗马城，让城中公民免费看马戏和吃面包。奥古斯都

图5 内蒙古居延汉简81.10
The Han Dynasty *Juyan* wooden slips, Inner Mongolia (no. 81.10)

之后渐渐改变这种状况，派遣税务官员去行省，向城镇收一定的税额，不再无限制地压榨。

秦汉中国的记录则清清楚楚，全国有多少开垦和未开垦的土地，有多少男女人口，有多大税出税入(图5~6)。

这是因为全帝国郡县必须"上计"，也就是地方须将每年人口、土地和财税等等情况层层上报。中央根据上报的数字，考核地方官员的优劣。近年在安徽、湖北、湖南，甚至今天的朝鲜（汉代的乐浪郡）出土不少秦汉时期写在竹木简牍上的地方行政文书，这些新资料一再证明秦汉上计制度通用于全帝国，数字基本可靠，可以和《汉书·地理志》等文献的记载相印证。地方官不免偷懒和造假，但整体而言，统计严密可靠的程度，在近世以前，可以说全世界独一无二。

五 民兵对比职业常备军：帝国防卫与政策

秦汉与罗马帝国军队的性质完全不同。罗马共和末，军队走向常备职业化，而汉代军队的基本性质比较像民兵。中国历朝历代，除了女真人的辽和金、蒙古人的元和满州人的清，多采取以兵农合一为特色的民兵制。汉代规定成年男子必须为天子老爷当兵，在地方上当一年正卒，到边塞当一年戍卒或到京师当卫卒。国家另有需要时，比如要征匈奴，中央任命将军，临时征召地方百姓参军；仗打完，将归于朝，兵归于农。这是百姓徭役的一部分。当兵除了有点口粮，没有工资。百姓苦哈哈，不觉得当兵是一种光荣，打起仗来多求保命，谈不上卖力(图7)。

罗马军队职业化之前，原本是以公民军为主，也就是所有成年男性公民都有义务执干戈以卫城邦。打完仗即种田的种田，牧羊的牧羊。可是共和中晚期，罗马争霸地中海的战事越来越长，比如跟迦太基的战争，一个战役常常数年不能结束，士兵被迫长期服役而渐渐职业化了。到了奥古斯都建立帝国之后，就彻底成了职业化军队。罗马也从征兵转向了募兵。共和时期许多罗马公民觉得当兵是光荣，是个好职业。在征服战争中可以分得战利品；如果跟对了军头，可以分享更多的财富。苏拉、西泽和安东尼都是著名的军头。他们为了争夺政治权力自己招募军队，军队效忠他们私人，而不再效忠罗马城邦。这样的军队已失去过去公民军的性质，也谈不上什么义务了。

职业化的罗马士兵要服役20~25年，等于从年轻一直当兵到老。训练非常严格，机动性高，战斗力非常强。他们按月领饷，随着年资和功劳，可以升迁或得奖赏。如果能够活到退伍期限，可以得到土地、公民权和退伍金等等回报。作为一个长期存在的部队，他们自身有很多需要，会自备工匠做很多杂务。但他们不像汉代的军队亦兵亦农，"三时务农而一时讲武"。他们一年到头忙着军事训练，罗马将军的练兵书里有句名言叫："不能让士兵闲着。"总之，它是一个长期性，有年资、升迁和奖惩的职业。

罗马军队的一大问题是不事生产，构成帝国财政上极大的负担。古代农业社会的生产力有限，要靠巨大的劳动力投入来维持。国家如果养一批人不生产而专门消耗，这会对财政造成极为沉重的负担。罗马帝国皇帝靠枪杆子掌权，

图6 安徽天长汉墓出土局部"户籍"
"Household registration records" unearthed at the Tianchang Tombs, Anhui Province

图7 四川成都出土汉代佩刀持臿陶俑
Han Dynasty armed clay figures unearthed in Sichuan, Chengdu Province

图8 罗马18军团司令墓碑，公元2世纪
Tombstone of the Commander of the 18th Roman Legion, 2nd century AD

图9 罗马禁卫军士兵石刻
Stone carving, Roman Praetorian Guard

图10 陕西靖边杨桥畔东汉墓壁画中的农人
Farmer depicted in mural found in Eastern Han Dynasty tomb in Yangqiaoban, Jingbian, Shaanxi Province

最伤脑筋的事就是应付军队的一般开销和无厌的需索。罗马的禁卫军和地方军团不断拥立和篡弑皇帝(图8~9)。很多皇帝自己就曾是军团司令，被拥立登位。因为职业化、服役时间长，军队成了一个极为强固的利益团体，罗马社会没有可以跟军队抗衡的其他利益团体。所以罗马军队可以在罗马政治史上扮演举足轻重的角色。我们今天说枪杆子里出政权，罗马是最典型的例子。

这样的情形却不见于秦汉，只有到了东汉晚期，因为长期跟匈奴和羌人作战以及黄巾之乱，才制造出长期拥有军队的军阀。像董卓、孙权这样的人掌握了军队，最后导致汉代结束。但在汉代四百年大部分时期，军队多半临时征召，大将也是临时任命，打完仗军队就解散，将和兵之间没有长久强固的联系。这当然有好处。中国皇帝不喜欢将和兵长期黏在一起，形成对皇权的威胁。

六　齐民对比公民：百姓的地位和角色

对绝大部分传统中国的老百姓来说，很难想象自己有什么所谓的"政治权利"。即便像孟老夫子这样主张民权的人，经常说"民为贵，社稷次之，君为轻"、"天视自我民视，天听自我民听"，好像强调了老百姓的重要性。可是，说到底他还是把人分成两种：一种是劳心者，治理众人；一种是劳力者，只配被统治。他主张百姓有权去推翻桀纣这样的暴君，但在他眼中，一般百姓缺乏圣人般的真知灼见，只可乐终，不可虑始，并没有能力成为统治的主体。百姓只配劳动生产以供养治人者(图10)，等待圣王带给他们太平的日子。

孟老夫子当然还说过人人皆可为尧舜，奈何像尧舜这样的圣王五百年才会出现一次。圣王没出现的日子，怎么办？他没给答案。除了他，先秦诸子也都没有想过：老百姓可不可以据自己的好恶，以制度性的手段更换他们不喜欢的统治者？可不可以不像周革商命那样，人头落地，血流漂杵？先秦诸子虽然主张仁民爱物，以民为本，但压根不认为凡民百姓有能力自治或治人，也压根没有公民治国或公民权的概念。千百年来的中国百姓只是不停完粮纳税，做个逆来顺受的羔羊而已。

罗马人很早就接触到位于意大利半岛南部希腊人所建的殖民城邦，学习了希腊公民治理城邦的观念。城邦公民是政治权力的主体，有权参加城邦管理，投票选举官员，也有权放逐他们。公元前6~5世纪的雅典就曾发展出一套陶片流放制，只要有六千公民投票，不受欢迎的执政者就会被逐出雅典十年(图11)。罗马人在共和晚期可能受到希腊流放制的启发，元老院可以投票，宣布某人为"公敌"，置他于罗马法律保护之外。公敌如果不自动离开罗马，流亡它地，人人得而诛之，财产也会被充公。这个办法在共和晚期虽然沦为政客政争的工具，不论如何，公民大会或流放制，这些理论上用以保障公民权益的制度，是孟子和所有先秦政治思想家都不曾想过或提出过的。背后意识形态的不同，由此可以看得明明白白。

七　秦汉和罗马帝国对后世的影响

秦汉影响后世中国极为深远。尽管秦始皇本人的历史形象很负面，他的一些作为，比如说统一文字，毫无疑问对维系中国长久的一统起了决定性的作用。修长城当然耗竭民力，但保证了中国农耕地带的安全，历朝历代都靠着长城抵御北方的游牧民族，一直到抗战时期，西北军大刀队还依靠长城抵抗日本人。秦统一后，消除战国以来各国间的关津壁垒，大修直道，把很多过去割裂的道路联系起来，成就一个全帝国性的道路系统，这就好像罗马人在帝国内大修道路一样；罗马帝国之内"条条大路通罗马"，秦汉帝国之内也是条条大路通咸阳、长安或洛阳。欧洲一直到中古，甚至到近代前期，还在使用不少罗马时代修筑的道路。秦汉时代的道路有不少一直沿用到明清。

此外，前面提到过，秦帝国的官僚体系是从春秋战国时期发展扩大而来，已经经过了长期的试验。秦在征服过程中，以法为治，提高效率，体系趋于完善。秦一统中国后的官僚制度，相对于当时世界上的其他统治体系来说，无疑是最严密，最庞大，也最有效率。汉制承秦，但记取秦朝短命的教训，刻意除去了秦制中的严苛，增多了合乎人性的

成份，例如强调施政须爱惜民力，平民俊秀可为卿相，减少了社会上下层之间的距离和矛盾。因为这些改进，自秦汉以来的政治体制才能大体维持了两千年。长远来看，秦的统一有不可否认的功劳。不过，当时的百姓付出的代价太过高昂则是无庸怀疑的事实。秦十来年就被推翻，这绝对合乎情理和正义。后世的人可以轻易不付代价地颂扬秦政，可是不也应该自问：如果活在秦始皇时代的是自己，愿意吗?

罗马人没有像秦汉一样，留下可长可久的官僚体制。罗马帝国崩溃后，没有人再能用罗马人的方式统一地中海世界。不过罗马人建立的和平（pax Romana）和宽容的文化宗教政策提供了基督教成长的温床，也成就了以罗马为首的教会体系。基督教会主宰欧洲上千年，这个影响不可谓不大。此外，罗马自共和时代以来，经无数皇帝、律师和法学专家不断努力，建立起从理论到实务兼具，十分完善的法典以及司法体系，奠下西方法治的基础。这个贡献无与伦比。

图11 雅典广场出土流放政要之投票用陶片
Ostraka Unearthed in the Agora of Athens

中文参考书目：

邢义田编译：《古罗马的荣光——罗马史资料选译（I、II）》，远流出版社，1998年，台北。

邢义田译著：《西洋古代史参考资料（一）》，联经出版社，1987年，台北。

邢义田：《天下一家：皇帝、官僚与社会》，中华书局，2011年，北京。

邢义田：《治国安邦：法制、行政与军事》，中华书局，2011年，北京。

References Across Distances: the Qin and Han Dynasties Vis-à-Vis the Roman Empire

(abridged)

Fellow Institute of History and Philology, Academica Sinica, Taiwan   Hsing I-tien

1. Form of Rule in the Qin/Han Dynasties and in the Roman Empire

The system of rule in China following the founding of the Qin Dynasty both inherited characteristics of preceding systems as well as took on innovative new elements. Qin Shihuang established commanderies and counties all over his empire and abolished the prior system of individual feudal states, calling himself *Huangdi* or "Emperor". On the other hand, he continued to believe in the Zhou Dynasty concept that the legitimacy of rule was decreed by Heaven and not by the ruled. In the Mediterranean, the Roman Empire took the reins of what was a long-existent and traditional city-state system, believing that the citizens of the state were its masters and that the legitimacy of rule came from the consent and recognition of all the state's citizens. Rome had been a city-state since the Republican era and already had a functioning citizen assembly and Senate mechanism. Even after Augustus' rule the position of the Emperor had to be recognized by the Senate before he could be deemed as the legitimate ruler. Further, the Emperor's powers were also regulated by the laws promulgated by the Senate.

2. Rule of Man versus Rule of Law: Power Dynamics

While the Qin and Han Dynasties claimed to rule along the letter of the law, in reality the Emperor had the final say in all matters great and small. The so-called rule of law in these cases was manifested in the systematic use of harsh penalties on officials and the common people while the Emperor remained above the law. One key characteristic of the system is the lack of any institutional limit on the Emperor's power. On the other hand, in Roman politics the Emperor's powers were bounded by the law. The powers enjoyed by the Roman Emperor had to be conferred individually by the Senate through legislation. The *"lex regia"* passed by the Senate proved to be a strong mechanism in Rome.

3. Unification versus Tolerance: Cultural Policies

Both the Qin/Han Dynasties and the Roman Empire were comparatively tolerant of foreign races and cultures. Apart from the implementation of the commandery/county administrative system, the Chinese dynasties also established *"dao"* and *"shubang"* provisions which allowed 'barbarian regions' to be run autonomously after they pledged fealty to the central government. The Roman Empire adopted a similarly open policy. While the multitude of city-states dotted around the Mediterranean was required to pay taxes to Rome and pay homage to the Roman Emperor, they were allowed to keep their respective customs and faiths. The Roman governor was only responsible for tax collection and the maintenance of public safety and civil order, with all other matters handled by the municipal authorities in each provincial capital. However, the Romans did not have a standardized system of writing. The Western half of the Empire used Latin while the Hellenized Eastern half of the Empire continued to use Greek. As such, the Romans did not think of themselves as cultural missionaries, instead actively pursuing study of the Greek language and Hellenistic culture.

4. Rigor versus Flexibility: Officialdom and Human Resource Control

Compared to that of Qin and Han China, the system of rule employed by the Roman Empire was comparatively more loosely-controlled. Unlike the former, the Romans did not have a gigantic bureaucratic system in place, and it was not until the third century AD that they began to establish a more substantial bureaucratic structure. Prior to this development the Romans had relied on a system of city self-rule with no national system of tax collection or land and citizen registration. By contrast, Qin and Han China had meticulously kept records with the merits of local officials evaluated on the basis of centrally collected data. Broadly speaking, the level of detail in data collection in Qin and Han China was unprecedented until modern times.

5. Conscripted Armies versus Professional Military: Matters of Defense

The nature of the military in Qin/Han China and in the Roman Empire was completely different. In Han China, the army was largely a conscript army, with a stipulation that adult males had to serve two years of military service for the Son of Heaven. When the state was in need the central government would authorize its generals to recruit among the local populace to boost the army's numbers. Once the war was over, the general would return to the royal court while the conscripts would return to their farms. Over the vast majority of the four-hundred-year history of the Han Dynasty, both armies and generals were generally recruited temporarily as needed, and there were no deep long-term relationships between commanders and troops. While the Roman Army was initially made up of citizen soldiers, by the late Republican era the army had gradually transformed into a professional outfit due to frequent wars and lengthened periods of service for soldiers. Following the establishment of the Roman Empire by Augustus, the army was fully professionalized and existed no longer in the service of Rome but in the service of its own leader. The Roman army became a strong interest group within Roman politics, with the Praetorian Guards and local military groups constantly enthroning and violently dethroning Emperors, creating political instability.

6. Common People versus Citizens: the Place and Role of the People

In traditional Chinese political thought, the common folk were not considered to be capable of self-governance or ruling. Further, there was no concept of democracy or citizen rights in this tradition. The Romans learnt about democracy from the Greeks and sought to protect citizens' rights at least in theory with the Senate and citizen assembly mechanisms. These were unheard of in traditional Chinese political thought.

7. The Influence and Impact of the Qin/Han Dynasties and the Roman Empire on Later Generations

The Qin and Han Dynasties went on to have a profound impact on China. The standardized system of writing ensured the longevity of a unified China and the Great Wall guaranteed the safety of China's farming regions. After China was unified under the Qin Dynasty a national road system was built, similar to what was implemented by the Romans across the Empire. Qin and Han China established a large and rigorous bureaucratic system that remained in use in its basic form for almost two millennia. In Rome, the peaceful and tolerant cultural policies of the Romans created an environment conducive for the growth of Christianity and paved the way for Rome to become the center of Catholicism. Rome also made an unparalleled contribution to the world in that its complete legislative and law enforcement structures laid down the foundation for Western rule of law.

写实之道——罗马帝国的肖像雕塑艺术

湖北美术学院副教授　左奇志

图1　母狼，罗马卡皮托林山博物馆藏
She-wolf of Rome, Capitoline Museums, Rome

图2　维伊的阿波罗，约公元前550~520年，罗马伊特鲁利亚博物馆藏
Apollo of Vei, National Etruscan Museum, Rome

> 要估价罗马艺术领域的遗产，最好是通过它的雕刻。
>
> ——杰弗里·韦维尔《罗马的遗产·艺术》[1]

一　罗马艺术的背景

罗马民族发源于意大利半岛的台伯河边，最初只是沿台伯河岸诸山丘的一些村落联盟。意大利半岛的地理特征对罗马历史的发展历程影响非常大。与贫瘠的希腊不同，意大利土地肥沃，林木丰富，气候湿润，阳光充足，农业成为这个民族发展的基础。虽然意大利半岛的海岸线漫长，但良港之地不多，因此贸易并不发达，使罗马民族很少能享受到与其他民族在贸易交往中所能得到的文化刺激。相反，丰腴的土地和漫长低平的海岸常常遭到来自海上的觊觎和侵袭。几乎从定居意大利开始，罗马人就不得不以军事和武力来保卫自己的发展成果。特殊的地理地势条件促成了古代罗马民族崇尚武力的性格的形成。在罗马民族起源的传说中，罗马人相信他们的祖先是战神之子。事实上罗马人也比邻近民族如伊特鲁利亚人（Etruscans）和沃斯基人（volsci）更加勇猛和冷酷无情。他们对邻近部落进行无休止的征服，只有当边境牢牢控制在自己手中时，罗马人才会感到安全。

古罗马诗人维吉尔（Vergil，公元前70~19年）的《埃涅阿斯纪》描述了特洛伊王室成员埃涅阿斯从特洛伊逃出，来到拉丁海岸，成为罗马人祖先的故事。埃涅阿斯的后代创立了阿尔巴·隆加城。传说阿尔巴·隆迦（Alba Longa）的公主与战神马尔斯（Mars）生下了双胞胎儿子罗慕洛（Romulus）和罗姆斯(Remus)。他们在婴儿时期遭受篡位斗争的牵连，被抛弃在台伯河。漂到岸边的婴儿被一只母狼发现并用乳汁哺育了他们。陈列在罗马的卡皮托林山（The Capitoline Hill）博物馆中的雕刻"母狼"（图1），据传是伊特鲁利亚人的作品。[2]两兄弟于公元前753年建造了罗马城。它处于台伯河岸边的七座小山丘上，据易守难攻之势。罗马城一开始就建立在武力和杀戮之上。性格暴烈好斗的两兄弟在建城时发生口角，罗慕洛拔剑杀死了弟弟罗姆斯，成为了罗马城的第一位国王。凭借优势的战略地位，罗马逐渐把邻近几个最重要的城邦置于自己的统治之下。到了公元前6世纪，成为了邻近地区的主宰。公元前146年，希腊本土被罗马征服。公元前30年，罗马击败了托勒密王朝。自此，原来为希腊所统治的广大地区，包括希腊本土，全部归入罗马版图。罗马取代以前希腊的地位，成为西方政治、文化的中心。罗马历史学家李维（Titus Livius，公元前59 年~公元17年）曾经写道："如果一个民族有权宣称拥有神圣的祖先，那么一定是我们自己。罗马人民在战争中所赢得的荣耀之伟大，以至于当罗马人宣布战神是自己的鼻祖时，全世界都理应接受。"[3]

二 伊特鲁利亚文化的影响

罗马文化是在伊特鲁利亚人的影响下开始的。伊特鲁利亚人的来源至今不明，学者大多认为他们来自小亚细亚，约在公元前6世纪建立了一个扩展到意大利北部和中部地区的城市联盟。其全盛时期，曾统治罗马人长达一个世纪之久。伊特鲁利亚人与希腊人和迦太基人有着频繁的交往，文化艺术深受希腊影响，同时又具有自身的特点。他们拥有丰富的想象力和创造力，具有非凡的艺术才能，创造了光辉的文化，在建筑、雕刻、壁画、工艺等方面都有突出的成就。在罗马最初建立的一百年间，无论工程建筑、生产技术、工艺风格还是典章礼仪都受其影响。伊特鲁利亚人的宗教信仰和艺术风格等方面也受希腊的影响，对罗马人来说他们起到了文明中转站的作用。他们带给罗马既有自己的，也有从希腊移植过来的因素。他们给罗马人留下了大量遗产，如：穿托加袍的习惯、[4]建造大型建筑的技术基础——拱券结构、角斗这一残酷的娱乐方式以及以动物内脏和飞鸟占卜的方法等。

在雕塑上，罗马人受伊特鲁利亚人影响也很深。罗马早先似乎没有自己的雕刻家，在共和时期早期，罗马的统治者聘请伊特鲁利亚工匠为他们塑造天神朱庇特（Jupiter）神像，安放在卡皮托林山（Capitoline Hill）的神庙里。

"维伊的阿波罗"是神庙装饰雕塑（图2），原是维伊神庙顶部装饰雕塑中的一个，公元前6世纪末这里是伊特鲁利亚雕塑艺术的中心。这尊雕像从题材看显然受希腊神话的影响，阿波罗向前迈出了一步，上身略向前倾，面带希腊雕塑古风式的微笑，给人一种古拙的感觉。然而薄薄地覆盖在身体上的衣纹，处理技巧轻松，富于图案化和装饰韵律，是伊特鲁利亚特色。人物形象和姿态比希腊古风时期的雕塑更加活泼，一扫希腊古风的呆板和拘谨，具有伊特鲁利亚文化特有的亲切感。伊特鲁利亚人对对象的敏锐观察力和精确表现力使罗马雕塑深受其益。

这尊半身铜像被认为是罗马共和国的传奇创始人布鲁图（Lucius Junius Brutus）的肖像（图3）。布鲁图于公元前509年领导罗马人推翻了伊特鲁利亚国王塔克文的暴政统治。雕像融合了希腊、罗马和伊特鲁利亚的因素。炯炯有神的目光，挺直的鼻子，紧闭的嘴唇，严肃、坚毅的神情都以希腊式理想化的手法表现出了人物意志坚强、勇敢果断的性格。眼球用象牙和玻璃制作，为的是追求真实感。头发、眉毛、胡须受伊特鲁利亚影响，在追求真实的基础上具有程式化、图案化的表现特点。

这尊身穿托加袍的真人大小的演讲者雕像出土于伊特鲁利亚地区（图4）。上面刻有伊特鲁利亚的文字和Aule Metele之名。后人猜测这可能就是他人的名字。他大概是当时的一位官员。这件作品突出之处在于其严谨而平实的特质。人物姿态和衣纹处理方法是希腊式的，稍大于正常比例的手和面部的简约处理则有伊特鲁利亚手法特征。

从公元前2世纪起，罗马艺术逐渐摆脱伊特鲁利亚文化的影响而出形成自己

图3 执政官布鲁图，约公元前3世纪(头部为古代的，胸部是后来加上去的)，罗马卡皮托林博物馆藏
Lucius Junius Brutus, Capitoline Museums,, Rome

图4 演说者，公元前2世纪，佛罗伦萨国立考古博物馆藏
Orator, Nationa Archeological Museum, Florence

图5 奥古斯都像，梵蒂冈博物馆藏
Augustus, Musei Vaticani

图6 持矛者（罗马复制品），约公元前440年，那不勒斯国立考古博物馆藏
Doryphorus, National Archaeological Museum, Naples

的特色，而雕塑是最具代表性的方面。

三　希腊艺术的影响

希腊艺术对除了经伊特鲁利亚人中转外，它也直接影响到罗马艺术。到公元前3世纪，罗马人开始征服希腊后，希腊对罗马人的影响取代了伊特鲁利亚人。拉丁诗人贺拉斯（Horace，公元前65~8年）说过："被征服的希腊，反而征服了粗鲁、无文明的征服者，把艺术带到了拉丁姆。"[5]

早在公元前3世纪末期罗马人便开始搜集希腊雕塑。随着东征西讨，罗马人把希腊以及其他地区的许多雕刻作品当成战利品运回罗马。那些曾经用来供奉神的雕塑被罗马贵族当成奢侈品来装点他们的别墅和豪宅，以抬高身份。西塞罗就曾想在雅典找一个朋友帮他搜集雕像来装饰他在罗马郊外的房子。据说公元前146年希腊被征服后，仅仅德尔斐（Delphi）神殿一处就被劫走约500尊雕像。一大批供奉在希腊神庙中的雕刻被当做陈设品买了回来。即便这样，希腊雕塑在罗马仍供不应求。于是大量的仿制品诞生了。为罗马人复制和创作雕刻品的常常是罗马征服地区的那些受过良好教育的雕塑家和工匠，他们被当做奴隶或人质集中到了罗马。后来，因为市场的庞大，吸引了一批大希腊地区的雕塑家前往罗马进行雕塑创作。比如原居住在意大利南部属希腊统治区的雕塑家帕斯特勒斯（Pasiteles），就取得了罗马公民的身份并在罗马进行创作。[6]一批旨在培养雕塑人才的雕塑学校也应运而生。这些都使得希腊化时代的艺术风格继续在罗马得到继承和发展。

罗马人对雕塑的疯狂爱好导致雕塑

的泛滥："公元4世纪的罗马是一座雕刻之城。据说当时城内的雕刻比人还要多，而据估计，当时罗马城内的人口大约为100万。"[7]时至今日，历经两千年历史的淘洗和破坏，意大利现今仍存有数量惊人的罗马雕像。可见造像行业在当时的风靡程度。

这种风靡导致一个结果，就是雕塑的市场化。罗马全身像的雕塑往往是在复制的希腊原作躯干上加一个头像。那些躯干是在工厂批量制作的，可以随意购买，各种姿势、类型和尺寸都有，每个躯干的脖颈上都有一个安装头像的接口。买家只要定制相应的头部即可。甚至罗马帝国杰出人物的雕像也用这种方法制作，如奥古斯都像（图5）借鉴了希腊古典时期的雕塑家波留克列特斯（Polyclitos）的经典作品"持矛者"（图6）的形象，只是将头稍抬，右手做出指挥的动作，并穿上了铠甲和衣服。而"持矛者"这一姿态在（图7）"捧着祖先头像的罗马人"中也能看到。再对比图7的衣纹，我们发现，在另一尊屋大维的全身像（图8）身上，衣纹与图7几乎如出一辙。可见那个时代的罗马全身像制作是希腊程式化的。这种程式化是何等普及，证实罗马人对待希腊艺术所持的无动于衷、理所当然的拿来主义态度。

从另一个方面看，罗马人对希腊人的继承又并非是毫无改变的照抄。讲求实际的罗马人不喜欢纯粹的唯美主义，对希腊人的幻想特性不感兴趣。他们对外来文化也是按照自己的需要加以扬弃，在建筑、绘画如此，在雕塑领域也是如此。

四　折衷主义风格的形成

罗马人对艺术品持一种实用主义的

态度，因受到伊特鲁利亚、希腊甚至埃及等多种文化的影响，就很难在罗马艺术中找到一种比较统一的视觉语言，帝国时期的作品尤其如此。

罗马艺术之前的其他文明的艺术，如埃及和希腊的艺术，它们的阶段和风格界定都很清楚，罗马艺术则不然。早在公元前6世纪前后，罗马的王政时代，意大利半岛上就居住着多个民族。如南部的那不勒斯、帕埃斯图姆（Paestum）居住的都是希腊人移民，北部则居住着伊特鲁利亚人等。在罗马文明初期，伊特鲁利亚、希腊和埃及亚历山大地区，都直接影响了罗马艺术，而希腊文化的影响最为突出。西塞罗（Marcus Tullius Cicero，公元前106~43年）曾评价到："罗马人的审美是以希腊人的审美情趣、技艺修养、优美典雅为特点，并与他们自身传统的实用观点相结合。"[8]到了帝国时期，随着不断的征服，罗马疆域扩大，民族益众，艺术家及其作品都广为流动。罗马文明对外来文化有极强的汲取能力，造成了其风格的多样性和混合性，罗马帝国的艺术也就呈现出兼收并蓄的折衷主义特征。

五 罗马雕塑的特征

1. 现实主义特征

对希腊人而言，"美"与"善"的观念可以相互转换。苏格拉底认为艺术家们应该专心致志地表现"善"和"美"的事物，艺术应该反映灵魂之美。在希腊人看来，肉体美和精神美之间几乎没有区别。荷马史诗中的英雄都是美的，而所有反派角色都是丑的或畸形的。因此，希腊雕塑，尤其是希腊化

时期的雕塑完美体现了这种精神与肉体之美的高度统一（图7）。

与希腊化时期主流的雕塑"善"与"美"的统一不同，在公元前4世纪末期和公元前3世纪，希腊雕塑发展出了一种新风格，即逼真风格。在雕像"巴克特的欧西德莫斯"（Euthydemus I）中（图8），我们看到了一种惊人的坦率。这位在公元前230年僭取希腊-巴克特里亚王国王位的统治者，长着一对三角眼和一个大大的酒糟鼻，那满脸的横肉、粗壮的脖颈和向下撇的嘴角都在暗示其发迹手段的不端。这种逼真风格在"狄摩西尼（Demosthenes）像"中则真实地再现了这位精神强大的希腊政治家孱弱的身体（图9）。

在希腊雕塑中写实的和理想化两种风格并存，显而易见希腊人更偏爱理想化的风格。罗马人与希腊人则正好相反。早期罗马民族依靠农业为生，在与自然抗争的过程中，培养了对客观事物冷静和求实的精神。多年的征战，实用性的军事技术和地理测绘及工程技术都得到了相应的发展。在哲学领域，罗马人的哲学更注重实用，而不像希腊人那样穷究宇宙的本源和人生的根底，他们希望哲学能服务于某种行为准则和对国家的治理。罗马虽有神话，但与丰富多彩的希腊神话相比要贫乏得多。他们的神话与生活关系很密切，每个地方或场所都有自己的神，如家神、灶神、囤神、门神等，而田地、山林、泉水、河流、山岗都有神祇居住。同希腊文化接触后，罗马的神就同希腊的神融合了。如天神朱庇特、天后朱诺、月神和狩猎女神狄安娜以及爱与美之神维纳斯等，都承袭了希腊神话的形象和传说。可见罗马人缺乏丰富的想象

图7 胜利女神像，希腊化时期，卢浮宫藏（于萨莫色雷斯岛（Samothrace）发现）
Winged Victory of Samothrace, Louvre, Paris

图8 巴克特的欧西德莫斯，罗马阿尔巴尼别墅藏
Euthydemus Bactrian, Villa Albani, Rome

图9 狄摩西尼像，梵蒂冈博物馆藏
Demosthenes, Musei Vaticani

图10　捧着祖先头像的罗马人，公元前1世纪末，罗马卡皮托林博物馆藏
A Roman man holding busts of his ancestors, Capitoline Museums, Rome

图11　罗马人头像，公元前80~50年，罗马帕拉佐·托卢尼亚博物馆藏
Head of a Roman patrician, Torlonia Museum, Rome

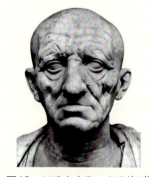

图12　罗马人头像，公元前1世纪，纽约大都会艺术博物馆藏
Portrait bust of a man, Metropolitan Museum of Art, New york

力。他们的文学以写实和叙事性为主要特征，艺术也不像希腊人那样具有充满幻想的史诗性。因此，罗马雕塑在不同时期不同需求的情况下，写实和理想化风格交替共存的过程中，写实的风格是占据主导地位的。

罗马人的全身像受希腊人影响如此之深，因此并不能代表罗马雕塑的最高成就和特色。而胸像这种艺术样式可算是罗马人的发明。以前人像只有全身像和胸像柱两种，[9]虽然幸存下来的罗马雕塑的作者常常是些希腊雕塑家，但他们的工作多是在富有的罗马资助人的影响下进行的。订件者的口味和要求无疑会影响到艺术家的创作。罗马传统的家族观念和祖像制作传统无疑是重要的影响。而罗马民族的好战性格和农业传统带来的务实性格为其注入了重要特征。

罗马人有保存祖先遗像的风俗，它始于某种原始的信仰，认为逼真的形象中寄托着灵魂。这一风俗在古埃及、伊特鲁利亚和古希腊也有，但在罗马尤为突出。这些像有的就是直接从死者面部蜡模翻制的面具，有的则是根据这种面模制作的酷似死者的雕像。罗马人把翻制的祖先面模称为"祖像"（imagines）。

罗马人的第一批青铜雕像就是运用希腊人和伊特鲁利亚人的翻铸青铜技术，直接用面具翻铸而成。这种雕像固然缺乏艺术创造性，但却肖似，由此奠定了罗马肖像雕塑特别注重人物面部刻画的特点。这与古希腊雕塑注重人物姿态动作，相对忽视面部刻画的传统正好相反。

罗马人的家族观念极强。他们把以父亲为家长的家庭观念应用于整个国家共同体，强调家庭和祖先的荣耀。罗马家庭把供奉祖先的半身肖像的神龛放在大厅最重要的位置。与中国人相似的是，罗马人认为与祖先肖似是一件极为荣耀的事。希腊作家波利比乌斯（Polybius，约公元前200~118年）写道："当家族中地位煊赫之人去世时，已逝家长的面具就会出现在葬礼上，长相最接近已逝家长的人才可以佩戴。对于渴望赢得荣誉和被施与美德的年轻人来说，还有比获此殊荣更加难忘的吗？"[10]因此肖像雕塑成为罗马独特葬仪中不可缺少的组成部分。

"捧着祖先头像的罗马人"（图10），表现的就是罗马人葬仪中出现的情节。一位身穿托加袍的罗马人，自豪地手捧着祖先的遗像，可能是他的父亲和祖父。三人的发型都是共和时期标志性的短发。从容貌上看，三人有明显的相似性这组雕像通体使用写实手法，着重刻画头部，身体繁复的衣褶质感很强，明显受到希腊时代雕塑的影响，而头部强调的真实感却是希腊雕塑所没有的。因此，一件希腊全身像雕塑缺失头部通常并不影响其观赏性，但一件罗马全身像雕塑若没有了头部则会大大损失其艺术价值。

a. 真实主义：[11]男性雕像

从罗马共和时期开始。罗马的（男性）个人雕像的特点就是不掩饰人物身体和面貌上的缺陷，即所谓的"真实主义"（veristic）。或"极端写实主义"[12]（extreme realism）的风格。这是一种严峻的现实主义的表达。严酷的内部和外部环境，不断征伐的经历，使罗马人建立起他们的价值观念：身为男性公民，必须身负严肃的军事责任。在罗马，凡是有一定财产的男性公民都有服兵役的义务，尤其是贵族。[13]因此罗马人认为：一个高贵的人，其面部特征是一个人的年龄和智慧的最好反映。岁月和艰苦的人生经历刻画在面部的皱纹，正是人生经历最有价值的宝贵表征——年龄的增加意味着生活的成就。正是基于这种信念，我们才能看到在众多现存的罗马肖像雕塑上所表现出来的毫无粉饰的沧桑感和严峻的面容：凹陷的面颊、如同刀刻一般的肌肉纹路和皮肤皱褶（图11、12）。而这种极端写实的面容也传达出了罗马人的价值取向：尊贵、正直和沉稳。因此在有的作品中，这种沧桑感甚至还会在一定程度上被放大和夸张（图13）。

这种对真实感的追求在对大人物形象的刻画上也是毫不含糊的。盖乌斯·马略（Gaius Marius，公元前157~86年）是罗马著名的军事统帅和政治家（图14），他的父亲是罗马郊外的佃农，其低微的出身一直为元老院诟病。这尊马略的雕像毫无粉饰地表现了这位统帅的质朴形象：厚而突出的下唇，光秃秃的前额，耷拉着的眉毛和疲软无力的油腻腻的细发——显然他对自己的外貌是否光鲜毫不在意。只有紧皱的眉头和专注的目光透露出这位意志坚定的领袖的气质。

真实主义带来罗马雕塑的一个显著特点——人物面貌的写实性。两千多年过去了，我们仍然可以通过这些雕塑看到那个时代很多人的样貌。比如马略和凯撒的秃顶，庞贝的小眼睛和圆脸，韦帕芗的四方脸和慈祥的气质，卡拉卡拉的紧绷的神经……就像贡布里希（E. H. Gombrich，1909-2001)所说："……我们都很熟悉庞培、奥古斯都、提图斯或尼禄，几乎就像是在新闻片中见过他们的面孔一样，。尽管如此，这些罗马肖像却毫无猥琐之处。艺术家设法成功地实现了既逼真又不平凡。"[14]

在尤里乌斯·凯撒（Gaius Julius Caesar，公元前100~44年）的雕像中（图15~16），我们几乎都能看到他那著名的秃顶，即使有的雕像对此稍加掩饰，但仍可看出发际线很高，头发稀疏。据说凯撒很在意他的秃顶，元老院允许凯撒在任何时候都可以佩戴桂冠，就像凯撒金币中显示的那样，这让他很高兴，因为这样就可以遮住它们。此外，凯撒的雕像还有着瘦长的面颊、宽阔的额头、高高的颧骨、犀利的目光、鹰钩鼻子和紧抿着的薄嘴唇。这些特征都能帮助我们辨认出这位伟大

图13　罗马人头像，纽约大都会艺术博物馆藏
Portrait bust of a man, Metropolitan Museum of Art, New york

图14　盖乌斯·马略像，罗马梵蒂冈博物馆藏
Gaius Marius, Vatican Museums

图15　尤里乌斯·凯撒像，那不勒斯国立考古博物馆藏
Gaius Julius Caesar, National Archaeological Museum, Naples

图16　尤里乌斯·凯撒像，公元1世纪中期，柏林老博物馆藏
Gaius Julius Caesar, Altes Museum, Berlin.

图17　庞贝像，丹麦新嘉士伯博物馆藏
Pompey, New Carlsberg Museum

图18　庞贝像（庞贝死后的雕像，可能是一件帝国时期的复制品），丹麦麦新嘉士伯博物馆藏
Pompey, New Carlsberg Museum

图19 盖乌斯·屋大维像，佛罗伦萨国立考古博物馆藏
Caracalla, Nationa Archeological Museum, Florence

图20 作为祭司的盖乌斯·屋大维像，公元前10年~公元10年，罗马国立博物馆藏
Augusts as a veiled priest, National Museum of Rome, Rome

图21 卡拉卡拉像，那不勒斯国立考古博物馆藏
Caracalla, National Archaeological Museum, Naples

图22 卡拉卡拉像，佛罗伦萨国立考古博物馆藏
Caracalla, Nationa Archaeological Museum, Florence

图23 韦帕芗像，罗马国家博物馆藏
Head of Vespasian, National Museum of Rome, Rome

图24 韦帕芗像，丹麦新嘉士伯博物馆藏
Head of Vespasian, New Carlsberg Museum

的统帅。

被称为罗马前三巨头之一，凯撒曾经的密友和合作者庞贝（Pompey，公元前106~48年），长着一张与凯撒完全不同的脸（图17、18）。与轮廓清晰，具有天然领袖气质的凯撒相比，庞贝的面容似乎更适合做一名戏剧表演中的小丑而不是一位政治家。他有着一副圆圆的面庞，丰茂而柔软的头发在额顶上卷起一个小涡。两只小眼睛似乎总透着笑意，圆圆的鼻头下有一张小小的嘴。虽然面容甚至称得上是和善，但总让人感觉在他的面容后面还有另一张脸。

在现存可见的奥古斯都（屋大维）的雕像中（图19、20），他的样子总是那样年轻和英俊。他的形象几乎是我们可以看到的罗马皇帝中最正常和有魅力的一个。那双表情严肃而坦诚的大眼睛，配上平滑的眉毛，几乎带有孩子气。这个不到33岁就成为罗马世界主人的人，他的脸在雕像中是属于未成年人的，虽然他的各种身份都被表现出来：既是军人指挥和元首（图5）、又是大祭司（图20）。最初创作这种形象可能是为了纪念他所带来的新的和平和繁荣，但这种形象在他漫长的执政生涯中一以贯之几乎从来没有改变。要注意的是，与其他罗马帝王的肖像相比，奥古斯都的像经过了一定程度的美化——从现存雕像的相似程度上看，我们仍相信这是基于他真实模样基础上的美化。

卡拉卡拉（Caracalla，公元186~217年）是罗马历史上几位最为臭名昭著的暴君之一（图21、22）。他为了巩固自己的王位，杀死了自己的亲弟弟塞普提米乌斯·盖塔（Septimius Geta），并把盖塔的支持者清洗一空。他流放自己的妻子，最后还将她杀害。卡拉卡拉在位期间的雕像不少，从现存的作品看，卡拉卡拉似乎并未干涉艺术家的创作自由——卡拉卡拉像是罗马肖像艺术中最具个性的代表。它们无一例外地忠实记录了卡拉卡拉那并不优美的容貌和气质。比如他那非洲人一般紧贴头皮的浓密卷曲而纠结的头发和络腮胡子、粗壮有力的脖颈。尤其统一的是他那紧蹙的眉头，我们可以相信这是他的习惯表情，因为长期的紧蹙，使眉弓处形成了刀刻一般的痕迹。这些雕像让人们相信自己看到的是一个被情绪所控制的随时暴怒的人。但另一方面，在他蛮横的外表下，紧张和不安也一览无遗：他的头突然向一方转动，以及肩膀倾斜的方式，似乎时刻怀疑背后隐藏着危险。卡拉卡拉的紧张是不无道理的：仅仅在位8年，31岁被自己的近卫刺杀身亡。

韦帕芗（Vespasian，公元9~79年）是尼禄死后结束帝位纷争上台的一位皇帝（图23、24），史上对这位皇帝多有正面评价。在韦帕芗的雕像中我们可以看到他的这些特征：貌不惊人（尤其是老年）的一张方圆脸，略微嫌短，头发不多，眼角下垂，嘴唇内陷。气质上韦帕芗相当平易，没有丝毫跋扈之气，老年时代的像更显慈祥。正如贡布里希所言"韦帕芗的胸像丝毫没有讨好之处——根本无意于把他表现为神。他的形象有如富有的银行家或航运公司老板。"[15]

b. 温和的写实：女性雕像

在罗马这样一个典型的父权社会中，罗马妇女的社会地位无疑是十分低下的，她们甚至连自己的名字都没有。只是在自己的父姓后加一个阴性的词尾来构成。如朱莉娅（julia）来自尤里乌斯(julius)，克劳迪娅（Claudia）来自克劳迪乌斯（Claudius）等。一家中如果有两个女儿，常常这样区别：大朱莉娅、小朱莉娅，依此类推。男人认为女人应该养育孩子、管理家庭奴隶，闲暇之时进行纺织。就算是奥古斯都的孙女阿格里皮娜和安东尼娅这样的身份高贵并富有的女人也要学习纺织。在观看角斗表演时，妇女只能与平民坐在在最后一排。

虽然有种种限制，但女性在公共生活中仍然扮演者重要角色。尤其是上流社会的妇女甚至比希腊时期雅典妇女拥有更高的地位。她们通常受到良好的教育，可以自由地从事文化艺术活动，可以经营自己的生意，有时可以在神庙中担任女祭司。皇族的女性与其丈夫一样，肖像可以出现在钱币上（图25）。有些女人通过给丈夫和儿子施加影响力来行使权力。比如著名的小阿格里皮娜毒死了自己的丈夫从而让儿子尼禄当上了皇帝。也因为希望继续控制尼禄而送了命。

古罗马的女性雕像与男性雕像相比，虽然也秉承了"真实主义"的传统，但要柔和许多。个性气质、情感的表现的同时伴随着时尚更迭的记录。

奥古斯都的皇后利维娅·杜路莎·奥古斯塔 (Livia Drusa Augusta，公元前58~29年）是奥古斯都（屋大维）的第三任妻子（图26），她是罗马帝国早期最有权力的妇女。凯撒抛弃前妻将她从自己的丈夫身边夺走，并与她共同生活了五十多年。她是奥古斯都的忠实顾问，并多次以实际执政的身份主宰帝国政治。她的两个儿子后来都成为帝国的皇帝。奥古斯都时代的雕像倾向于理想化，所以作为罗马的第一位皇后，利维娅的肖像一方面是写实的：清秀的小脸，秀气的五官。另一方面又体现了公众所期待的所有美德：美丽、高贵、谦逊和端庄。

利维娅创造了一个新的发型，额头中间的头发做成一个高高的卷，两侧的头发以松散的波浪状向后梳理，最后做成一个髻固定于脑后，皇后的这个发型立即风靡整个帝国，妇女们人人效仿，哪怕年老妇女也不例外（图27）。这尊老妇像虽然梳着利维娅式的发型，但造型风格上显然遵循的是共和时期的真实风格。由于苍老而骨骼突出的面容，稀疏的头发，严肃的面容都与早期罗马雕塑如出一辙。

图25 哈德良皇后萨宾那金币
A Roman Gold Aureus of Sabina, Wife of Hadrian

图26 利维娅像，巴尔的摩沃尔特斯艺术博物馆藏
Baltimore, The Walters Art Museum, Baltimore

图27 老妇像，公元前1世纪末，罗马国家博物馆藏
Portrait of Old Woman, National Museum of Rome, Rome

图28 小阿格里庇娜像，公元15~59年，佛罗伦萨国立考古博物馆藏
Portrait of Agrippina Minor, National Archeological Museum, Florence

图29 弗拉维时代的女子胸像，公元70~80年，佛洛伦萨国家考古博物馆藏
Bust of a Flavian Woman, National Archeological Museum, Florence

图30 罗马妇女胸像，约公元90年，罗马首都博物馆藏
Female portrait, Capitoline Museum, Rome

图31 萨宾娜像，罗马国家博物馆马西莫宫藏
Sabina, Palazzo Massimo, Roma

本次展览中的小阿格里庇娜像是一件十分精致的作品（图28）。小阿格里庇娜是尼禄的母亲，她一手将尼禄扶上王位。这尊雕像把小阿格里庇娜表现为一位长相端庄甜美的女性。中分的卷发向两边分开，在头上形成一个个规整的小涡卷，显然是一种程式化的处理手法。

本次展览中另有一件成年女子的肖像（图29），女子头戴弗拉维王朝（Flavian dynasty，公元69~96年）极为流行的涡状发圈式的假发发冠，艺术家用小钻头钻出这些圆孔以表现小发圈，这是罗马雕塑造型上的新手法。钻孔的手法在弗拉维时代得到进一步的发展，逐渐成熟，最终达到图30那样对繁复造型掌控自如的程度。此后不久钻孔术也运用到雕刻肖像的瞳孔上。[16]

公元1世纪下半叶，罗马的肖像雕刻已取得了高度成就，尤其是在弗拉维时期。肖像的多样化和写实主义手法已臻于完美。这尊"罗马妇女半身像"尤其为人称道的是她额前堆起的假发发冠（图30），不再是像图29中显示的那样规整，而是波涛起伏，富有真发的质感。用钻头透空的雕刻使大理石表面出现丰富的光影变化，反衬出人物柔润光洁的脸部，令人过目不忘。据鉴定，这名罗马的名门闺秀可能是图拉真皇帝的侄女维莉娅·玛蒂迪亚。她那花费大量时间精心安置的豪华假发、颈项微转的姿态、矜持的面部表情，强调了其高贵的身份和冷漠的内心。

萨宾娜（Vibia Sabin，公元83~136或137年）是哈德良皇帝的皇后（图31），此像约作于公元117~134年。雕塑面貌清丽端庄，富有教养，稍显倔强。根据哈德良皇帝的生平记载，皇后可能常遭冷落，因而此像没有任何骄横之态，显得郁郁寡欢，观之令人有黯然神伤之感。与帝国初建时期贵族们的高昂自足之像比较，有种含蓄孤高的气质和丰富沉静的美感。哈德良皇帝执政时期大兴希腊风，对个体内心体验的微妙表达反而减少，因此这尊雕像所表现的个性尤其难得。

尤利亚·多姆娜（Julia Domna 公元170~217年）是卡拉卡拉和盖塔的母亲（图32），塞维鲁皇帝的皇后。她聪敏美丽，热心支持各种艺术，身边聚集了不少文人雅士。卡拉卡拉被刺之后，多姆娜绝食而亡。这尊雕像展现了年轻的多姆娜温婉知性之美。高高的略有点弯曲的鼻梁和嘴角又透露出她隐藏的个性，眼神则藏着一丝忧郁，似乎预示了儿子和自己的悲惨结局。头上披下的厚厚波浪形的假发稍显沉重。

2．理想主义特征

写实主义雕塑虽然成为主流，但那些政治和军事首领仍希望雕塑家们以神像作为范本来创作他们的形象，以向臣民宣扬他们具有神一般的容貌和力量。每当罗马的统治者强调复古，强调英雄主义，强调采用希腊手法时，罗马肖像雕刻中的美化成分就明显加强。比如屋大维执政时期，提倡复古主义，要求文学艺术为帝王歌功颂德，在奥古斯都时代的雕塑中都可以看到这一倾向。因此，在罗马肖像艺术的发展中，写实和美化两种倾向始终是并行着，罗马雕像艺术中还有不少强调人物英雄气概的理想化、唯美主义的作品。

在哈德良时期，一味模仿希腊"古典风格"的罗马雕塑走上了追求柔和、纤细和典雅的格调形式主义，已无活力。

屋大维被元老院封为"奥古斯都"称号后，就开始被神化，死后也成为罗马神灵。屋大维的形象被罗马人进行理想化地处理也不足为怪。图5是一个广为人知的奥古斯都像，缺乏艺术想象力的罗马人，借鉴希腊雕塑家波留克列特斯的经典作品"持矛者"（图6）的形象来塑造了他，仅稍微变化了一下姿态。奥古斯都有帝王身份，所以不能裸体，于是给他身披铠甲，为了强化其神性，让他光着脚，并在右腿的支撑处加上了象征其高贵出身的丘比特。

同样，创作于1世纪，在现藏于卢浮宫的"利维娅像"（Livia Drusilla，公元前58 年~公元29年）则毫无掩饰地将屋大维的皇后表现为大地与丰收女神的模样（图33）。她头戴花冠，左手持丰饶角，右手持麦穗，身躯丰满富态，面庞圆润，一派丰饶之相。独特的发型则提示人们她就是利维娅。这类形象无疑也是源自古希腊时代，如克菲索多妥斯（Kephisodotos，约公元前400 ~360年）在公元前370年所创作的"埃伦娜与普鲁多斯"（Eirene, Ploutos）（图34），只是气势更雍容端庄、更符合利维娅母仪天下的身份。

马可·奥里略皇帝（Marcus Aurelius，公元前161~180 年）是罗马帝国最伟大的皇帝之一，他一生四处征战，疲于奔命。在他执政时期，罗马肖像雕刻更注重内心的刻画，因此被称作："情绪雕像"。"马可·奥里略骑马像"是古代最重要的骑马像，其脸部表现出内省和沉思，带着忧郁和伤感（图35）。

康茂德（Commodus，公元161~192年）像是罗马雕像中最精致的雕像作品（图36）。它与罗马早期那些强调男性社会责任感的雕像完全背道而驰。这尊像把他刻画成希腊神话英雄赫拉克勒斯的模样，一手持棒，另一手拿着苹果。象牙般光滑的脸上长着精致的胡须，精心整理过的卷发一丝不乱，虽头戴赫拉克勒斯的战利品狮子皮，却毫无力度和野性，整个雕像是在炫耀这位喜爱决斗的皇帝高高在上的优越感。该像精致有余，但早期罗马雕塑的力量感和严肃性已经荡然无存了。

哈德良皇帝热爱希腊文化。据说他的希腊语比母语还要纯熟。他的行宫里里外外都摆满希腊雕像。在男宠安提诺乌斯（Antinous，公元110或115~130年）不幸溺亡之后（图37），哈德良将他神化，在帝国境内树

图32　多姆娜像，约公元213年，德国慕尼黑古代雕塑博物馆藏
Julia Domna, Glyptothek, Munich

图33　扮作丰收女神的利维娅，公元1世纪，巴黎卢浮宫藏
Livia as Demeter, Louvre, Paris

图34　埃伦娜与普鲁多斯（罗马摹制品），公元前370年，德国慕尼黑古代雕塑博物馆藏
Eirene, Ploutos, Glyptothek, Munich

图35　马可·奥里略骑马像，罗马卡皮托林广场
Equestrian Statue of Marcus Aurelius, Piazza del Campidoglio, Rome

图36　扮成赫拉克勒斯的康茂德，公元190 ~192年，罗马卡皮托林广场
Equestrian Statue of Marcus Aurelius, Piazza del Campidoglio, Rome

图37　安提诺乌斯，那不勒斯国立考古博物馆藏
Antinous, National Archaeological Museum, Naples

立了大量他的雕像。这些安提诺乌斯的雕像都显示了娴熟的技艺，是罗马艺术在希腊文化影响下所创作的最具理想化的作品。安提诺乌斯的头像被嫁接在各种神祇的身躯上，赫尔墨斯，狄尼俄索斯，奥西里斯……，并相应改变了身躯的比例。这种混搭的结果是造就了罗马艺术中一个新的艺术典型——雕像具有健美的运动员式的体魄和忧郁柔弱的气质，希腊英雄式已难看见，这个新典型兆示了罗马艺术在高峰后的衰落。

六　结语

罗马艺术尤其是雕塑艺术是在多种文化如埃及文化、伊特鲁利亚文化、尤其是希腊文化的影响下发展起来的。罗马人生活环境以及特质使其雕塑艺术呈现出写实主义的主要特征。

写实性的胸像无疑是罗马雕塑艺术最重要的成就。罗马人创造了这一艺术形式，并赋予了它独有的文化功能。从文化背景看，这一因为纪念祖先而发展起来的艺术形式，基于对真实性的追求，使罗马雕塑艺术摆脱了希腊艺术的影响而确立了写实性特性。在希腊艺术里，艺术家首先关心的是一件雕塑应该是什么样，而不是这个人（模特）实际上是什么样，所以希腊艺术追求的是一种带有典型意义的理想化的表达。而对罗马人而言，一件雕塑品的成功或者被社会认可就是肖似，肖像必须具有"他"所独有的样貌、个性与气质，哪怕这样貌和个性有时并不优雅、美好。从对凯撒的秃顶到卡拉卡拉的残暴性格的真实记录上，我们都可以看到这一点。罗马人的雕像真实地再现了"人"，而没有重复希腊人的"神化"

或"美化"的旧途。因此，罗马人的肖像超越了希腊人，是真正的肖像。

从屋大维建立罗马帝国到公元 244 年元老院推举的最后一位皇帝戈尔迪安三世（Gordianus III，公元238~244年）因战而死的二百多年，这是罗马帝国黄金时代，也是罗马雕塑创作的高峰时期。它持续性地影响了欧洲后世的艺术创作。如罗马雕塑对意大利文艺复兴的影响怎样强调都不过分，它们不仅给吉布尔提、多纳太罗和米开朗基罗那样的雕刻家，而且给乔托、曼坦尼亚、达·芬奇和拉斐尔那样的画家提供了灵感。以马可·奥里略骑马像为例，这尊曾被误认为是第一位使基督教合法化的皇帝君士坦丁的像而幸存下来的雕像，成为后世无数君王骑马像的灵感源泉。[17] 到了17世纪，无论是在阿尼巴·卡拉奇、普桑的绘画还是贝尼尼创作的那些胸像中，我们都可以见到罗马雕塑给予他们的灵感。而19世纪盛行的，新古典主义无论从题材还是造型方法的选择上，都与罗马艺术有着至关重要联系。罗马艺术实际上影响了整个欧洲大陆的艺术品位，这种影响还将以不同的形式源源不断地传递下去。

注 释：

1. 杰弗里·韦维尔：《艺术》，理查德·詹金森编《罗马的遗产》，上海人民出版社，2002年，页361。

2. 母狼身下的婴孩是由文艺复兴时期的雕塑家、画家波拉约洛（Antonio Pollaiuolo，1431~1498年），增补上去的。"母狼"的铸造年代一直存在争议。罗马官方2012年6月对外承认，最新的年代鉴定结果显示，它是在1021~1153年间铸造的。在铸造方法上，这个时期的青铜铸造法与伊特鲁利亚时期也存在差异。后者的青铜雕塑多是分范铸造，最后拼合。而"母狼"青铜像则是整体范铸，有明显中世纪技术的痕迹。现在通过最新的年代测定技术鉴定后，研究者认为有95.4%的把握，可断定这件青铜塑像是11~12世纪的作品。研究者指出，这件作品很可能是中世纪对伊特鲁利亚时期原作的复制品。由于母狼的形象也曾出现在古罗马的钱币和其他艺术形式上，因此"母狼"青铜雕刻的断代并不影响母狼传说来自古代的事实（http://roll.sohu.com/20120630/n346942426.shtml）。

3. 彼得·克里斯普著：《艺术为证之古代罗马》，天津教育出版社，2011年，页8。

4. 托加袍是一种男子穿着的长形服装，经过复杂的折叠后包裹在身体上，遮盖左臂而露出右臂。罗马人在托加袍中还要加穿一件短袖长袍。托加袍相当于罗马男子的正式服装。

5. 邵大箴：《古代希腊罗马美术》，中国人民大学出版社，2004年，页185。

6. Martin Henig. *A Handbook of Roman Art : A Survey of the Visual Arts of the Roman World*, Phaidon Press Limited ,1983, p.180

7. 杰弗里·韦维尔：《艺术》，理查德·詹金森编《罗马的遗产》，上海人民出版社，2002年，页362。

8. 李贤辉：《西方艺术风格》，http://vr.theatre.ntu.edu.tw/fineart/th9_1000/open-12-broadcast.htm.

9. 一种置于方形石柱之上的头像，最初的胸像柱都是赫尔墨斯的头像，后来也有名人像。

10. 彼得·克里斯普著：《艺术为证之古代罗马》，天津教育出版社，2011年，页28。

11. *Rome Portrait Sculpture. The Stylistic Cycle.*参见http://www.metmuseum.org/toah/hd/ropo2/hd_ropo2.htm.

12. Tim Cornell、John Matthews. *Atlas of the Roman World*, Phaidon Press Limited, 1982, p.180

13. 邢义田：《古罗马的荣光——罗马史料选译》远流出版社，1998年，页546

14. 贡布里希：《艺术的故事》，生活·读书·新知三联书店，1999年，页121。

15. 贡布里希著：《艺术的故事》，生活·读书·新知三联书店，1999年，页121。

16. 罗马人从希腊人那里学会在雕像上着色，眼球和眉毛也用色彩表现，或用有色宝石来镶嵌，如图3"布鲁图像"中的眼球就是用玻璃和象牙所制。随着钻孔技术的运用，逐渐产生以钻孔来表现瞳孔的技巧。这一技巧运用的效果在图32"多姆娜像"中可以见到。说明弗拉维王朝之后，原来靠涂色来增加雕塑艺术表现力的办法逐渐让位于以造型手段来获取丰富光影变化的方法。这是雕塑语言上的一大进步。

17. 多纳太罗在帕多瓦创作的"格太梅拉达骑马像"（公元1443~1453年），委罗基奥在威尼斯创作的"巴托罗缪·科来奥尼骑马像"（公元1488年），其灵感都来自于马可·奥里略骑马像。

The Art of Realism: Sculptural Art in the Roman Empire

(abridged)

Assistant Professor, Hubei Academy of Fine Arts   Zuo Qizhi

1. Background

The Romans originated from the banks of the river Tiber on the Italian peninsula, where the fertile lands and long, flat coastline attracted waves of raiders and invaders. The region's particular terrain led to the development of a militaristic culture among ancient Romans.

i. The Influence of Etruscan Culture

Roman culture had its beginnings in the Etruscan peoples who were profoundly influenced by the ancient Greeks. They brought both native Etruscan elements and Greek influences to Rome. Keen observation and accurate representation skills were a major contribution of the Etruscans to Roman sculpture.

ii. The Influence of Hellenistic Art

In the third century BCE, following the conquest of Greece, the influence of Hellenistic culture on Rome eventually exceeded that of the Etruscans. Demand in Rome for Hellenistic sculpture grossly outstripped supply, and a great number of imitations began to appear on the market. The influence of Hellenistic art was such that oftentimes Roman full-body sculptures consisted of a head sculpture transplanted on top of an imitation Greek body. The ancient Romans were not keen on aestheticism and thus dealt with Hellenistic art according to their needs.

iii. The Development of the Eclectic Style

The Romans were influenced by the Etruscans, the Greeks and even ancient Egyptian culture, and bore a practical attitude with regards to works of art. Therefore, it is difficult to identify a relatively uniform visual language in Roman art, especially so in artworks from the Roman Empire. Roman civilization had the capacity to learn from foreign cultures and adapt influences from such cultures to their use. As such, the Roman style was full of diversity and the mix of cultural influences within also articulated the possibility of co-existence. This is why the art of the Roman Empire may be described as eclectic in nature.

2. Characteristics of Roman Sculpture

i. The Realists

There were two stylistic tendencies in Hellenistic sculpture: the realist and the stylized approach. The Romans later took on the realist approach. Bust sculpture was the greatest contribution to sculptural art made by the ancient Romans. The Romans had the custom of preserving their ancestors' portraits through portrait masks known as *imagines*. The masks were then used to cast copper statues, which led to the establishment of the Roman portrait sculpture tradition of paying particular attention to facial features.

a. Sculptures of Male Figures

Beginning with the era of the Roman Republic, the key feature of Roman sculptures of male figures was not to gloss over flaws in the body and face of the subject in what was known as the *veristic* style. The Romans believed that an individual's facial features were the best reflection of his age and wisdom.

b. Sculptures of Female Figures

The women of Rome occupied a very low position in society. Compared to sculptures of male figures, Roman sculptures of female figures though realistic were also a lot softer.

By the second half of the first century CE the makers of Roman sculpture of human figures were already highly accomplished, creating an incredible array of figures and executing the realist style to perfection.

ii. The Idealists

Although realist sculpture was well-established in the mainstream of Roman sculptural arts, whenever Roman rulers needed to exalt the heroic, sculptures became markedly more stylized. Therefore, there are also a number of highly-idealized and aesthetic works in

Roman portrait art. By Hadrian's reign, Roman sculpture that imitated Hellenistic "Classical" work and which pursued the mild, slender and elegant formalist style had gone out of fashion.

3.Conclusion

Roman art, in particular Roman sculptural art, developed under the influence of a mix of cultures, in particular that of the Greeks. The Romans' way of life and their cultural characteristics led to the creation of sculpture works that were highly realist in execution.

Realist busts of human figures were undoubtedly the most important accomplishment of Roman sculptural art. This was an art form invented by the Romans, who also endowed the bust with a specific cultural function. Roman sculpture successfully represented the "human" in the human figure instead of replicating the "deifying" or "stylized" approaches of the ancient Greeks. In this regard, Roman sculpture had surpassed Greek sculpture in that its human figures were truly representative of the individual portrayed.

Roman sculpture had a profound impact on the Italian Renaissance. Inspiration drawn from Roman sculpture can be seen clearly in busts of seventeenth-century artists. Even today, Roman art continues to be the source of inspiration for all kinds of art forms, ensuring that its influence will continue to live on into the future in various ways.

以公平正义之名——罗马法与罗马公民

湖北省博物馆研究员　王纪潮

古希腊、古罗马文明是现代西方文明的基石。从对世界的影响上看，古希腊给世界留下了民主、科学与哲学，而古罗马则留下了法律。在欧洲近代化过程中，罗马法中的平等、公正至上和保护私产等一些具有普世价值的原则成为新兴阶级的有力武器，推动了西方人文主义的发展。中世纪以来的西方各种政体要维持长久统治，无一例外地都得高举"以人为本"的旗帜，正是罗马人在历史上第一次以法律形式保护个人自由和私产的成果。"罗马法的复兴"也与"文艺复兴"、"宗教改革"并称为"欧洲三大思想运动"，奠定了西方现代法治社会的基础。德国学者耶林（Rodolf von Ihering，公元1818～1892年）说，罗马帝国曾三次征服世界，第一次以武力，第二次以宗教，第三次以法律，唯有法律征服世界是最为持久的征服。[1]因此可以说在罗马帝国的众多遗产中，没有一项比罗马法更重要。因"辉煌时代——罗马帝国文物展"之故，本文对罗马法与罗马公民略作论述。

一　罗马法源流

罗马法是奴隶制国家的法律，起源于罗马社会早先的习惯法。法学界一般把它限定在罗马共和（公元前509～31年）到尤士丁尼（Justinian，也译查士丁尼，公元526～565年在位）时代颁布的法典。也有人认为罗马法体系一个动态的法律概念，应从罗马建城（公元前753年）始，是古罗马法律原则、法律制度和法律规范的总和。[2]

按照普鲁塔克（Plutarchus，公元46~125年）的说法，罗马人是特洛伊战争中率众逃到拉丁姆地区的武士艾涅阿斯（Aeneas）[3]的后裔，经历15代君主之后由罗慕洛兄弟（Romulus）率众于公元前753年在罗马建城。[4]之后经过七王共250年的"王政时期"。在第六位君王塞尔维·图里乌斯（Servius Tullius，公元前578～535年）进行的改革中，罗马社会的血缘组织解体，出现了国家，这也是罗马法起点的标志。

罗马早期的法律有神法（fas）、习惯法。贵族、宗教领袖掌控法律的解释权，没有统一的法律权威。罗马王政时期政治有多种成分：1.由贵族组成的库里亚大会（Comitia Curiata）可选举国王、制定法律（lex）。2.由库里亚大会选举的王（rex）。王是终身制，除不得世袭外，他是宗教、军事和司法的最高首领，这与先秦时期的诸侯没有大的区别。3.由氏族领袖组成的元老院（Senatus）。库里亚大会通过的法律或王的法令须元老院批准。4.库里亚大会任命祭司（pontefici）和占卜官（auguri），祭司也掌握法律。5.图里乌斯实行改革后，罗马人按财产多寡划分服兵役的公民等级，组成了193个百人团（Comitia Centuriati），有权决定战争和纳税等事项，它后来取代了库里亚大会的大部分权力和职能。罗马的每种政治势力都可以对法律施加影响，如文献记载有占卜的影响判案的事例。罗马人迷信占卜的好处是对法律起了制衡作用。

罗马法是在贵族与平民、罗马人与外邦人的斗争和利益博弈中发展起来的。罗马的城邦制度是贵族与平民的二元结构，城邦各阶级的争斗、各种利益关系的调整以不能损害城邦的统一为最高原则。在罗马共和时期，贵族集团为加强统治废除了王，改由百人团选出任期只一年的两名执政官（consules）或执法官（magistratus）来代替。此后因事务繁多，先后增设执政官各种职官，如事务官（quaestores，公元前449年）、监察官（censores，公元前443～435年）、市政官（aediles curules，公元前367年）、负责处理罗马人事物的大法官（Praetor，公元前367年）和负责处理罗马人与外邦以及外邦人之间的事务的外务大法官（praetor peregrinus，公元前242年）等。与中国的专制集权不同的是，这些执政官、大法官、市政官、监察官都是独立行使职权。平民则于公元前494年组织平民议会（Concilia tributa plebis），选举具有两名平民为神圣不可侵犯的护民官(Tribune)。《瓦勒里和奥拉兹法》（Lex Valeria Horatia）规定，护民官有否决权，以帮助平民抗拒当局，元老院不得逮捕他们。公元前289～286年颁布的《霍尔滕西法》（Lex Hortensia）又规定，平民议会通过的决议（plebiscitum）百人团大会（后又改为经元老院）批准后也正式成为法（Lex），对全体罗马市民生效。护民官的神圣性和否决权源自远古的传统，这一防止公共权力滥用的武器推动了罗马国家的发展。[5]

罗马法由习惯法发展到成文法是平民与贵族的斗争结果，标志是公元前449年由十人委员会完成的《十二表法》。它是罗马第一个由人制定的法（ius），其内容涉及到传唤、审理、执行、家长权、赔偿、继承与监护、所有权与占有、房屋与土地、私犯（delictum）、公法等方面。《十二表法》破除了法律神授，以成文法的形式打破贵族或祭司对法律的垄断，人民（populus）的最后决定具有法律效力。《十二表法》作了罪、刑罚的定义，阐明了财产权、个人权利和诉讼程序，明确规定罗马人在"私法"领域一律平等。《十二表法》的内容已经反映出罗马法尊重人性、保障私权的原则，这乃是日后罗马法的基础，比如第四表规定胎儿享有继承权，第九表规定不得无罪而诛等。[6]《十二表法》中区别对待奴隶与平民是当时罗马处于奴隶制社会的反映，但保护罗马城邦的发展，

维护社会公平正义的超阶级性是它的进步所在。如英国法学家梅因（H. S. Maine，公元1822～1888年）所说，《十二表法》的贡献是以条文形式保护社会不受特权寡头政治的欺压，保证国家制度不被腐败。[7]

《十二表法》自公布到尤士丁尼大帝编纂法典时（公元529～534年）的千余年中，历代统治者从未明文废止，只是随着政治结构和经济发展的实际予以调整和修改。随着罗马的扩展和经济的繁荣，罗马也由单一的城邦国家变成横跨欧、亚、非三洲的帝国。早期简单的法律也无法适应需要，于是在《十二表法》之外，贵族议会、行政部门、民意团体的各种政策、决议也陆续成为罗马法的来源。如公元前27年，屋大维被元老院奉为"奥古斯都"（元首），形式上存在的民众会议因立法权转归元老院，成了皇帝的橡皮图章。皇帝和元老院共同管理国家，皇帝居于主导地位，元老院有行政、立法和司法权，其决议(Senatusconsulta)在公元2世纪就成为法律。概况起来罗马法的来源有元老院通过的决议、经元老院批准实施的各种民意团体会议的决议、各种长官公告（Edicta magistratuum）、皇帝敕令（Constitutions principum）和法学家的解释（Interpretatio prudentium）等。

公元284年，罗马皇帝戴克里先（Diocletianus，公元284～305年）即位，以往皇帝自称"元首"还保留一丝民主政治的意味，他却自称"主"和"神"（Dominus et deus）。皇帝此后拥有绝对的权力，元老院的权力萎缩，成为无足轻重的城市议会，罗马由此变成君主专制制度。公元330年，君士坦丁皇帝（Constantinus I Magnus，公元306～337年）因意大利财赋枯竭，在拜占庭建立"新罗马"，帝国在行政上开始分为东、西两部。公元476年西罗马帝国灭亡，但罗马法的完善和汇纂工作仍在进行，到公元565年尤士丁尼大帝去世才告一段落。

尤士丁尼时期对大部分罗马法进行了重新整理汇总，编纂了集罗马法之大成的《民法大全》（Corpus Iuris Civilis），它包括《法典》（Codex，哈德良皇帝以后的各代皇帝敕令）、《学说汇纂》（Digesta，帝政时代法律学者们对法律的解答和著述）、《法学阶梯》（Iustiniani Institutiones，法学基础教材）和

《新律》（*Novellae Constitutiones Justiniani*，尤士丁尼时期的法律）四个部分。《民法大全》系统地搜集、整理了罗马共和时期至当时所有的法律和法学著作，具有法律概念和术语严谨、简明的特点，尤其是确认契约生效须当事人同意、自由民在"私法"上的形式上平等和财产无限制私有等原则，成为后世法律遵循的原则。今天世界上起源于欧洲的两大法系一是产生于英国的"普通法"，范围及于大部分讲英语的国家，一是产生于古罗马的"大陆法"，它覆盖了几乎所有的欧洲国家，其他地区包括我国和日本都受其影响。

二 罗马法特点

罗马法分为公法（*ius publicum*）、私法（*ius privatum*）。按尤士丁尼的说法，涉及罗马帝国政体为公法，涉及个人利益为私法。私法又包括自然法（*ius naturalis*）、万民法（*ius gentium*）和市民法（*ius civile*）。自然法是自然界法律，不独人类所特有，如男女结合为婚姻。它依据的是"所有的人是自然平等的"（*omnes homines natural equales sunt*）推定；市民法是罗马市民之间的法律，旨在确定市民之间的关系；万民法是出自"自然理性而为全人类制定的法"，旨在调整罗马人与外国人关系。[8]罗马法学家乌尔比安（Domitius Ulpianus，公元170？~228年）说，公法涉及城邦组织结构，是有关罗马国家稳定的法，[9]但在罗马法的发展中公法却远不如私法重要。罗马法的目的要为整个罗马世界建立都适用的一般性法律，它从《十二表法》到《尤士丁尼法典》经历了一千余年，又是在多民族融合中形成的，其多样、纷繁自不待言，但所具有统一性和连续性也是显而易见，这就是立法的核心是以公平和正义为原则来保障私人权利，这个原则一直贯穿于罗马私法中。

从宏观上看，罗马法受到希腊的影响。希腊人认为法律是针对人类对不公正的恐惧而设，但把正义与正确混为一谈。罗马人认为正义不是规则的对错，而是要求相同规则适用相同境遇的所有人。罗马人认为，法律是理性、正义的同义词，法律是用一般性法规解决个案，它必须符合公众普遍接受的道德观念，也就是罗马

法必须政治正确。从细节和操作层面上看，比如罗马法庭的要件必须是程序完备和有辩护律师，这也是体现公平的制度设计，这一制度设计成为推动罗马法进步的两个发动机。

罗马法的核心是其公平性、正义性。在词源上，罗马人的法（*ius*）有两层意义，在外部意义上是要求人们遵守的规范。如市民法的"*civile*"一词源于*civitas*（城邦），"城邦"在罗马的含义就有"有秩序的民族"之意。在目的意义上，罗马人使用*aequitas*(公正)一词来阐明法的宗旨，所谓公正就是个人的行为是有条件和有限度的原则，它考虑了个人与群体中他人的关系，对每个人都是一样。[10]个人行为的有条件和有限性是罗马法发展过程中的重要原则。乌尔比安说，研究法（*ius*）的人首先要懂得这个词从"正义"一词而来，正如塞尔苏斯所做的恰当定义："法是善和公正的艺术"。[11]罗马法的价值正在于使罗马人知道法与非法的界限，知道如何去做。

与世界上其他古代法律比较，罗马法有三个特点：一是人定法而不是神意法，二是罗马法重实际，三是罗马私法发达。[12]在任何古代社会法律的发展过程中，神意、神判、宗教和习惯势力退出法律是迟早的事，如郑国、晋国的铸刑鼎。但罗马法与时俱进，更注重实际。《十二表法》的第十二表已有后法优于前法的规定，这一原则至今为现代法律采用。尤其是罗马私法中有关所有权、债权、婚姻、继承权等条文，不仅概念清晰，用词严谨简明，其所蕴涵的平等、公正至上的法律原则使它在今天都有强大的生命力。

罗马私法分为人法、物法和诉讼法三部分。人法是身份法，涉及人的权利能力和行为能力、法律地位、各种权利的取得和丧失以及婚姻等方面的法律。罗马法中"人"的概念却是不断完善的。罗马法规定，权利义务主体只能是人，但并非一切人都是权利主体。罗马人有"*homo*"、"*caput*"和"*persona*"三个"人"的概念。*Homo*是自然人，却不一定是权利义务主体，比如奴隶。*Caput*是法律上的人格。*Persona*由演员角色引伸而来，指某种身份，后用来指权利义务主体的各种身份。罗马法意义上的人还必须具是自由的（*status libertatis*），在市民法里还必须有市民身份（*status* *civitati*）。早先只有贵族家长是权利义务主体，其他家族成员和平民都不是。儿子与奴隶都是家父的财产，可以生杀予夺，只是在公法上儿子有投票权。[13]随着战争和罗马疆域的扩大，权利义务主体逐渐扩大到平民，在《十二表法》中已经承认平民是权利义务主体。到罗马帝国初期，家族的男性子嗣开始普遍享有公权和财产权，妇女、拉丁人和外国人也逐渐取得了部分公私权利。公元212年，卡拉卡拉皇帝（Caracalla，公元186~217年）（见P76图版）颁布著名的"安托尼亚那敕令"（*Constitutio Antoniana*）之后，所有罗马帝国境内的居民都获得市民权，甚至奴隶也逐渐享有限制的私权。权利义务主体之"人"的范围从贵族家长扩展到几乎全体自由人，由此可见随着罗马帝国的发展，罗马法中的"人"的定义也在不断调整。

罗马法以确定和保护罗马公民的权利为目的。奴隶之外，"人生而自由"是罗马法对作为法律对象之人的基本原则，即使奴隶，其身份也非终身不变，他有一定法律地位，甚至有财产继承权。如奴隶可以完成要式买卖、让渡（作为接受人）、要式口约（受承诺人），只是不能作为法律关系的一方当事人。梅因指出，罗马法受"自然法"理论的影响，[14]把奴隶当作财产的趋势逐渐停止。甚至凡是深受罗马法影响并准许有奴隶的地方，其奴隶的状态从来不是那么悲惨。"我们有大量的证据，证明在美国，凡是以高度罗马化的路易斯安那州法典为其法律基础的那些州中，黑种人的命运及其前途，在许多重大方面都比以英国普通法为其基础的制度之下的要好得多。"[15]

罗马法的权利主体是人，一切权利也因人而设。但人必须有自由权、市民权和家族权。自由权主要因出生而取得（父母是自由人，出生的子女也是自由人），被主人释放的奴隶也可以获得。市民权专属罗马市民，有公权（选举权、被选举权）、私权（婚姻权、财产权、遗嘱权和诉讼权等），这个权利从胎儿直到死亡。当时罗马民间有"胎儿或者即将出生的婴儿视同已出生儿"的俗语。[16]胎儿的继承权在《十二表法》已明确规定，罗马法采用"子女身份从母"的原则，母亲怀孕时是自由人，分娩时成为女奴，也不影响所生子女为自由人。"胎儿的利益视为已经出生"这一规定实际上是保护私人财产权。这一著名原则为日后各国民法遵循，实行罗马法的国家很难发生强制引产和溺婴的事情，这也是得益于胎儿在法律上是人以及具有财产继承权的规定。

罗马私法的大部分是物法，个人权利通过物权法、继承法和债权法这三方面的法律得到确认和保障。物权是权利义务主体直接行使于物上之权利。继承法与公民身份和婚姻有关。债权法以"概括继承"（即继承人必须继承所有遗产和债务）原则。[17]罗马法中的物权分为所有权和他物权，所有权是核心，它包括占有、使用、收益、处分、禁止他人对其所有物为任何行为，他物权是对他人所有物直接享有的权利，不能脱离所有权存在。西谚"风能进，雨能进，国王不能进"，依据的就是罗马私法规定所有权具有绝对性、排他性、永续性，这是"普天之下莫非王土"东方专制体系下的法律无法比拟的。

罗马法还有一个重要特点就是契约发达。罗马法的契约是逐步发展完善的。罗马法早期契约(即"耐克逊"，*Nexum*）的缔结多依据信任和友情制定。在《十二表法》中就有了要式口约(*stipulatio*)，以程式化的词句相互问答。如第六表规定，"当有偿还借贷债务或让渡的契约行为时，口头的约定具有约束力。"[18]随着经济贸易的发展，先后出现了四种实物契约、四种合意契约（*consensus*）和文字契约。契约的核心是"诚信"（*fides bona*），在扩张中的罗马世界里，"典型地体现着诚信效力的合意契约(尤其是合意的买卖契约)，恰恰是罗马人的一种创造，在其他地中海民族的法中均不包括这样规则。"[19]如果没有以"合意"为核心的合意契约的完善和发展，罗马帝国经济的强大是无法想象的。

三 罗马法与罗马公民

罗马不是一天建成的，罗马法也不是一天完成的。我们知道今天的"民法"是适用于全体公民之法。民法一词即来源于罗马的"市民法"（*ius civile*）。*Civile*一词是城邦，含有秩序之义。罗马的市民法最早只有贵族才是全权公民，享有各种政治经济权利，相当于今天的公民权。到公元221年卡拉卡拉皇帝取消罗马市民与臣民的区别，授予帝国境内所有居民公民权，罗马法中的市民法与万民法界限就逐渐取消，罗马法也具有了世界性意义。[20]罗马帝国最强盛时，覆盖了从亚得里亚海到幼发拉底河的广大地区，所有被征服的人民都想成为"罗马人"[21]。这和其他任何文明被征服者抗拒征服者完全不一样，对被征服者来说，罗马帝国就是共同的祖国（communis patria）。吉本（Edward Gibbon，公元1737~1794年）指出，罗马人认为他们的文明优于任何文明，被征服国家的精英都会拥抱罗马的价值观和生活方式。在克劳迪乌斯皇帝（Tiberius Claudius Drusus Germanicus，公元前10 ~公元54年）时期，罗马公民约694万，加上统治区域的妇女、儿童和奴隶，总人口数在1.2亿左右，远远超过中国西汉时期的人口总数。"被征服的民族完全和一个伟大的人民融合在一起，便完全放弃重新获得独立的希望，不，甚至连这种愿望也不存在了。他们几乎已不再感觉到罗马的存在与他们自身的存在有什么区别。"[22]那么，罗马的魅力在哪里？其实最根本的魅力就是罗马的公民身份，而罗马法的进步正是围绕扩大罗马人或罗马公民的权利和义务在展开。

罗马与希腊一样是由城邦共和国发展起来，但希腊没有发展出帝国，吉本认为原因在于希腊狭隘的"不容忍外族血统参入的偏狭政策，阻止了雅典与斯巴达的繁荣，并加速了它们的灭亡。"[23]罗马在发展中一改希腊的做法，不断扩大罗马人或者罗马公民的范围，使之最终形成伟大的帝国。其大致有四个阶段：第一阶段是从罗马城邦建城到公元前381年，授予拉丁同盟首领图斯库姆(Tusculum)罗马公民权。第二阶段是拉丁战争结束后（公元前338年），罗马成为意大利半岛的主人，使大约1/4的意大利居民获得公民权。第三阶段是到公元前90年后，所有意大利人都有了罗马公民权。第四阶段在罗马内战之后，把公民权普遍授予行省居民。

罗马市民法中的权利或者说公民权（civitas）是罗马人在政治、法律和财产上的特权（见P256图版）。罗马公民权利主要有投票权（ius suffragiorum）、荣誉权（ius honorum）、交易权（ius commercii）、通婚权（ius connubii）、迁徙权（ius migrationis）、遗嘱权（testamentio factio）、诉讼权（actio）等，还附属有受审权（罗马公民定罪必须通过正式审判，且有辩护权）、刑事豁免权、某些税种的免税权等。罗马的女性和拉丁公民（Latini）没有政治权利但有财产权。罗马行省居民（Provinciales）仅拥有万民法所授予的有限权利。奴隶是财产，但有机会被解放成为自由民，其解放证书由主人颁发，也有皇帝特许颁发。这些权利简单归纳就是有政治权利，比如可以成为公务员，可以批评政府不受跨省逮捕；有经济权利，比如可以分得征服的土地，在上面建私房不会被强拆；有司法权利，比如不用担心起诉官员会败诉，被起诉时可以找律师为自己辩护，不用担心发生躲猫猫死一类倒霉的事情。《圣经·使徒行传》有一则使徒保罗在耶路撒冷被抓住遭受鞭打的记载。保罗质问军官：没有罪证，你们就敢鞭打罗马人，有这样的法律吗？这个例子说明罗马公民是当时社会的有尊严的上等人。正是罗马法有保护公民权利之用，有公平正义之实，被征服者愿意把罗马当成共同的祖国。

罗马法的发展、罗马公民权利的扩大与罗马帝国的扩张是同步的。罗马人通过授予的公民权赢得了盟友和征服地区民众的拥护，逐渐完成占领区的罗马化进程。公民权实际上成为罗马共同体不断壮大的人权武器。罗马早期用授予罗马公民权的方式鼓励外邦人为罗马服役和富人投资罗马。以拉丁人为例，在罗马卫队服役6年（后改为3年）、或建造一艘装载8.75万升的船为罗马运送了6年的小麦、或有20万以上塞斯特斯（sesterces）的钱并在罗马建有房屋、或是在罗马城经营磨坊每天磨了100莫迪小麦[24]都可以成为罗马人。[25]这些与今天一些国家制定的技术移民、投资移民的规定没有什么两样，目的是扩大罗马的兵源和财富。如拉丁同盟战争后，罗马公民人数就从公元前339年的16.5万扩大到公元前319年的25万。

广泛授予公民权带来了好处主要有：一、扩大了兵源，为帝国扩张形成良性循环。罗马军队的主力一向由公民组成，具有罗马公民权才可以获得土地。帝国的扩张可以使他们获得更多土地，更多的公民就意味着更多的兵源和需要更多的土地。《十二表法》的产生，也是因为贵族需要平民的支持长期进行战争的结果。罗马每当兵源不足时，就会采用授予行省居民或外国人以公民权。凯撒为创建高卢兵团就是这样干的。另外罗马也授予参加辅助武装的外国人以公民身份，只要他服役满25年。二、促进了经济的繁荣。罗马是以农民为主体的城邦。公民权的扩大，包括给予奴隶公民权，促进了罗马由城邦发展为帝国，并促进了各地区经济文化的发展。三、在政治上巩固了罗马帝国的社会基础。

罗马人是一种法律身份，罗马法也是一个开放性的法。它的开放性使它具有了世界性，它不根据人的出生而是依据人的意愿，不分肤色、种族、贵贱把各地的人们甚至是奴隶都变成罗马人，变成罗马公民。希腊学者Dionigo di Alicarnasso说：罗马人注定要成为最伟大的民族……，因为他们慷慨地把避难权授予那些需要庇护的人，把罗马市民权授予那些在战争中英勇作战的人，把市民权授予被解放的奴隶，不蔑视任何人。"[26]罗马法以体现"人民的权力"为整个法律体制不可变更的核心，人们也在罗马法的框架内生存和寻求正义。正如西塞罗说，正义是在法律中发现，"因为法律是一种自然力。它是聪明人的理智和理性，是衡量正义非正义的标准。"[27]成为罗马人就意味着在法律上能够得到正义的保护，帝国的各色人等对自己拥有罗马人的身份与有荣焉也在情理之中，这和今天许多人以成为美国人为荣倒是十分的相似。

四 结 语

罗马法是奴隶制社会的产物，除开把奴隶作为财产看待一类身份性的压迫条文之外，就"罗马人"的权利而言，它是当时世界上最好的法律。恩格斯曾说："罗马法是纯粹私有制占统治的社会的生产条件和冲突的十分经典性的法律表现，以致一切后来的法律都不能对它作任何实质性的修改。"[28]《十二表法》公布后一直到优士丁尼编纂法典的近千年中，罗马的历代统治者从来都没有以明文直接废止它。罗马法尤其是罗马私法的完备体系一直影响到今天的大陆法，这是罗马帝国的伟大贡献。

罗马法以公平正义之名而立，其《自然法》依据的就是"平等"、"自由"、"理性"，这日后成为人权运动的法律武器。在《市民法》中，法既然是"善"

与"公正"的艺术，它自必鼓励更多的公民用法律武器来保障自己的权利。在《万民法》中，罗马人摒弃希腊人的法律"平等"概念而引入以"正义、良心和公正"为原则的"衡平"（equitas）概念，主张在法律和公平发生冲突时公平优先。它依据"自然"固有秩序、等差之事实，使《万国法》成为处理各国之间的法律关系方便工具，也成为日后英国《衡平法》的来源。

罗马法的《契约法》的进步具有里程碑的意义。契约由《十二表法》的"耐克逊（Nexum）发端，到《法学阶梯》的诺成契约（Contractus consensu），契约作为当事人合意的产物具有法律效力，已基本具备了现代民法的"契约自由"原则。梅因的名言说："所有进步社会的运动，到此处为止，都是一个'从身份到契约'的运动。"[29]罗马法的"契约自由"原则对人类社会的进步所起的作用也是无法估量的。

值得一提的是，在罗马帝国，"法律就必定是（国家）最大的善之一。"[30]罗马帝国上至君主，下至平民都极为看重罗马法。西塞罗说，当时罗马最优秀之人的职能就是向人们解释法律。法律也非君主随意制定，法学家的法律解释也能成为法律。罗马帝国的优秀学者以法律为终身事业者比比皆是。我国仅秦汉时期儒生经、律兼修，曹魏以降，经与律学渐分，律令逐渐沦为寒门技艺。[31]东西方的法律史虽不能完全对应比照，但中国的士大夫轻律重经的事实表明，他们在儒学的浸淫下无法成为关注公平正义、保护个人权利的知识分子，只能是天命、王道、皇权的仆人。

注 释：

1. 周枏：《罗马法原论（上册）》，商务印书馆，1994年，页10。

2. 桑德罗·斯奇巴尼（Sandro Schipani）著，张礼洪译：《罗马法体系的典型特征》，《法学》2006年第12期。

3. 特洛伊的英雄，罗马诗人维吉尔曾以此创作长诗《伊尼德》。

4. 普鲁塔克：《希腊罗马名人传（上册）》，商务印书馆，1995年，页41~51。

5. 朱塞佩·格罗索（Giuseppe Grosso）：《罗马法史》，中国政法大学出版社，1994年，页78。

6. 邢义田编译：《古罗马的荣光——罗马史料选译（I）》，远流出版社，1998年，页113~126。

7. 梅因（H. S. Maine）：《古代法》，商务印书馆，1959年，页9。

8. 查士丁尼：《法学总论》，商务印书馆，1984年，页6~7。

9. 朱塞佩·格罗索：《罗马法史》，中国政法大学出版社，1994年，页109。

10. 彭梵得（pietro Bonfante）：《罗马法教科书》，中国政法大学出版社，1996年，页4。

11. R. H. 巴洛基：《罗马人》，上海人民出版社，2000年，页229。

12. 周枏：《罗马法原论（上册）》，商务印书馆，1994年，页9。

13. 巴里·尼古拉斯：《罗马法概论》，法律出版社，2004年，页70。

14. 罗马法深受希腊斯多噶学派的影响。斯多噶学派的认为"自然"是一切事务的逻辑和秩序，是理性体系。"自然法"就是将自然理性注入人心的道德法。罗马法的"平等"、"权利"、"统一"等概念都源于此。

15. 梅因：《古代法》，商务印书馆，1959年，页95。

16. 彭梵得：《罗马法教科书》，中国政法大学出版社，1996年，页30。

17. 有学者认为，罗马私法的物权其实是财产（拥有）和债物（应当拥有），继承并不属于财产。尼古拉斯：《罗马法概论·物法》，法律出版社，2004年。

18. 邢义田编译：《古罗马的荣光——罗马史料选译（I）》，远流出版社，1998年，页119。

19. 朱塞佩·格罗索（Giuseppe Grosso）：《罗马法史》，中国政法大学出版社，1994年，页237。

20. 拉卡拉授予非罗马人以市民权，有出于税收方面的考虑，因为罗马市民要交5~10%的遗产税和解放奴隶税，另有宗教方面的考虑，希望行省居民信仰罗马教，以抵制基督教的传播。

21. "'罗马人'是一个法律概念，任何种族的人都可能成为罗马公民。"理查德·詹金斯（Richard Jenkyns）：《罗马的遗产》，上海人民出版社，2002年，页8。

22. 爱德华·吉本（Edward Gibbon）：《罗马帝国衰亡史(上册)》，商务印书馆，1997年，页41~42。

23. 爱德华·吉本：《罗马帝国衰亡史(上册)》，页32。

24. 1塞斯特斯＝400as铜币，1莫迪（*ModiiI*）8.91公升。

25. 盖尤斯：《法学阶梯》，中国政法大学出版社，1996年，页10。

26. 同注2。

27. 西塞罗：《法律篇》，商务印书馆，1999年，页152。

28. 恩格斯：《论封建制度的瓦解和民族国家的产生》，《马克思恩格斯全集（卷21）》，人民出版社，1965年，页454。

29. 梅因：《古代法》，商务印书馆，1959年，页97。

30. 西塞罗：《法律篇》，商务印书馆，1999年，页182。

31. 邢义田：《秦汉的律令学》，《治国安邦》，中华书局，2011年，页61。

In the Name of Fairness and Justice: The Laws of Rome and the Roman Citizenry

(abridged)

Researcher, Hubei Provincial Museum   Wang Jichao

The ancient Greek and Roman civilizations are the foundation of modern Western civilization. In terms of their impact on the world, ancient Greece has left us with the legacy of democracy, science and philosophy, while the basis for modern legal systems came from ancient Rome. In the more recent modernization process of Europe, "the resurgence of Roman law" was one of the "three major thought movements of Europe" along with the Renaissance and the Reformation, thereby forming the foundation of modern Western society.

1. The Origins of Roman Law

Roman law was the product of a slave-owning society and arose from the early customs of Roman society, and is the amalgam of the legal principles, structure and customs of ancient Rome. In early Rome, there was both divine law *(fas)* and customary law. The nobles and religious leaders held the right of interpretation of the law in an environment with no central legal authority. Roman law then evolved from customary law to statutory law as a result of conflict between the plebeians and the patricians, with a landmark change occurring in 449 BCE with the Law of the Twelve Tables completed by a committee of ten men. The Twelve Tables were a reflection of the Roman principles of respect for humanity and individual privacy, which later became the pillars of Roman law. Justinian Rome saw an overhaul of the majority of existing Roman law with the completion of the Body of Civil Law *(Corpus Iuris Civilis)* which was grounded in legal concepts and rigorously utilized technical terms that were clear and concise. In particular, the Roman requirement that the validity of a contract is dependent on the relevant Parties' agreement, the understanding that free individuals were equal under "private law", and the principle of the private ownership of property in perpetuity were all concepts that were retained in the legal systems of later generations.

2. Characteristics of Roman Law

Roman law comprised public laws *(ius publicum)*, laws which concerned the body politic of the Roman Empire, and private laws *(ius privatum)*, which had to do with the individual's interests. The fundamental basis for Roman law was fairness and justice, the principle of which may be discerned across Roman private law. Compared to other legal systems found in the ancient world, Roman law had three distinguishing characteristics. First, Roman laws were secular laws rather than divine laws. Second, Roman law had an emphasis on the practical. Third, Roman private law was highly developed. This was especially true with statutes on rights of ownership, debts, marriage and property inheritance, which were conceptually clear and used technical terms in a rigorous manner. The principles of fairness and justice underlying these laws ensure that these laws continue to find life in the world today.

Roman law was written to confirm and protect the rights of Roman citizens. With the exception of slaves, the basic belief underlying Roman law was "beings are born free". In fact, even slaves had a certain legal position within Roman society, and were even given property inheritance rights.

A large part of Roman private law was dedicated to material law, and an individual's rights to property, inheritance and debts were guaranteed. There is a Western saying that goes: "the wind may enter, the rain may enter, but the King may not", which refers to the absolute, exclusive and perpetual nature of citizens' rights in ancient Rome. This is something that was never found in the autocracies of the East. Roman law is also known for the advanced development of contract law. Good faith, or *fides bona*, was regarded as the cornerstone of the contract, and the advanced state of Roman contract law was one factor in the prosperity of the Roman Empire.

3. Roman Law and the Roman Citizenry

Rome was not built in a single day, and it was the same with Roman law. What was so attractive about ancient Rome? The appeal lay in the identity of the Roman citizen, for the evolution of Roman law centered on the rights and obligations of Roman citizens and Greater Romans alike. Roman law protected the rights of its citizens and promoted fairness and justice. Becoming a Roman meant receiving just protection under the laws of the Empire, encouraging conquered peoples to regard Rome as their common homeland.

4. Conclusion

Roman law was the product of a slave-owning society, and apart from the oppressive clauses targeted at slaves who were regarded as mere property, "Romans" enjoyed the best legal protection for their time. Roman law was promulgated in the name of fairness and justice, and its contribution in terms of the principles of "Contract Law" and "Freedom of Contract" to the progress of human society cannot be underestimated.

It is worth mentioning that in the Roman Empire the best scholars often made their lifelong careers in law-related vocations. On the other hand, in China only scholars during the Qin and Han Dynasties were required to read both the Confucian classics as well as legal texts. After the Six Dynasties period, it was only the poor who undertook legal studies. Although it is not possible to conduct a direct comparison between Western and Eastern legal systems, it is fair to say that China's scholars did not put a premium on legal thinking, preferring to expend their energies on Confucian thought instead. As such, they were not intelligentsia who defended fairness and justice as well as individual human rights; instead, they remained the faithful servants of the Divine, the King and his powers.

罗马帝国之城市建筑

佛罗伦萨大学 建筑系教授　欧金尼奥·马特拉

　　帝国时期的罗马文化精髓莫过于其建筑艺术与城市构造。公元前31年，马克·安东尼（Mark Antony）败于阿克提姆岬（Actium）战役，从此独裁式统治的稳固政权开始形成。这就是历史上赫赫有名的罗马帝国。帝王一人独揽大权后对包括建筑在内的诸多领域有着深远的影响，明显的一点就是越来越多的资源可以有组织地为公众提供资助。

　　在建筑领域，举国上下大规模施行公共建筑项目。其中，修复和完善尤利乌斯·凯撒（Julius Caesar）时代的遗留工程成为首要之举。作为歌颂君权的重要手段，修建工程中对公共设施、市民工程以及宗教场所都赋予了象征性元素。这对稳固政体意义重大。也因如此，帝国时期的建筑物并无特定风格，而是直接借鉴并融合了古希腊时期的古典传统建筑和意大利伊特鲁利亚艺术细节。

　　历史学家一致认为，"奥古斯都古典主义"（Augustan classicism）有效扼制了上世纪共和体制下兴起的自主创新。于强盛的帝国统治期间完工的建筑虽气势恢宏，设计独特，但其真正新意并不体现于个体建筑物本身，而是它们于城市格局中的传播和组织影响力。单一建筑比不上公共建筑汇聚产生的宏伟气势，然而帝国时期所建城市同性质的结构体现了罗马帝国非同凡响的主导地位。迄今为止，这点仍能在诸多国家与其各异的文化中感受一二。此外，建筑方面，城市基础设施的建设是体现罗马帝国权势的最好佐证之一：桥梁、渡槽以及道路至今都能显现出古代公共建筑群卓尔不凡的价值。

　　在罗马帝国不断扩张期间，罗马城始终是罗马不容置疑的政权中心。扩张使得欧洲、北非以及小亚细亚区域的每个角落都烙上了罗马的印记。殖民城市、自由城市和纳贡城市，这些不同类型城市的历史沉淀铸就了罗马帝国的特色。据估计，罗马帝国在衰退之前拥有大约5600个独立城邦。正是于罗马帝国统治时期，随着城市概念的逐步形成，西方人历史上第一次体会到了所谓的开放世界，即法律和秩序优先及所有人都享有公民权益的概念。

　　罗马城市的文明形成源于两大艺术源流：伊特鲁利亚（Etruscan）文化和希腊（Hellenic）文化。在融合了伊特鲁利亚人的建筑技术和古希腊建筑成就之后，罗马进行了自主创新，并塑造出一个宏伟国度的非凡城市形象。通过吸收临近北部地区的伊特鲁利亚文明，罗马文化将宗教信仰和对神的情感与城市建设和发展联系在一起。每座城市建立之前，都会请祭司进行预言讲道，并利用犁沟出城市的边界。

　　此外，城市建设根据基本方位点来定向，以符合自然规律。

　　城市呈方形建设，布局特色是将南北走向的大道（cardo）和东西走向的大道（decumano）作为主干道。Cardo和decumano在城市中心地带交汇，从而引申出"中心"的概念。市中心矗立着宗教建筑和广场，类似于集市（Agora）广场和雅典卫城的罗马建筑交相辉映，彰显宏伟气势。迄今帝国麾下区域的许多其他城市，仍能体现罗马城市规划的精髓。阿尔吉利亚提姆加德市规整，棋盘式格局分布，柱廊环绕大街，两条主要道路Cardo和decumano十字相交，交汇处建有广场，剧院，公共休闲场所，典型的城市布局尽显无遗，因此被称之为"规整的生活场所"。

从英国的切斯特（Chester）到小亚细亚的安提俄克（Antioch）和以弗所（Ephesus），此种类型的规划在整个帝国随处可见。城市的理想规模为2400×1600英尺。出于防御目的，城市规模不能超出该范围。新城按照最多容纳50,000人口的标准来建设。

罗马城的建设使得城市与农村环境间的平衡恰到好处，而确定这些城市规模和居民容纳数的理想数值，是其取得成功的主要因素之一。在很多地区，城市周边的疆土也纳入"几何化"的城市布局范围，同时布局也勾勒了城市外围田地的划分和道路的方向和线性设计。罗马式的区划法"centuriation"这种城市布局体系使得意大利东部的达尔马提亚（Dalmatic）以及北非景观迄今仍保持一致。

罗马城市规划有着非常鲜明的历史烙印，其主导地位也保持了几个世纪。虽然欧洲城市空间布局历经了各类变迁，但直到18世纪才涌现出大量实质性的艺术创新。毫无疑问，尽管沿习了古希腊的建筑艺术，但罗马建筑的重要性和价值并不在于建筑本身的华丽，罗马城本身足以证明这一点，工程师的杰出才华与军队的支持完美结合，铸就了众多辉煌雄伟的公共建筑。

建于公元前6世纪的大型污水处理系统马克西姆下水道规模庞大，是古代罗马最为宏伟的建筑工程之一。帝国时期的罗马已发展成为拥有百万居民的大都市，而该下水道也紧跟其脚步发挥其重要的作用。该建筑修建非常牢固，即使今天也仍在投入使用。

很多历史学家指出，希腊人建造城市注重其美观性和军事防御，而罗马人更多注重铺路和水源供应、排污体系的建设。公元前321年，克劳迪乌斯负责修建了罗马第一条真正意义上的道路——阿庇安古道（The Appian Way）。帝国时代统治期间，所有的城市道路都由石头铺设。罗马工程师的预期方案，如通过水平层面划分区域来分离行人和车辆，在若干世纪后，被列奥纳多·达·芬奇作为基本规范所采用。不是所有的城市要素都由罗马人发明，其中有不少要素在罗马帝国建立之前已经得到广泛的应用。而罗马帝国的优势在于让这些要素成为城市建设须具备的"最低要求"。

总而言之，正因为罗马帝国的城市建设或扩张，不同文化因有相似的空间特征才得以在城市环境下和谐共存。事实上，如今已统一在欧盟名下的昔日各国，其有利条件之一是都有着共同的特征。

Architecture and the City in the Roman Empire

Eugenio Martera, Professor, Faculty of Architecture, University of Florence

The architectural works and structure of a city were important aspects of Roman culture during the Imperial period. With the victory over Mark Antony at the battle of Actium in 31 BCE, a stable political system was established based on an authoritarian structure historically defined as the Roman Empire. Power concentrated solely in the hands of the Emperor alone led to important consequences also in the field of architecture, with increased and institutionalized recourse to public patronage.

In the architectural field, a large-scale program of public works was implemented, initially with the resumption and completion of the sites and projects inherited from Julius Caesar. Public, civic and religious buildings were infused with symbolic significance and played an important role in political stabilization. Also for these reasons, the architecture of the period, although not definable as a single style, showed a marked classical and traditional tendency seen in the recurrent reproduction of Greek models and in recourse to Italic and Etruscan detail.

Historians agree on the observation that "Augustan classicism" did much to curb the autonomous innovation that took place during the last century of the Republic. Although often remarkable, it was not the single architectural works realized throughout the vast empire that represented true innovation, but rather their diffusion and organization in the form of a city. The combined power of public works, rather than their individual aspect, and the homogeneous structure of cities built during the Imperial period that still today represent an exceptional common denominator in so great a number of different countries and cultures. Moreover, one of the best examples of the power of Imperial Rome in architecture can be seen in structures which do not represent power, but rather embody the city's infrastructure: bridges, aqueducts and roads that still today provide outstanding insight into the value attributed to public works in ancient times.

The Roman Empire originated from the expansion of the city of Rome, which remained the sole, undisputed center of power. The characteristics of this expansion left the mark of the city of Rome everywhere in Europe, North Africa and Asia Minor. The Empire was characterized by the foundation of different types of cities: colonial cities, free cities, tributary cities. It is estimated that just before its decline, the Roman Empire consisted of approximately 5600 separate civic units. In the history of the formation of the concept of a city, it can be said that during the Roman Empire, western man, for the first time, perceived an open world in which law and order prevailed and the concept of citizenship was a privilege shared by all.

The origins of the Roman city derived directly from two important civilizations: Etruscan and Hellenic. From each it inherited various characteristics, but produced an autonomous and singular model that, as we have seen, gave rise to the urban image of a very vast area. Roman culture drew on the Etruscan civilization in nearby northern areas for religious implications and superstitions connected with the foundation and development of its cities. Before each city was founded, presages were interpreted and the city boundaries were traced with a plough of a priest.

In addition, the city was oriented according to the cardinal points so as to relate to a universal order.

Cities were rectangular in shape and the urban layout featured two main roads known as the *cardo* and *decumano*, respectively running from north to south and east to west. The *cardo* and *decumano* intersected in the center of the city, giving rise to the concept of a "center", where stood the religious buildings and the forum, the Roman equivalent of the *agora* and the *acropolis* united in a single space. The merits of Roman town planning can still be seen today in many towns throughout the areas united by the Empire. The city of Timgad, with its checkerboard layout, portico-covered avenues, and the presence at the *cardo* and *decumano* crossroads of the forum, theater and public conveniences, represents a typical city layout intended as "a structured living place".

This typology can be seen all over the empire, from Chester in England to Antioch and Ephesus in Asia Minor. The ideal size was 2400 by 1600 feet. Anything larger was considered detrimental for defensive purposes. New cities were built to accommodate a maximum population of 50,000.

The definition of these optimal measurements was one of the main values of a Roman city which, of this size and with this number of inhabitants, succeeded in keeping an excellent balance between the urban and rural environment. In many areas, the "geometrization" of the urban layout also regarded the territory surrounding the city, and outlined the division of fields and the direction and linearity of the roads outside the city. This system of "centuriation" still today unifies the landscapes of Italy, Dalmatia and North Africa.

Thus, the main characteristics of a Roman city were so dominant that they remained unaltered for many centuries and it can be said that although European urban space underwent various changes, it was not subject to any substantial innovations until the 1700s. Without a doubt, the importance and value of Roman architecture cannot be attributed to works of great aesthetic value even though of unequivocal Hellenistic derivation. For proof of this, suffice it to examine the city of Rome itself, where the work of engineers and the military combined masterfully to produce great public works.

One of the greatest feats of Roman engineering is considered to be the *Cloaca Maxima*, the great sewage system built in the VI century BCE on such a monumental scale that it was still functional even when Rome became a metropolis of 1 million inhabitants during the Empire. It was so sturdily built that even today, great stretches of it are still in use.

Many historians have pointed out how, in building a city, the Greeks were concerned above all with aesthetics and fortifications, while the Romans were more concerned with paving roads and supplying the city with adequate water and sewage systems. In 321 BCE, Appius Claudius had the first authentic Roman road built, the Appian Way, and during the Imperial period almost all city roads were paved. Roman engineers anticipated solutions postulated many centuries later by Leonardo da Vinci such as separating vehicular from pedestrian traffic through differentiating levels. Not all these urban endowments were of Roman invention; many had already been applied in times and places preceding Imperial Rome. The merit of the Roman Empire was that of having made them the "minimum requirements" for a city.

To conclude, thanks to cities founded or expanded during the Roman Empire, a great number of different cultures now live in urban environments with similar spatial characteristics. In fact, one of the benefits of the unity of those countries that have today been brought together under the name of Europe is precisely that of having this characteristic in common.

希贝尔尼亚 HIBERNI
不列颠 BRITAIN
伦敦 LONDON
日耳曼海 GERMAN OCEAN
莱茵河 RHINE
维斯杜拉河 VISTULA
大西洋 ATLANTICA OCEAN
科隆 COLOGNE
梅兹 METZ
日耳曼 GERMAN
卢瓦尔河 LOIRE
高卢 GAUL
多瑙河 DANUBE
里昂 LYON
阿尔卑斯山 ALPS
波河 PO
伊利里库姆 ILLYRICUM
达西 DAC
隆河 RHONE
意大利 ITALY
萨洛纳 SALONA
塔古斯河 TAGUS
科西嘉 CORSICA
亚得里亚海 ADRIATIC SEA
默西 MERC
罗马 ROME
色雷 THR
西班牙 SPAIN
撒丁 SARDINIA
腓立比 PHILIP
第勒尼安海 TYRRHENIAN SEA
马其顿 MACEDONIA
爱琴海 AEGEAN SEA
毛里塔尼亚 MAURITANIA
迦太基 CARTHAGE
西西里 SICILY
叙拉古 SYRACUSE
雅典 ATHENS
努米底亚 NUMIDIA
地中海 MEDITERRANENA SEA
克里特 CRET
阿非利加 AFRICA
昔兰尼 CYRENE
昔兰尼加 CYRENAICA

凯撒时代(公元前44年)的罗马帝国
Roman Empire to death of Caesar, 44BCE

奥古斯都时代(公元14年)的罗马帝国
Roman Empire to death of Augustus,14CE

图拉真时代（公元117年）的罗马帝国
Roman Empire to death of Trajan,117CE

罗马帝国的领土
Temporarily ruled territory of the Roman Empire

罗马帝国疆域图
MAP OF THE ROMAN EMPIRE

　　罗马在共和国最后的两百年得以最强势的扩张。在图拉真皇帝时期(公元98~117年)达到了鼎盛。在其极度的扩张后，罗马帝国的疆域北面包括不列颠与莱茵河以西、多瑙河以南所有的欧洲大陆，以及亚洲幼发拉底河以西的大部分、北非的沿海区域和所有的地中海岛屿。

　　The Rome achieved most of its expansion during the last two centuries of the Republic, and reached its greatest extent under the emperor Trajan (98-117 CE). At its maximum expansion, the Roman Empire encompassed Britain in the North, all of continental Europe west of the Rine and south of the Danube, most of Asis west of the Euphrates River, the coastal areas of Northern Africa and all the Mediterranean islands.

图 版
PLATES

导 言

佛罗伦萨国家考古博物馆馆长　吉斯皮娜·卡洛塔·钱菲诺尼

　　为了让人们了解和欣赏源于意大利的伟大文明，我们特举办罗马帝国文化、艺术展以飨公众。举办者相信，文物本身所包含的视觉信息是传达展览所蕴含的史实和文献意义的最佳方式。

　　此次展览最重要的目标是加深人们对罗马帝国时期的了解和兴趣，我们将竭尽所能为您呈现古罗马文化的璀璨历史。

　　得益于考古的研究成果，我们如今已拥有大量可供呈现罗马文化的艺术遗产。我们从中选择出最为人珍视的艺术品并将其呈现于您的眼前。通过展示最有文化特色和艺术特点的文物，我们能揭示出罗马文明的一般面貌和特质。此展览为公众提供尽可能全面了解罗马文明的艺术品和古罗马世界的机会。

　　展览的宗旨是传达明确清晰的信息。为此，我们精心挑选能明确呈现帝国时代下古罗马生活和艺术精髓的文物。另外，承办方必须格外注意文物的陈列顺序和环境布局，使之有内在的逻辑联系和易于观看。对于大量封存多年的文物来说，此次展览是极富新意的，也正因为如此，应予以极大的关注和赞赏。

　　此次展览重点展示从公元前1世纪到公元3世纪中叶罗马帝国巅峰时期的君主文化。公元前27年，罗马时代真正的转折点"罗马纪元（Urbe）"出现了。这一年，罗马元老院授予屋大维以奥古斯都的尊号，屋大维即为罗马帝国的开国皇帝。罗马黄金时代从此拉开帷幕。然而，公元244年，由元老院推举的最后一位皇帝戈尔迪安三世死去，罗马帝国随之衰落。这是罗马霸权终结的明显标志。自此，罗马城和意大利不再是帝国政治和经济的中心。其实，衰落趋势的征兆早在塞维鲁王朝便已出现，公众和社会生活的新观念和新方式在那时候开始在帝国内部流行。戴克里先（公元284～305年）统治时期，这一系列的变革削弱了帝国基础，对整个帝国政治和社会结构的转变具有深刻影响。随着罗马帝国的衰落，蛮夷国家日益强大，并形成了欧洲中世纪的国家雏形。

　　此次罗马帝国展共收集展品近300件，主要来自托斯卡纳各博物馆，尤其是意大利佛罗伦萨国家考古博物馆。展品分6个主题，其中有大量成套的硬币、陶器、瓦器、玻璃器、雕像、瓮罐和精美的石棺雕刻、大理石雕塑及小青铜器和珠宝。

　　我要强调的是，此次展览我们主要关注的是挑选最具代表性的罗马艺术文化品，它们在体现罗马帝国整体风貌上，远胜于那些反映军事或意识形态的器物。此次展览所涵盖的罗马帝国时代的文物事实上已不仅只是罗马及其居民艺术品位的反映，也是融合了不同文化和不同历史时期遗产的整个罗马帝国的文化遗产。

后世欧洲艺术文化的发展正是因汲取了罗马文明的独特之处，罗马文明也因此被视为共同的历史根源。罗马艺术决定了整个欧洲大陆的艺术品位，推动了各地的艺术创作。罗马艺术除了那些固有的、无可争议的价值之外，也因帝国内不同文化的融合保留了独有的鲜明特色，具有极高的普世价值和历史意义。

实际上，罗马艺术主要突出的特点是折中主义。它糅合了古意大利、伊特鲁利亚和希腊元素于一体，最终形成其无可挑剔的独特风格。此外，罗马艺术作品采用现实主义手法，并讨厌过于理想化、符号化或程式化的风格。罗马艺术形式风格多样，不能简单地归结为罗马帝国年复一年的自然发展，而是罗马帝国强势扩张的产物。

在帝国时代，随着罗马军团驰骋疆土，罗马帝国的霸权扩展到整个西方文明世界。与此同时，罗马文明因融合其被征服地的文化差异而变得日益庞杂。

古罗马人不喜欢纯粹的唯美主义，无用之物在他们看来是不可思议的。在他们数量庞大的艺术遗产中，即使是奢侈手工艺品也有不同功用。考古学家发现了大量使用贵金属或青铜制作、饰有精致图案及采用模子制作的精美陶瓶，大量的小雕像、宝石和浮雕宝石。除物品本身的美学价值，罗马人喜爱这些并非其美学价值而是看重它们所象征的权力和财富。

在帝国时代前期，一些袖珍艺术品，如雕刻宝石、金属浮雕工艺品和带浮雕的陶器在艺术表达上的呈现已至巅峰。

在雕塑和浅浮雕艺术品中，肖像是罗马艺术最具特色的组成部分。这些雕像的制作目的是为歌颂罗马社会精英，或置于丧葬的场合。

在这里我想强调一下本展览所展示物品的另一重要意义：这些物品都拥有伟大的艺术和历史价值。认识当下的唯一方式是了解我们的历史，因此我们都负有不可推卸的责任去保护和保留这些文化和艺术遗产，因为他们让我们能够重新审视和构建我们文明的不同阶段。

INTRODUCTION

Giuseppina Carlotta Cianferoni, Director of Museo Archeologico Nazionale di Firenze

The proposal for an exhibition dedicated to the culture and art of Imperial Rome came from the desire to increase awareness and appreciation of this great civilisation that originated in ancient Italy. This project was organized with the conviction that the visual messages contained within artifacts are absolutely the most efficient instrument for conveying the meaning of the information and documentation contained within the exhibition.

It seemed to us that the most important objective of this exhibition should be to create a picture of ancient Roman culture during the Imperial age that is as complete and detailed as possible, in order to create a deeper understanding and appreciation of the period.

Thanks to archaeological research, we now have at our disposal a huge artistic legacy that enables us to choose among its works of art, those pieces that can be definitely regarded as the most significant ones. By exhibiting them, we can address both general themes and specific aspects of the Roman civilisation focusing on its most characteristic cultural and artistic features. This exhibition offers the public the opportunity to become acquainted with the outstanding artistic production of this civilisation, while also providing a general overview of the ancient Rome world.

With the criteria to give clear and direct pieces of information, we have chosen to exhibit objects that can readily depict and convey the essence of ancient Rome life and art during the Imperial age. Great attention has been paid to the arrangement of the artifacts and their order is intended to form a neat, logical framework. This context has given new meaning to a large number of the objects that have not been exhibited for many years and that, on the contrary, deserve greater attention and admiration.

The exhibition focuses on the Roman culture of the Emperors and, in particular, on those centuries when Rome was at the apex of its powers, that it is to say from the 1st century BCE to the middle of the 3rd century CE. 27 BCE can be considered the real turning point in the history of the "Urbe". In that year, indeed, the Roman Senate conferred the title of Augustus upon Octavian and elected him first Roman Emperor. This was the beginning of the golden age of Rome. On the contrary, the decline on the Roman Empire began in 244 CE when Gordianus III, the last Emperor elected by the Senate, died. This occurrence clearly marked the end of Roman hegemony. From that year on, Rome and Italy ceased to be the center of the political and economic power of the Empire. The first signs of this trend can be traced back to the Severan Dynasty when new ideas and new ways of conceiving of both public and social life began to impose themselves. During the reign of Diocletian (284 - 305 CE), these changes deeply affected and transformed the political and social structure of the whole Empire undermining its foundation. After the fall of Roman Empire, barbarian states strengthened and formed the basis of the future national states that shaped the Middle Ages in Europe.

This exhibition, Imperial Rome, assembles three hundred objects, primarily belonging to museums in Tuscany and in particular, the National Museum of Archaeology of Florence, Italy. Among the objects, are a large suite of coins, pieces of pottery, earthenware and glassware, portraits, urns, sarcophagus reliefs, marble statues, small bronzes and jewellery. They are distributed in six thematic sections.

Let me stress once again that one of our main concerns in the selection of the objects for this exhibition, was to focus attention on the strength of what can be called the Roman artistic culture that succeeded in unifying the extensive empire better that any army or ideology. Indeed, above all during the Imperial Age that is encompassed in this exhibition, Roman fine arts gradually ceased being simply the artistic expression of Rome and its inhabitants and evolved into the heritage of the entire Empire, melding together different cultural and historical legacies.

European artistic cultures owe much of their future development to this unique feature of Roman civilization that they all regard as the common historical root. Roman art shaped the taste of an entire continent and gave impetus to local artisan productions. Besides its intrinsic and undisputed value, Roman art is also universally and historically significant because it preserves the unique and distinctive features of all the different cultures annexed in the Empire.

In fact, the main and outstanding peculiarity of Roman Art is its eclecticism that succeeded in synthesizing Italic, Etruscan and Greek elements in a perfect and unique style. Moreover, Roman works of art are characterised by a well-balanced realism averse to any excessive idealization, symbolism or stylisation. Roman Art shows a great variety of forms and styles that cannot simply be ascribed to its natural chronological development but that are the outcome of the Roman expansionary attitude.

Indeed while its Legions conquered territories and spread Rome hegemony to the entire western civilised world during the Imperial Age, the Roman civilisation absorbed the different cultures it came into contact with, becoming more rich and heterogeneous.

The ancient Romans did not love pure aestheticism; the idea of objects being an end in themselves was simply inconceivable. Among their huge artistic legacy, even luxury handicrafts have different significance. Archaeologists have brought to light a large number of wonderful vases made of precious metals or bronze and decorated with refined figurative patterns together with ceramic ones manufactured on their model, and a large number of little statues, gemstones and cameos. Romans appreciated all these objects not for their aesthetic value but because they represented and emphasized the power and wealth of their owners.

During the first half of the Imperial Age, some of the so called minor arts such as glyptics, toreutics and ceramics in relief, came to the height of their artistic expressiveness.

As far as sculpture and bas-reliefs are concerned, portraits are the most distinctive attribute of Roman art. They were intended to celebrate eminent figures of Roman society or to be inserted into funerary contexts.

Please let me stress another important aspect of the objects displayed in this exhibition: they are all of great artistic and historical value. The only way to understand the present is to know our history; for this reason we all have a responsibility to protect and preserve the cultural and artistic heritage that allows us to reconsider and reconstruct the different phases of our civilisation.

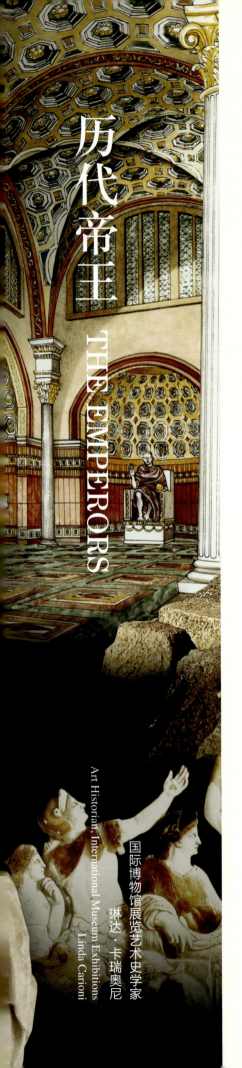

历代帝王

THE EMPERORS

国际博物馆展览艺术史学家
Art Historian, International Museum Exhibitions

琳达·卡瑞奥尼
Linda Carioni

公元前8世纪，罗马发源于台伯河岸边的一个小村庄。罗马帝国时代公元前27年至公元前4世纪中期左右，罗马的政治、经济、军事力量已然在西方文明世界中占主导地位。而在罗马帝国势力范围扩大的同时，其文化影响也得到了最大化。

公元前5世纪，罗马共和国成立。在元老院（相当于现在的参议院）的领导下，罗马成立了自己的政治体制，同时在地中海地区进行军事扩张。然而，公元前1世纪，元老院执政危机引发了罗马内战。这场意义非凡的争战导致罗马共和国走向消亡。罗马帝国应运而生。罗马成功地扩张了其领地后，面临着由元老院代表的旧统治阶级和为平民阶级伸张民权和政治权利的新兴社会力量之间的冲突。最终，拥有军队支持的平民利益获得了胜利。公元前60年，元老院被迫承认了由凯撒、庞培和克拉苏组成的"前三头同盟"（Triumvirate）的合法地位。尤利乌斯·凯撒不断征服外族领地的行为招致了同僚和元老院的憎恨。公元前45年，他最终击败了所有反对他的人，施行了独裁统治。在元老院的存亡之际，他们于公元前44年3月15日密谋刺杀了凯撒，但这个举动并不足以改变共和国的命运。由马克·安东尼、屋大维和雷必达组成的"后三头同盟"（Second Triumvirate）诞生了，新的矛盾随之产生。公元前30年，屋大维在亚克提姆海战中大获全胜，事件也以马克·安东尼和克利奥帕特拉在亚历山大的自杀而告终。

公元前27年，屋大维接受了元老院赐予的荣誉"奥古斯都"，成为了第一位罗马皇帝。依循罗马共和国的形式和传统，他务实地回应着罗马当时所存在的各种问题，并确保其统辖范围有着长期稳定性和繁荣昌盛。他的权力涉及到整个罗马领土和所有城中最高的统帅和官员。此权利虽永久，却也需要每年由元老院授予。然而他真正的力量却源自于其个人魅力所奠定，也因此赋予了他日后无与伦比的声望。像所有罗马人一样，他也有三个名字，其中"凯撒大帝·奥古斯都"的称号最得日后帝王们的高度赞誉。他还有一个由罗马人民自己命名的民间称号"元首"，意为罗马第一公民，以区别于首个专制政府的第一个皇帝称号。奥古斯都所取得的成就和罗马人的社会快速发展，必然使奥古斯都文化在整个地中海国家广为传播。

虽然他无子嗣，然而他那至高无上的地位驱使着他必须选择一位接班人。这位接班人必须秉承一直在建立的帝国基质，就是奉行在百年后将由有血统的继承者来继承王朝统治。他选择的包括提比略，帝国的第二位皇帝朱里亚·克劳迪乌斯皇帝。其他还有残酷疯狂的卡里古拉，并吞了英国的干将克劳迪乌斯和因火烧罗马事件而遗臭万年的尼禄。

当尼禄自杀时，提图斯在东欧。公元69年，罗马帝国处在逆转期，在埃及，叙利亚和多瑙河的罗马军团拥立韦帕芗为皇帝。他的两个儿子，提图斯和图密善也将继任帝位，三人执政期间称为弗拉维王朝。他们成功的统治了罗马，恢复了国家的财政稳定，并大规模修建了罗马斗兽场等公共建筑。

公元2世纪被认为是拥有众多杰出帝王的时代，例如图拉真、哈德良、安托尼乌斯·皮乌斯和马可·奥里略。公元180年，马可·奥里略 的去世标志着这一时代的结束，从某方面来说，也象征着衰亡的开始。他那腐败无能的儿子康茂德继承了王位，于公元193年被暗杀，从而吹响了南北战争的号角。

塞普蒂米乌斯·塞维鲁从南北战争中胜出，并建立了一个军事独裁的王朝。而他的儿子卡拉卡拉是一位凶残的暴君，随后被他自己的部下刺杀。接下去的两位塞弗伦斯帝王都落得了类似的下场。这个模式从公元235年的最后一位帝王沿袭到284年戴克里先重建帝国。在北非，一些对王座虎视眈眈的国家层出不穷，高卢和叙利亚频频发动国内战争，日耳曼部落始终在北部边境步步逼近，波斯在东部边境时有威胁。

历经了这三个世纪的众多起起落落之后，罗马居民和其他奴隶既经历过纷争、遭受过暴行，也享受过一时繁荣。他们沉浸于战争胜利带来的喜悦中，或受帝王的命令而行动。由于朱利尤斯·凯撒被暗杀，罗马进入了君士坦丁一世的统治时期。他是第一位信仰基督教的罗马帝土，曾一度想将拜占庭设为首都。而罗马城依然维持它的中心地位，不光是地理位置上而言的帝国中心，同时也是人们信仰中奉为圣地的城市。

Although Rome began as a small village of huts near the banks of the Tiber River in the 8th century BCE, it was during the age of Imperial Rome from 27 BCE to about the mid 4th century CE that Rome as the dominant political, economic and military power of the western civilized world, also achieved its utmost cultural impact throughout the vast sphere of Roman influence.

In the 5th century BCE, the Republic of Rome was founded. Led by its Senate, Rome was empowered by its political institutions at home and military expansion throughout the Mediterranean region. In the I century BCE, however, a profound crisis of Senate authority led to civil war and resulted in the birth of the Roman Empire and the death of the republic. Due to the success of its expansion into the provinces, Rome faced conflict between the ruling class of the past, embodied by the Senate, and emerging social forces that urged for civil and political rights for the plebian (general citizenry) class. Eventually, plebian interests with the support of the army took over and in 60 BCE, the Senate was forced to recognize the legitimacy of the first ruling Triumvirate, consisting of Caesar, Pompey and Crasso. Resplendent in his power derived from foreign conquests, Julius Caesar aroused the antipathy of both his fellow consuls and the Senate. He eventually defeated his enemies in 45 BCE and imposed authoritarian rule. In a last gasp of vitality, the Senate conspired to assassinate Caesar in 44 BCE on the Ides of March (March 15), but that event did not alter the republic's fate. The creation of a second Triumvirate, composed of Mark Antony, Octavian and Lepidus, led to a new conflict that would only end with the unequivocal victory of Octavian at Actium and the suicide of Mark Antony and Cleopatra in Alexandria in 30 BCE.

Through honours bestowed by the Senate including the name, Augustus, Octavian became the first Roman Emperor in 27 BCE. Respecting republican forms and traditions, his pragmatic responses to the problems of Rome and its provinces ensured stability, continuity and prosperity. Wisely, his power although perpetual, was annually bestowed, including *imperium proconsulare majus* (high command and governorship) of the city and all Roman territories. His real power, however, laid in his charisma that conferred unrivalled prestige. Like all Romans, he carried three names, but his, Imperator Caesar Augustus held such magic that later emperors would appropriate them as titles. His unofficial title, *princeps* (Prince), a term bestowed by the people of Rome and meaning first citizen, distinguished him as the first Emperor and his government as the first principate. The accomplishments of Augustus and Rome's predominance made inevitable the diffusion of Augustan culture throughout the Mediterranean world.

Although he had no son, again his unassailable position entitled him to select a successor thus establishing a system of Imperial adoptions that allowed dynastic rule that in later centuries would be by bloodline. His choice was Tiberius, the second of the Julio-Claudian emperors. Others included the cruel and insane Caligula, the capable Claudius who annexed Britain, and the notorious Nero, held accountable by history for the burning of Rome.

Titus Flavius Vespasian was in the East when Nero committed suicide. As the situation in Rome deteriorated during 69 CE, the Roman legions in Egypt, Syria and the Danube declared for Vespasian. Assured of their support, Vespasian marched on Rome where he was hailed as the new emperor. His two sons, Titus and Domitian, would follow him to the throne and the three of them represent the Flavian dynasty. They ruled successfully, restored fiscal stability and were responsible for massive public building projects such as the Colosseum in Rome.

The second century CE is considered the era of the good emperors - Trajan, Hadrian, Antoninus Pius and Marcus Aurelius. The death of Marcus Aurelius in 180 CE signals the end of the era and in some ways, the beginning of the decline. He was succeeded by his son, Commodus, corrupt and inept, whose assassination in 193 CE led to civil war.

Septimius Severus emerged victorious from the civil wars and installed a dynastic, military dictatorship. His son, Caracalla, a cruel tyrant, was assassinated by his own officers. The two Severan emperors that followed met similar ends. This was to be the pattern from the last Severans in 235 CE until Diocletian restructured the Empire in 284. Rival candidates for the throne and revolts in North Africa, Gaul and Syria meant almost constant civil wars. And all the while, Germanic tribes were pressing in on the northern frontier and Persians were threatening the eastern frontier.

Throughout the many ups and downs in the course of these three centuries, citizens of Rome and other subjugated populations of the Empire endured periods of strife, suffered atrocities, enjoyed periods of prosperity, rejoiced in military triumphs at the mercy and whim, sometimes the guidance and caution, of its emperors. From the climatic assassination of Julius Caesar to the rule of Constantine I, the first Roman emperor to convert to Christianity, who would make Byzantium his capital, the city of Rome would remain the pivotal center, both in the tangible sense as center of the Empire, but also in an intangible concept represented by the deification of the city.

奥古斯都石像
Portrait of Augustus

奥古斯都时期（公元前27年~公元14年）
大理石
高40厘米
佛罗伦萨国家考古博物馆

Reign of Augustus (27 BCE —14 CE)
Marble
H. 40 cm
National Archeological Museum, Florence

从面部特征上可以辨认出这是奥古斯都的肖像，尺寸要比同类型画像稍大，暗示这也许是一件死后的肖像。
花冠上镶有一块经雕琢的宝石或刻有浮雕的贝壳（在奥古斯都的前额中心）。由宝石装饰的橡树和花冠是皇帝的标志，从奥古斯都到君士坦丁，许多皇帝的肖像中都有所表现。学者猜想花冠是克罗那花冠（城市花冠），但是尖状的树叶包围着圆形的花朵显示出这是月桂树的花冠。这是唯一所知的描绘奥古斯都戴有头饰的圆雕塑像，此类肖像在货币和珠宝上也很常见。

Recognizable from the facial features as a portrait of Augustus, the dimensions are slightly larger than other examples of the same type, suggesting that it may be a posthumous portrait.
A gemstone or a cameo was probably set in the hole in the wreath (in the middle of Augustus' forehead). Oak and laurel wreaths embellished by a jewel were imperial insignia and are present in portraits of several emperors from Augustus to Constantine. Many scholars have supposed the wreath to be the *corona civica* (civic wreath), but the foliage of pointed leaves interlaced with round flowers suggests that it is a laurel wreath.
This is the only known full relief sculpture that depicts Augustus wearing such a headdress, but this kind of portrait is quite common on coins and jewels.

屋大维(凯撒·奥古斯都) OCTAVIAN (CAESAR AUGUSTUS)

公元前30年，马克·安东尼和克利奥佩特拉在亚克兴角(希腊外海)被奥古斯都击败，这两个情人自杀。之后，奥古斯都统治了罗马五十五年。在经历了一个世纪的政治动荡之后，他为罗马帝国带来了稳定、和平和繁荣。

奥古斯都小心翼翼地隐藏起他的个人野心，把自己伪装成一个重建共和国的君主。他改革了政府，为自己及继任者的独裁统治而将相应规条制度化。他更喜欢"第一公民"（princeps）的称号，以及后来被称作元首制的那段帝国统治时期。

奥古斯都拓展了帝国的边界，并直接管理文化事务，美化罗马，声称接手的是一个砖城，而留下的是一个大理石城。他的成就和罗马的优势地位使奥古斯都文化——奥古斯都时代，在整个地中海地区传播开来成为必然。

After the defeat of the armies of Mark Antony and Cleopatra at Actium (off the coast of Greece) and the subsequent suicides of the two lovers in 30 BCE, Augustus ruled for the next forty-five years. He and brought stability, peace and prosperity to the empire after a century of political turmoil.

Under the guise of restoring the Republic, and taking care to avoid the appearance of personal ambition, Augustus revolutionized the government and institutionalized dictatorial rule for himself and his successors. He preferred the title *princeps* (first citizen), and the period of imperial rule that followed is known as the Principate.

Augustus expanded the frontiers of the empire, took a direct interest in cultural affairs, and beautified Rome, claiming to have found a city of brick but left a city of marble. His accomplishments and Rome's predominance made inevitable the diffusion of Augustan culture—the Age of Augustus—throughout the Mediterranean world.

图拉真石像
Portrait of Trajan

图拉真时期（公元98~117年）
大理石
高27厘米
佛罗伦萨国家考古博物馆

Reign of Trajan (98–117 CE)
Marble
H. 27 cm
National Archeological Museum, Florence

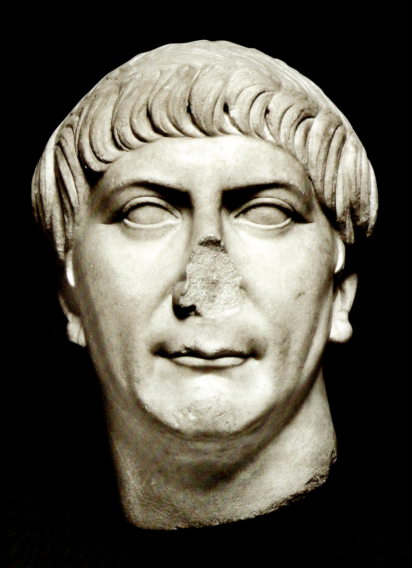

图拉真是一位非常成功且受欢迎的皇帝，留下了许多雕像。他低眉、直发、隆准（此件已残），嘴唇宽而薄。他于公元53年出生于西班牙的意大利卡市，他成为上日耳曼省的总督，后被涅尔瓦皇帝收养，被任命为下一任皇帝。

Trajan was a very successful and popular emperor, and many of his portraits have survived. He is identifiable by his low brow, hair brushed down in bangs, pointed nose (missing in this portrait), and wide, thin lips. Born in 53 CE in the Spanish city of Italica, Trajan was serving as governor of Upper Germany when Nerva, by adopting him, designated him as the next emperor.

哈德良石像
Portrait of Hadrian

哈德良时期（公元117~138年）
大理石
高70厘米，宽60厘米
佛罗伦萨国家考古博物馆

Reign of Hadrian (117–138 CE)
Marble
H. 70 cm, W. 60 cm
National Archeological Museum, Florence

哈德良是首位以络腮胡形象
出现在雕像中的皇帝，也许
反映了他喜欢所有希腊的东
西。古代传说另有他以胡子
掩饰脸上缺陷的解释。图拉
真和哈德良都来自同一个西
班牙的城市。图拉真的妻子
普洛蒂娜钟爱哈德良，
怂恿哈德良娶了图拉真的
侄女薇薇·沙比娜，使图拉
真在死前收养哈德良，并
任命他继位。

Hadrian was the first emperor to be
depicted in portraits wearing a full
beard, possibly reflecting his love for
all things Greek. One ancient source
gives a different explanation—the
beard covered blemishes on his
face. Trajan and Hadrian were
cousins and from the same Spanish
city, but apparently it was Trajan's
wife Plotina who took a special
interest in Hadrian. She encouraged
Hadrian's marriage to Trajan's niece
Vivia Sabina, and may have been
largely responsible for Trajan's
deathbed adoption of Hadrian, which
designated Hadrian as the next
successor.

图拉真柱
Trajan's Column

卢修斯·维鲁斯石像
Portrait of Lucius Verus

卢修斯时期（公元161~166年）
大理石
高72厘米，宽62厘米
佛罗伦萨国家考古博物馆

Reign of Lucius (161–166 CE)
Marble
H. 72 cm, W. 62 cm
National Archeological Museum, Florence

这件半身像是卢修斯·维鲁斯最常见的形像，他是安东尼奥·派阿斯皇帝的养子。公元162~169年他与马可·奥里略共同担任皇帝。这件用钻头雕出的长卷须发的雕像详细地展现出卢修斯·维鲁斯的面貌。

This bust is an example of the most common portrait type of Lucius Verus, adopted son of the emperor Antoninus Pius and co-emperor with Marcus Aurelius from 162 to 169 CE. It shows Lucius Verus' rounded profile and long curly beard and hair rendered in sculpture by the use of a drill.

康茂德石像
Portrait Statue of Commodus

康茂德时期（公元180~192年）
大理石
高65厘米，宽30厘米
佛罗伦萨国家考古博物馆

Reign of Commodus (180-192 CE)
Marble
H. 65 cm, W. 30 cm
National Archeological Museum, Florence

由胡须可知，康茂德的这件
雕像的时间是其统治的后
期。康茂德显然自比希腊神
赫拉克勒斯，他的其他肖像
也和赫拉克勒斯的像一样，
有着狮皮和棍棒。

This portrait of Commodus can
be dated to the final years of his
reign because of the beard. Clearly
deranged, Commodus identified
himself with the Greek god Hercules
and other portraits depict him, like
Hercules, with a lion skin and club.

卡拉卡拉以暴君著称，其肖像也展示出这一性情。正如该像所示，他通常是皱着眉头、斜眼而视，一脸怒容。他宁可杀死自己的兄弟，也不愿与其共享王位。他的统治充斥着恐怖的氛围，他也在这种残酷的环境死去。

Caracalla gained the reputation as a cruel tyrant and his portraits display that disposition. Usually, as in this one, he has a threatening scowl, wrinkled brow, and sidelong glance. He killed his brother rather than share the throne, unleashed a reign of terror, and met his own death under brutal circumstances.

青年卡拉卡拉石像
Portrait of Young Caracalla

卡拉卡拉时期（公元211~217年）
大理石
高31厘米
佛罗伦萨国家考古博物馆

Reign of Caracalla (211—217 CE)
Marble
H. 31 cm
National Archeological Museum, Florence

铜任命表
Patronage Table

公元101年
青铜
长43.5厘米，宽 35.8厘米
佛罗伦萨国家考古博物馆

101 CE
Bronze
L. 43.5 cm, W. 35.8 cm
National Archeological Museum, Florence

碑文上刻有意大利拉齐奥区
弗莱底努姆市的参议院法
令，任命 *T. Pomponio Basso*
为守护神。

The inscription bears the ordinance
with which the Senate of Ferentinum,
a city of Lazio region of Italy,
appointed *T. Pomponio Basso* as
patron.

小阿格丽品娜石像
Portrait of Agrippina Minor

尼禄的统治时期（公元54~68年）
大理石
高21厘米
佛罗伦萨国家考古博物馆

Reign of Nero (54–68 CE)
Marble
H. 21 cm
National Archeological Museum, Florence

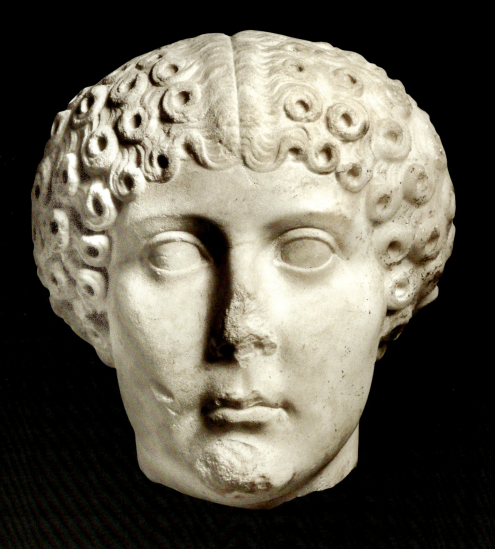

从发型就可以明显看出这是小阿格丽品娜的肖像。中分、四股扁平的卷发遮住耳朵。小阿格丽品娜是卡里古拉的姐姐，嫁给了克劳迪乌斯皇帝。克劳迪乌斯是她的叔叔，对双方来说都是第二次婚姻，通过支配克劳迪乌斯，她在帝国中有相当大的权力。她说服了克劳迪乌斯收养她与前夫的儿子尼禄，据传她为了让尼禄尽快继位而毒害了克劳迪乌斯。后来，尼禄将其杀死。

The hairstyle strongly suggests that this is a portrait of Agrippina the Younger. It is parted in the middle and arranged in four rows of flat curls that cover her ears. Agrippina the Younger was the sister of Caligula and married to the emperor Claudius. Claudius was her uncle, it was a second marriage for both, and by dominating Claudius she exercised considerable power in the empire. Also she persuaded Claudius to adopt Nero, her son by a previous marriage, and allegedly poisoned Claudius in order to hasten Nero's accession to the throne. Later Nero had her murdered.

朱里亚·克劳狄家族之子石像
Portrait of a Julio-Claudian Child

公元1世纪上半叶
大理石
高18.8厘米
佛罗伦萨国家考古博物馆

First half of the 1st century CE
Marble
H. 18.8 cm
National Archeological Museum, Florence

这个雕像是一个约两三岁的孩子。鉴于雕像的质量以及至少两个以上的副本,这个孩子极有可能来自朱里亚·克劳狄家族。孩子的发型暗示着这是在提比略统治后期或者卡里古拉的统治时期。

This statue portrays a child about two or three years old. Considering the quality of the portrait and the fact that there are at least two other copies of it, the child was probably someone from the Julio-Claudian family. The child's hair style, characterized by flat locks, suggests a date late in the reign of Tiberius or during the reign of Caligula.

朱里亚·克劳狄王子石像
Small statue of Julio-Claudian prince

朱里亚·克劳狄时期（公元前27年~公元68年）
大理石
高39.5厘米
佛罗伦萨国家考古博物馆

Julio-Claudian dynasty (27BCE – 68 CE)
Marble
H. 39.5 cm
National Archeological Museum, Florence

这个男性裸体的雕型再现了希腊雕刻家波利克里托斯的风格。通过脸部和发型特征判断它描绘的是朱里亚·克劳狄王朝的一位王子。家庭神龛通常把皇室成员和本土之神形象一起供奉。

This statuette of a nude male reproduces the style of the Greek sculptor Polykleitos. Judging by the treatment of the face and the hairstyle, it represents a prince of the Julio-Claudian dynasty. Family household shrines often included images of the Imperial family along with domestic deities.

妇女石像
Small Statue with Julio-Claudian Princess

朱里亚·克劳狄时期（公元前27~公元68年）
大理石
高40厘米
佛罗伦萨国家考古博物馆

Julio-Claudian Dynasty (27 BCE – 68 CE)
Marble
H. 40 cm
National Archeological Museum, Florence

这件基于希腊化艺术风格的雕像表明它是一名理想化的皇室女性。女子左脚朝前站立，左手托着一个球，右手握着的物件现已丢失。她身着带袖外衣的希玛申长袍，头戴半月形王冠。

The style of this statuette, which is based on Hellenistic Greek models, suggests that it is an idealized image of a female member of the Imperial family. The woman stands with her left leg forward. In her left hand she holds a sphere, while the object once held in her right hand is now lost. She wears a tunic with sleeves, a long *himation* (cloak), and on her head a half-moon diadem.

有权势的女性
POWERFUL WOMEN

古罗马时代人们通常希望妇女只关注家庭事务和照顾儿童。

但是也有例外。比较贫困的阶层的妇女由于需要出外工作，反而常常比那些富裕阶层的妇女拥有更多的社会自由。妇女在婚姻中可以将继承的财产和自有的财产区分开。

妇女有时也可以担任女祭司。权势者的母亲和妻子，特别是皇室家庭的某些妇女有时也会通过儿子和丈夫施加相当大的影响。皇室家庭中极具影响力的著名女性，包括奥古斯都的妻子、提比略的母亲利维娅、克劳迪乌斯皇帝的妻子和尼禄的母亲小阿格丽品娜。

Women in ancient Rome generally were expected to confine their attention to running the household and caring for children.

There were exceptions, however. Women of the poorer classes, with the necessity of working outside the home, often exercised more social freedom than those of wealthy families. Women could inherit property and own property separately in a marriage.

Women served occasionally as priestesses. Also mothers and wives of powerful men sometimes exercised considerable influence through their sons and husbands. This was especially true of certain women of the Imperial household. Notable among influential women of the Imperial household were Livia, wife of Augustus and mother of Tiberius; and Agrippina the Younger, wife of Claudius and mother of Nero.

钱币：不仅仅是货币　COINS: MORE THAN MONEY

　　钱币除了购买物品和积累财富的功能之外，还被赋予了其他的用途。皇帝们通过发行有自己形象的硬币，来维护他们的合法性和宣扬他们的权威。有时皇帝也利用硬币来传递其他信息——比如他们与某位特别的神或女神有特殊的联系、他们引以为荣的成就和宣告其配偶或亲属。

　　Coins served purposes other than purchasing goods and accumulating wealth. By issuing coins with their own image on them, the emperors were asserting their legitimacy and proclaiming their authority. Sometimes emperors used the coins to convey other messages as well—their special connection to a particular god or goddess, their pride with some achievement, their affirmation of a spouse or close relative.

奥古斯都"奥里斯"金币
Aureus of Augustus

公元前1世纪
黄金
重7.9克
佛罗伦萨国家考古博物馆

正面：奥古斯都头像（免冠）。
反面：摩羯座。

1st century BCE
Gold
W. 7.9 g
National Archeological Museum, Florence

Obverse: Head of Augustus (uncovered).
Reverse: Capricorn.

硬币背面展示了奥古斯都皇帝的星座。硬币有实际的经济用途，此外，其背面的装饰元素也说明了硬币的纪念意义。

The coin shows on the reverse the astrological sign of the Emperor Augustus. Coins had a practical and economic usage, however the decorative element on the reverse side testifies to how this one had also a celebrative function.

奥古斯都"迪纳厄斯"银币
Denarius of Augustus

公元前2世纪~公元11年
银
直径1.8厘米
锡耶纳国家考古博物馆

正面：戴月桂花冠的奥古斯都头像。
反面：身穿长袍，面蒙纱的盖尤斯和卢修斯·凯撒（Lucius Caesar）。

2nd century BCE – 11 CE
Silver
D. 1.8 cm
National Archeological Museum, Siena

Obverse: Head of Augustus with laurel wreath.
Reverse: Gaius and Lucius Caesar in togas with veiled heads.

盖尤斯和卢修斯是奥古斯都的孙子，是其女儿朱莉娅和他的密友兼盟友阿古利巴的儿子。奥古斯都把他们列为继承人，但均早逝。

Gaius and Lucius were Augustus' grandsons by his daughter Julia and his close friend and ally Agrippa. Augustus adopted them to be his heirs, but both died prematurely.

奥古斯都 "阿斯" 铜币
As of Augustus

公元前23年
青铜
直径3厘米
锡耶纳国家考古博物馆

正面：戴月桂花冠的奥古斯都头像。
反面：元老院。

23 BCE
Bronze
D. 3 cm
National Archeological Museum, Siena

Obverse: Head of Augustus crowned with laurel
wreath.
Reverse: S C.

SC为 "依据元老院指令"
（*Senatus Consulto*)的缩
写，指元老院已批准发行该
货币。

S C (*Senatus Consulto*, "By decree of
the Senate") indicates that the Senate
had given its approval for issuing the
coin.

提比略 "阿斯" 铜币
As of Tiberius

公元10~11年
青铜
直径2.8厘米
锡耶纳国家考古博物馆

正面：提比略的头像（免冠）。
反面：元老院。

10–11 CE
Bronze
D. 2.8 cm
National Archeological Museum, Siena

Obverse: Head of Tiberius
(uncovered).
Reverse: S C.

提比略 "奥里斯" 金币
Aureus of Tiberius

公元26~37年
黄金
直径1.8厘米
锡耶纳国家考古博物馆

正面：提比略头像，头戴月桂花冠。
反面：穿斗篷的女性坐在宝座上，左手持树枝，右手持权杖。

26-37 CE
Gold
D. 1.8 cm
National Archeological Museum, Siena

Obverse: Head of Tiberius with laurel wreath.
Reverse: Cloaked female figure, seated on a throne, with a branch in her left hand and a long scepter in her right.

该像表现了提比略的母亲利维娅扮作和平女神潘克斯。

The figure represents Tiberius' mother Livia as the goddess Pax (Peace).

提比略 "迪纳厄斯" 银币
Denarius of Tiberius

公元16~21年
银
直径1.8厘米
锡耶纳国家考古博物馆

正面：戴月桂花冠的提比略头像。
反面：和平女神利维娅。

16-21 CE
Silver
D. 1.8 cm
National Archeological Museum, Siena

Obverse: Head of Tiberius with laurel wreath.
Reverse: Livia as the goddess Pax (Peace).

德鲁苏斯 "阿斯" 铜币
As of Drusus

公元22~23年
青铜
直径2.5厘米
锡耶纳国家考古博物馆

正面：德鲁苏斯的头像。
反面：元老院。

22-23 CE
Bronze
D. 2.5 cm
National Archeological Museum, Siena

Obverse: Head of Drusus.
Reverse: S C.

德鲁苏斯是皇帝提比略的独子，在提比略领养的儿子格马尼库斯死后，他继承了王位。但是德鲁苏斯早于他父亲去世，很有可能是被他的妻子毒死。

Drusus was the emperor Tiberius' only son and, after the death of Germanicus whom Tiberias adopted, heir to the throne. But Dursus also died before his father, poisoned, possibly by his wife.

卡里古拉"阿斯"铜币
As of Caligula

公元37~38年
青铜
直径2.5厘米
锡耶纳国家考古博物馆

正面：卡里古拉头像（免冠）。
反面：左手持托盘、右手持权杖的维斯塔登位像。

37-38 CE
Bronze
D. 2.5 cm
National Archeological Museum, Siena

Obverse: Head of Caligula (uncovered).
Reverse: Vesta enthroned with a tray in her left hand and a long scepter in her right.

如古罗马宗教大祭司长所言，卡里古拉皇帝狂热崇拜象征罗马团结和力量的灶神维斯塔。卡里古拉将赋予维斯太的殊荣给予了祖母小安东尼娅（Antonia the Younger）和姐姐。

As *Pontifex Maximus* (chief priest), the emperor was closely bound to the cult of Vesta, goddess of the domestic hearth, and by extension, the goddess of the unity and the strength of Rome. Caligula gave the honors usually reserved for the priestesses of Vesta to his grandmother Antonia the Younger and to his sisters.

卡里古拉"塞斯特提"铜币
Sestertius of Caligula

公元37~38年
青铜
直径3.2厘米
锡耶纳国家考古博物馆

正面：戴月桂花冠的卡里古拉头像。
反面：三名女性人物站立于聚宝盆边，从铭文中可识别为卡里古拉的姐姐。

37-38 CE
Bronze
D. 3.2 cm
National Archeological Museum, Siena

Obverse: Head of Caligula with laurel wreath.
Reverse: Three female figures standing by a cornucopia, identifiable from the inscription as Caligula's sisters.

左边的是阿格莉皮娜斜靠在壁柱上；中间的是德鲁西拉，手捧祭神的酒碗；右边掌舵的是朱莉娅。她们是女神的化身。卡里古拉最喜爱的德鲁西拉代表和谐，阿格莉皮娜代表安全，朱莉娅代表财富（繁荣）。

Agrippina is on the left leaning on a pilaster; Drusilla in the middle holds a *patera* (shallow bowl for libations); and Julia on the right holds a ship's rudder. They are represented as the personifications of deities. Drusilla, Caligula' favorite, represents Concordia (Harmony), Agrippina represents Securitas (Security) and Julia represents Fortuna (Prosperity).

格马尼库斯"阿斯"铜币
As of Germanicus

公元41~54年
青铜
直径2.2厘米
锡耶纳国家考古博物馆

正面：格马尼库斯头像（免冠）。
反面：元老院。

41-54 CE
Bronze
D. 2.2 cm
National Archeological Museum,. Siena

Obverse: Head of Germanicus (uncovered).
Reverse: S C.

该铜币是克劳迪斯皇帝为纪念其兄弟格马尼库斯而铸。SC是"依据元老院指令"（Senatus Consulto）的缩写，指元老院批准发行该货币。

The emperor Claudius minted this coin commemorating his brother Germanicus. S C (*Senatus Consulto*, "By decree of the Senate") indicates that the Senate had approved the coin's issue.

克罗迪斯 "阿斯" 铜币
As of Claudius

公元42年后
青铜
直径2.2厘米
锡耶纳国家考古博物馆

正面：克罗迪斯头像 。
反面：带有奥古斯都之名的、象征自由的
拟人像., 传递皇帝能捍卫自由的信息。

After 42 CE
Bronze
D. 2.2 cm
National Archeological Museum, Siena

Obverse: Head of Claudius.
Reverse: Personification of Libertas
(Freedom) with the name Augustus,
conveying the message that the emperor
could guarantee freedom.

尼禄 "奥里斯" 金币
Aureus of Nero

公元54~68年
黄金
直径1.4厘米
锡耶纳国家考古博物馆

正面：尼禄头像。
反面：戎装的博洛尼亚。

54-68 CE
Gold
D. 1.4 cm
National Archeological Museum, Siena

Obverse: Head of Nero.
Reverse: Armed Virtus.

尼禄 "阿斯" 铜币
As of Nero

公元54~68年
青铜
直径2.8厘米
锡耶纳国家考古博物馆

正面：戴月桂皇冠的尼禄头像。
反面：戎装的罗马女神坐在武器与盔甲上，左
手持胜利女神的雕像，右手持长矛。

54-68 CE
Bronze
D. 2.8 cm
National Archeological Museum, Siena

Obverse: Head of Nero crowned with laurel.
Reverse: The goddess Roma, armed and
seated on weapons and body armor, holds a
statue of the goddess Nike (Victory) in her
left hand and a spear in her right.

该币铸造的原因可能是公元
64年罗马大火和重建。罗马
女神被塑造成像一位坐在一
堆武器上战斗的女神，她左
手持胜利女神，这一形象成
为之后铸币的传统。

The great fire of Rome in 64 CE and
rebuilding that followed may have
prompted the minting of this coin.
The way that Roma is depicted on
it—as a warrior goddess seated on
a pile of arms and holding Victory in
the palm of her left hand—became a
convention for coinage.

尼禄 "阿斯" 铜币
As of Nero

公元54~68年
青铜
直径2厘米
锡耶纳国家考古博物馆

正面：戴月桂花冠的尼禄头像。
反面：门紧闭着的杰纳斯庙。

54-68 CE
Bronze
D. 2 cm
National Archeological Museum, Siena

Obverse: Head of Nero with laurel wreath.
Reverse: Temple of Janus with closed doors.

该币发行是为了庆祝杰纳斯庙的关门（罗马无战事该门才关闭）和和平时期的到来。

The circulation of this coin celebrated the closing of the doors of the Temple of Janus (closed only when Rome fought no wars) and the beginning of a period of peace.

格尔巴 "阿斯" 铜币
As of Galba

公元68~69年
青铜
直径2厘米
锡耶纳国家考古博物馆

正面：戴月桂花冠的格尔巴头像。
反面：自由女神。

68-69 CE
Bronze
D. 2 cm
National Archeological Museum, Siena

Obverse: Head of Galba with laurel wreath.
Reverse: The goddess Libertas.

奥托 "塞斯特提" 铜币
Sestertius of Othon

公元69年
青铜
直径2.6厘米
锡耶纳国家考古博物馆

正面：奥托头像（免冠）。
反面：一个比其他人略大的人物，右手伸向三位武士。

69 CE
Bronze
D. 2.6 cm
National Archeological Museum, Siena

Obverse: Head of Otho (uncovered).
Reverse: One figure larger than the others, holding out his right hands toward three armed figures.

该币代表了奥托短暂执政的重要时刻,即他的军队发誓要对他忠诚之时。

This coin represents the important moment in Otho's brief reign when his troops swore their allegiance to him.

维特里乌斯"迪纳厄斯"银币
Denarius of Vitellius

公元69年
银
直径1.1厘米
锡耶纳国家考古博物馆

正面：戴月桂花冠的维特里乌斯头像。
反面：站立的自由之神，右手持毡帽，左手持权杖。

69 CE
Silver
D. 1.1 cm
National Archeological Museum, Siena

Obverse: Head of Vitellius with laurel wreath.
Reverse: Libertas standing with a *pileus* (felt hat) in his right hand and a long scepter in his left.

韦帕芗"迪纳厄斯"银币
Denarius of Vespasian

公元70年
银
直径1厘米
锡耶纳国家考古博物馆

正面：戴月桂花冠的韦帕芗头像。
反面：一位女人坐在胜利纪念品之下，象征着朱迪亚的化身。

70 CE
Silver
D. 1 cm
National Archeological Museum, Siena

Obverse: Head of Vespasian with laurel wreath.
Reverse: Personification of Judaea represented as a woman seated below the trophy.

该币是系列展现朱迪亚行省作为战败者的形象的一部分，描绘了胜利纪念品和囚犯。

This coin, part of a series of coins showing trophies and prisoners, depicts the province of Judaea as a defeated enemy.

韦帕芗"都庞地亚"银币
Dupondius of Vespasian

公元73年
银
直径2厘米
锡耶纳国家考古博物馆

正面：戴光芒皇冠的韦帕芗。
反面：站立着的女子右手持双蛇杖（象征和平），左手持聚宝盆，象征着幸运女神的化身。

73 CE
Silver
D. 2 cm
National Archeological Museum, Siena

Obverse: Head of Vespasian with radiant crown.
Reverse: Felicitas represented as a standing female figure with a caduceus (staff of peace) in her right hand and a cornucopia in her left.

该币传递了新执政家族弗拉维将带来和平与繁荣的讯息。

The message is that the new ruling family, the Flavians, bring peace and prosperity.

提图斯 "塞斯特提" 铜币
Sestertius of Titus

公元80年
青铜
直径2.5厘米
锡耶纳国家考古博物馆

正面：长胡子的提图斯头像，头戴月桂花冠。
反面：韦帕芗与提图斯握手，相对而站。他们共同举起在船舵上方的地球。

80 CE
Bronze
D. 2.5 cm
National Archeological Museum, Siena

Obverse: Head of Titus with beard and laurel wreath.
Reverse: Vespasian and Titus standing and facing each other with their right hands joined. They hold up a globe that is positioned above a ship's rudder.

该币展现的是公元79年韦帕芗死后成神，他赋予继任者提图斯统治世界的权力。地球仪和船舵象征罗马对大地和海洋的统治。

This coin shows Vespasian, who had become divine after his death in 79 CE, offering his successor Titus the rule of the world. The globe and the ship's rudder symbolize Rome's rule over the land and sea.

图密善 "迪纳厄斯" 银币
Denarius of Domitian

公元93年
银
直径1.1厘米
锡耶纳国家考古博物馆

正面：长胡子的图密善头像，头戴月桂花冠。
反面：图密善的守护女神密涅瓦正用右手扔标枪。

93 CE
Silver
D. 1.1 cm
National Archeological Museum, Siena

Obverse: Head of Domitian with a beard and laurel wreath.
Reverse: Minerva, the patron goddess of Domitian, throwing a spear with her right hand.

图密善 "塞斯特提" 铜币
Sestertius Di Domitian

公元92~94年
青铜
直径2.5厘米
锡耶纳国家考古博物馆

正面：长胡子的图密善头像，头戴月桂花冠。
反面：坐着的朱庇特，右手执胜利女神，左手持权杖。

92-94 CE
Bronze
D. 2.5 cm
National Archeological Museum, Siena

Obverse: Head of Domitian with beard and laurel wreath.
Reverse: Seated Jupiter holding a goddess Nike (Victory) in his right hand and a scepter in his left.

朱庇特的形象意味着发行该币的人把自己置于众神之父的保护下。胜利之神的象征有助于政治与战争中获得胜利。

The image of Jupiter on a coin meant that the person who issued the coin was placing himself under the protection of the father of the gods. This helped ensure success in politics and warfare, as symbolized by the depiction of Victory.

涅尔瓦"阿斯"铜币
As of Nerva

公元96年
青铜
直径1.8厘米
锡耶纳国家考古博物馆

正面：戴月桂花冠的涅尔瓦头像。
反面：右手相握。

96 CE
Bronze
D. 1.8 cm
National Archeological Museum, Siena

Obverse: Head of Nerva with laurel wreath.
Reverse: Two right hands joined together.

相握的右手象征着和谐，即图密善艰难执政后重获的和谐。

The joined right hands symbolize *concordia*, the harmony that was regained after the difficult reign of Domitian.

图拉真"迪纳厄斯"银币
Denarius of Trajan

公元107~111年
银
直径1.4厘米
锡耶纳国家考古博物馆

正面：头戴月桂花冠的图拉真半身像。
反面：武器战利品。

107–111 CE
Silver
D. 1.4 cm
National Archeological Museum, Siena

Obverse: Bust of Trajan with laurel wreath.
Reverse: Trophy of weapons.

战利品和盔甲是图拉真在公元101~102年和105~106年战胜达西亚人的象征。

The trophy and the armor are symbols of Trajan's military victories over the Dacians in 101-102 CE and 105-106 CE.

图拉真"塞斯特提"铜币
Sestertius of Trajan

公元104–111年
青铜
直径2.8厘米
锡耶纳国家考古博物馆

正面：头戴月桂花冠的图拉真半身像。
反面：达西亚人坐在武器的战利品之下。

104–111 CE
Bronze
D. 2.8 cm
National Archeological Museum, Siena

Obverse: Bust of Trajan with laurel wreath.
Reverse: Dacian seated at the foot of a trophy of weapons.

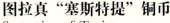

维比娅·萨宾娜 "塞斯特提" 铜币
Sestertius of Vibia Sabina

公元132~137年
青铜
直径2.8厘米
锡耶纳国家考古博物馆

正面：加冕的维比娅·萨宾娜半身像。
反面：敬意女神的化身以女性形象坐在宝座之上，右手持祭神酒碗，左手持权杖。

132–137 CE
Bronze
D. 2.8 cm
National Archeological Museum, Siena

Obverse: Bust of Vibia Sabina with diadem.
Reverse: The goddess Pietas represented as a female figure seated on a throne, holding a patera (shallow bowl for libations) in her right hand and a long scepter in her left.

安东尼·庇护 "杜邦迪斯" 铜币
Dupondius of Antoninus Pius

公元139年
青铜
直径1.8厘米
锡耶纳国家考古博物馆

正面：长胡子的安东尼·庇护头像，头戴月桂花冠。
反面：站立的女性形象，右手持树枝，左手捧聚宝盆 。

139 CE
Bronze
D. 1.8 cm
National Archeological Museum, Siena

Obverse: Head of Antoninus Pius with beard and laurel wreath.
Reverse: A standing female figure with a branch in her right hand and a cornucopia in her left.

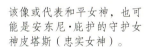

该像或代表和平女神，也可能是安东尼·庇护的守护女神皮塔斯（忠实女神）。

The figure may represent the goddess Pax (Peace), or perhaps Antoninus Pius' patron goddess Pietas (Duty).

安东尼·庇护 "迪纳厄斯" 银币
Denarius of Antoninus Pius

公元161年
银
直径1厘米
锡耶纳国家考古博物馆

正面：长胡子的安东尼·庇护神圣的头像。
反面：鹰。

161 CE
Silver
D. 1 cm
National Archeological Museum, Siena

Obverse: Bearded head of the divine Antoninus Pius.
Reverse: Eagle.

该币展现了神化后的皇帝安东尼·庇护。鹰作为朱庇特的信使，肩负着向天神贡献世间有价值之人的使命。

This coin shows the deification of emperor Antoninus Pius. The eagle, messenger of Jupiter, had the task of carrying worthy humans from earth to the kingdom of the gods.

马可·奥里略 "阿斯" 铜币
As of Marcus Aurelius

公元140~ 143年
青铜
直径2.8厘米
锡耶纳国家考古博物馆

正面：马可·奥里略头像。
反面：戎装的密涅瓦女神，挥舞标枪。

140-143 CE
Bronze
D. 2.8 cm
National Archeological Museum, Siena

Obverse: Head of Marcus Aurelius.
Reverse: The goddess Minerva armed and brandishing a javelin.

马可·奥里略 "迪纳厄斯" 银币
Denarius of Marcus Aurelius

公元161年
银
直径1.1厘米
锡耶纳国家考古博物馆

正面：长胡子的马可·奥里略头像。
反面：站立的女性右手持地球仪，左手持聚宝盆。

161 CE
Silver
D. 1.1 cm
National Archeological Museum, Siena

Obverse: Head of Marcus Aurelius with beard.
Reverse: Standing female figure with a globe in her extended right hand and cornucopia in her left.

该女性形象被认为是上帝普罗维登斯的化身，她率先决定让马可·奥里略继承帝位。该女神手持地球，象征着罗马在全世界的权力，聚宝盆（丰饶角）象征着新皇帝将带来的富足。

The female figure is thought to be a personification of divine Providence, who has predetermined the succession of Marcus Aurelius. The goddess holds the globe, a symbol of Rome's universal power, and the cornucopia, a symbol of abundance brought by the new emperor.

福斯蒂娜 "迪纳厄斯" 银币
Denarius of Faustina

公元161~176年
银
直径1.1厘米
锡耶纳国家考古博物馆

正面：福斯蒂娜的加冕半身像。
反面：萨鲁斯女神坐在宝座上。

161-176 CE
Silver
D. 1.1 cm
National Archeological Museum, Siena

Obverse: Bust of Faustina with crowned head.
Reverse: The goddess Salus (Salvation) seated on a throne.

小福斯蒂娜是安东尼·庇护和福斯蒂娜的女儿，皇帝马可·奥里略的妻子。

Faustina the younger, daughter of Antoninus Pius and Faustina the elder, was the wife of the emperor Marcus Aurelius.

卢修斯·维鲁斯 "迪纳厄斯" 银币
Denarius of Lucius Verus

公元163年
银
重24.65克
锡耶纳国家考古博物馆

正面：长胡子的卢修斯·维鲁斯半身像，头戴月桂花冠。
反面：站立的战神。

163 CE
Silver
W. 24.65 g
National Archeological Museum, Siena

Obverse: Bust of Lucius Verus with beard and laurel wreath.
Reverse: Standing Mars.

该币的战神形象是为纪念罗马于公元163年战胜亚美尼亚人的军事胜利。

The figure of Mars on this coin commemorates Rome's victorious military campaign against the Armenians in 163 CE.

康茂德 "迪纳厄斯" 银币
Denarius of Commodus

公元180年之前
银
直径1.1厘米
锡耶纳国家考古博物馆

正面：未蓄胡的康茂德免冠像。
反面：奠酒祭神的容器。

Before 180 CE
Silver
D. 1.1 cm
National Archeological Museum, Siena

Obverse: Uncovered and beardless head of Commodus.
Reverse: Vessel for pouring libations.

该币的发行流通为马可·奥里略，时间应在公元180年之前，此时康茂德成为唯一的皇帝。

This coin was struck and circulated by Marcus Aurelius, thus to be dated before 180 CE when Commodus became sole emperor.

康茂德 "迪纳厄斯" 银币
Denarius of Commodus

公元186年
银
直径1.1厘米
锡耶纳国家考古博物馆

正面：长胡子的康茂德头像，头戴月桂花冠。
反面：命运女神坐在宝座上，左手持聚宝盆，右手拿着在船舵上的地球仪。

186 CE
Silver
D. 1.1 cm
National Archeological Museum, Siena

Obverse: Head of Commodus with beard and laurel wreath.
Reverse: The goddess Fortuna Redux seated on a throne, holding a cornucopia in her left hand, and in her right a ship's rudder resting on a globe.

福特娜·雷德斯是命运女神，尤其能给家庭带来好运和平安。该币是为了纪念罗马军队从英国胜利归来而作。

Fortuna Redux was the goddess of Fortune, particularly the good fortune that brings one home safely, and the coin commemorated the Roman army's return after victories in Britain.

克丽丝皮娜 "阿斯" 铜币
As of Crispina

公元180~183年
青铜
直径2.5厘米
锡耶纳国家考古博物馆

正面：克丽丝皮娜的半身像。
反面：站立的朱诺。

180–183 CE
Bronze
D. 2.5 cm
National Archeological Museum, Siena

Obverse: Bust of Crispina.
Reverse: Standing Juno.

与婚姻仪式相联系的女神朱诺暗示该币的内容是在皇帝马可·奥里略死前康茂德与年轻的克丽丝皮娜举行婚礼。

The goddess Juno, associated with the rites of marriage, suggests that this coin relates to the marriage of Commodus to the young Crispina, which took place before the death of the emperor Marcus Aurelius.

卢修斯·维鲁斯和康茂德铜纪念章
Medallion with Lucius Verus and Commodus

马可·奥里略时期（公元161~180年）
青铜
直径2.1厘米
锡耶纳国家考古博物馆

正面：身披战袍的卢修斯·维鲁斯半身像。
反面：年轻的康茂德半身像，身披战袍。

Reign of Marcus Aurelius (161–180 CE)
Bronze
D. 2.1 cm
National Archeological Museum, Siena

Obverse: Bust of Annius Verus in military cloak.
Reverse: Bust of young Commodus in military cloak.

纪念章比货币大，用来纪念特定的政治、宗教和城邦事件。该纪念章有可能是马可·奥里略皇帝的两个儿子被给予凯撒称号时所铸，反映出对他们继承父位的期待。

Medallions were larger than coins, in order to better render subject matter, and were struck to commemorate specific political, religious or civil events. This medallion, which represents the two sons of the emperor Marcus Aurelius, was likely struck when the two boys were given the title of Caesar, anticipating that they would succeed their father.

马可·奥里略和康茂德铜纪念章
Medallion with Marcus Aurelius and Commodus

公元173年
青铜
直径2.8厘米
锡耶纳国家考古博物馆

正面：长胡子的马可·奥里略半身像，头戴月桂花冠，身穿古罗马胸甲手持盾牌。
反面：年轻的康茂德半身像，身着战袍和盔甲。

173 CE
Bronze
D. 2.8 cm
National Archeological Museum, Siena

Obverse: Bust of Marcus Aurelius with beard, laurel wreath, lorica (breast plate) and shield.
Reverse: Bust of young Commodus with *paludamentum* (military cloak) and armor.

该纪念章刻画了马可·奥里略皇帝和其子康茂德，在被授予凯撒头衔之时的情景，预示着康茂德会成为下一任皇帝。

This medallion portrays the emperor Marcus Aurelius and his son Commodus at a time when the latter had already been given the title of Caesar, anticipating that he would become the next emperor.

塞普蒂米乌斯·塞维鲁 "塞斯特提" 铜币
Sestertius of Septimius Severus

公元193年
青铜
重 26.45克
佛罗伦萨国家考古博物馆

正面：塞普蒂米乌斯·塞维鲁头像，头戴月桂花冠。
反面：位于两个战利品之间的军团鹰。

193 CE
Bronze
W. 26.45 g
National Archeological Museum, Florence

Obverse: Head of Septimius Severus with laurel wreath.
Reverse: Legionary eagle between two trophies.

塞普蒂米乌斯·塞维鲁 "奥里斯" 金币
Aureus of Septimius Severus

公元194年
黄金
直径2厘米
佛罗伦萨国家考古博物馆

正面：塞普蒂米乌斯·塞维鲁头像，头戴月桂花冠。
反面：胜利之神手持棕榈叶树枝与皇冠。

194 CE
Gold
D. 2 cm
National Archeological Museum, Florence

Obverse: Head of Septimius Severus with laurel wreath.
Reverse: Victory holding a palm bough and a crown.

朱利娅·当娜 "塞斯特提" 铜币
Sestertius of Julia Domna

公元211~217年
青铜
重27.05克
佛罗伦萨国家考古博物馆

正面：朱利娅·当娜的遮盖半身像。
反面：站立着的幸运女神在祭坛，手持神杖祭献。

211-217 CE
Bronze
W. 27.05 g
National Archeological Museum, Florence

Obverse: Draped bust of Julia Domna.
Reverse: Standing goddess Felicitas (Good Luck) holding a
caduceus (staff) and sacrificing at an altar.

卡拉卡拉 "奥里斯" 金币
Aureus of Caracalla

公元205年
黄金
直径2.2厘米
佛罗伦萨国家考古博物馆

正面：卡拉卡拉半身像。
反面：赤裸的战神，左肩披斗篷，手持树枝、权杖。

205 CE
Gold
D. 2.2 cm
National Archeological Museum, Florence

Obverse: Bust of Caracalla.
Reverse: Nude Mars with a cloak over his left shoulder, holding a tree branch and staff.

卡拉卡拉 "塞斯特提" 铜币
Sestertius of Caracalla

公元213年
青铜
直径3厘米
佛罗伦萨国家考古博物馆

正面：卡拉卡拉半身像，头戴月桂花冠。
反面：立于战车之上的胜利之神授予卡拉卡拉皇冠。

213 CE
Bronze
D. 3 cm
National Archeological Museum, Florence

Obverse: Bust of Caracalla with a laurel wreath.
Reverse: Caracalla being crowned by Victory who is on a chariot.

盖塔 "塞斯特提" 铜币
Sestertius of Geta

公元211年
青铜
直径3厘米
佛罗伦萨国家考古博物馆

正面：盖塔头像，头戴月桂花冠。
反面：坐兹女性手持权杖与聚宝盆。

211 CE
Bronze
D. 3 cm
National Archeological Museum, Florence

Obverse: Head of Geta with beard and laurel wreath.
Reverse: Seated female figure with a scepter and a cornucopia.

埃拉加巴卢斯 "塞斯特提" 铜币
Sestertius of Elioglabalus(Heliogabalus)

公元218~219年
青铜
直径3.5厘米
佛罗伦萨国家考古博物馆

正面：埃拉加巴卢斯的半身像，头戴月桂花冠。
反面：三个站立着的神明，手持天秤、聚宝盆，脚下有一堆钱币，是正义女神埃奎塔斯的化身。

218-219 CE
Bronze
D. 3.5 cm
National Archeological Museum, Florence

Obverse: Draped bust of Elagabalus with laurel wreath.
Reverse: Personifications of Aequitas (Fair Dealing): three standing deities, each holding a balance and a cornucopia with piles of coins at their feet.

亚历山大·塞维鲁 "奥里斯" 金币
Aureus of Alexander Severus

公元231~235年
黄金
直径2.2厘米
佛罗伦萨国家考古博物馆

正面：戴月桂花冠的亚历山大·塞维鲁头像。
反面：拿着算盘和羊角的自由女神。

231-235 CE
Gold
D. 2.2 cm
National Archeological Museum, Florence

Obverse: Head of Severus Alexander with laurel wreath.
Reverse: Libertas with an abacus and cornucopia.

亚历山大·塞维鲁 "塞斯特提" 铜币
Sestertius of Alexander Severus

公元222~231年
青铜
重20克
佛罗伦萨国家考古博物馆

正面：戴月桂花冠的亚历山大·塞维鲁头像。
反面：坐姿的罗马神带着盾牌，右手执胜利女神耐克，左手持权杖。

222-231 CE
Bronze
W. 20 g
National Archeological Museum, Florence
Obverse: Head of Alexander Severus with laurel wreath.
Reverse: Seated Roma with a shield, a Nike (Victory) in her right hand, and a scepter in her left.

马克西米努斯·色雷克斯 "塞斯特提" 铜币
Sestertius of Maximus Thrax

公元235~236年
青铜
重21.7克
佛罗伦萨国家考古博物馆

正面：戴月桂花冠的马克西米努斯·色雷克斯头像。
反面：前进中的胜利之神头戴皇冠、手持棕榈叶树枝。

235–236 CE
Bronze
W. 21.7 g
National Archeological Museum, Florence

Obverse: Head of Maximinus Thrax with laurel wreath.
Reverse: Advancing goddess Victory carrying a crown and a palm bough.

马克西米努斯·色雷克斯是来自色雷斯的一名士兵，从辅助兵一路晋升。公元235年，亚历山大·塞维鲁被暗杀之后，他被军队拥立为皇帝。马克西米努斯异常强大，在被刺杀以前，他捍卫王位长达三年之久。北非城市蒂斯德鲁斯（现在位于突尼斯的埃尔杰姆）曾爆发了针对马克西米努斯·色雷克斯所实行政策的反叛，虽然失败，但为他倒台奠定了基础。

Maximinus, a soldier from Thrace who had worked his way up from the auxiliary ranks, was acclaimed emperor by the army following the assassination of Alexander Severus in 235 CE. He was an unusually large man, and managed to survive as emperor for three years before being assassinated. A rebellion against Maximinus Thrax's policies that erupted in the North African city of Thysdrus (present-day El-Djem in Tunisia) failed, but it set the stage for his downfall.

戈狄亚努斯三世 "坤喀留斯" 金币
Quinquarius of Gordianus III

公元241~243年
黄金
直径1.8厘米
佛罗伦萨国家考古博物馆

正面：戴月桂花冠的戈狄亚努斯三世头像。
反面：平躺的赫拉克勒斯。

241–243 CE
Gold
D. 1.8 cm
National Archeological Museum, Florence

Obverse: Head of Gordanius III with laurel wreath.
Reverse: Resting Hercules.

罗马禁卫军选择由戈狄亚努斯三世继承马克西米努斯·色雷克斯。戈狄亚努斯当时年仅13岁，是阿非利加省年迈总督的孙子，在蒂斯德鲁斯抗议时期被宣布为皇帝。他努力生存直至19岁时被暗杀。

The Praetorian Guard selected Gordian III to succeed Maximinus Thrax. Gordian was 13 years old at the time, and grandson of the elderly proconsul of the Province of Africa who had been proclaimed emperor during the failed Thysdrus rebellion. He managed to survive until he was 19 before assassination.

戈狄亚努斯三世 "塞斯特提" 铜币
Sestertius of Gordianus III

公元240年
青铜
直径3.4厘米
佛罗伦萨国家考古博物馆

正面：戈狄亚努斯三世的头像。
反面：端坐的阿波罗右手持一根树枝，左手握里拉琴。

240 CE
Bronze
D. 3.4 cm
National Archeological Museum, Florence

Obverse: Head of Gordanius III.
Reverse: Seated Apollo with a tree branch in his right hand and a lyre in his left.

安东尼娅 "阿斯" 铜币
As of Antonia

公元1世纪中叶
青铜
直径2.8厘米
锡耶纳国家考古博物馆

正面：安东尼娅的头像。
反面：站立的男性人物。

Mid-1st century CE
Bronze
D. 2.8 cm
National Archeological Museum, Siena

Obverse: Head of Antonia.
Reverse: Standing male figure.

小安东尼娅是马克·安东尼和屋大维的女儿，克劳迪乌斯皇帝的母亲和卡里古拉皇帝的祖母。她以美貌和高尚的品德而著名，在克劳迪乌斯早期的统治时期，曾以她之名义发行货币。货币反面的男性很有可能就是克劳迪乌斯本人。

Antonia the Younger was the daughter of Mark Anthony and Octavia, mother of the emperor Claudius, and grandmother of Caligula. Renowned for her beauty and virtue, Claudius issued coins in her behalf early in his reign. The male depicted on the reverse is probably Claudius.

大阿格丽品娜 "塞斯特提" 铜币
Sestertius of Agrippina Major

公元37~41年
青铜
直径3.2厘米
锡耶纳国家考古博物馆

正面：身穿披风的阿格丽皮娜半身像。
反面：由骡子拉动的战车。

37–41 CE
Bronze
D. 3.2 cm
National Archeological Museum, Siena

Obverse: Bust of Agrippina wearing a cloak.
Reverse: Chariot drawn by mules.

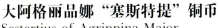

据史学家苏维托尼乌斯所述，卡里古拉每年举办庆典纪念他的母亲大阿格丽品娜。这些庆典包括各种竞赛和仪式，比如骡子拉战车比赛。

According to the author Suetonius, Caligula held annual public festivals in honor of his mother Agrippina the Elder. These festivals included various contests and rituals, including a race of chariots drawn by mules.

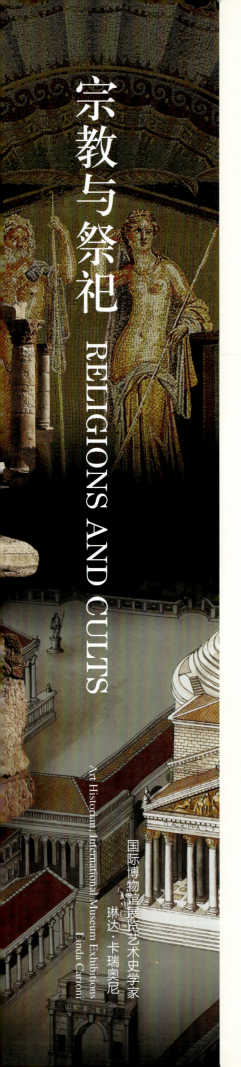

宗教与祭祀

RELIGIONS AND CULTS

国际博物馆展览艺术史学家
琳达·卡瑞奥尼
Art Historian International Museum Exhibitions
Linda Carioni

　　早期的罗马人和之前的希腊人一样，信奉一些"至高神"，祭拜的仪式与他们所处的环境和农业种植周期息息相关。这些神灵未被明确地人格化，因为他们没有与之相关的神话故事，也没有伴侣和子嗣，但他们拥有超能力，能够应朝拜者的召唤造福人类。重要的神灵有战神马尔斯（Mars）以及在和平年代等同于火星的奎里纳斯（Quirinus）。罗马神灵的首领是天神朱庇特（Jupiter），他如同希腊神灵中的宙斯（Zeus）。他是掌管天气的神灵，能为干旱地区带来雨水。因此，人们在意大利的山顶祭拜他。所有经受过闪电的地区都成了他的领地。朱庇特也是代表着道德理念的神灵，他带领着各位英雄履行职责。

　　罗马帝国时代的神灵论是多种宗教信仰交替混合的产物。事实上，宗教的宽容和同化正是罗马文明的特征。宗教信仰多是来自意大利南部的希腊殖民地，其他的则是在古伊特鲁尼亚或拉丁（Latin）部落中根深蒂固的宗教信仰。受到伊特鲁利亚的希腊文化影响，朱庇特还被赋予了伴侣朱诺（Juno）和密涅瓦（Minerva），即赫拉和雅典娜。供奉三位神灵的庙宇高耸于古罗马城市广场，并且屹立了整个帝国时期。维纳斯、福耳图那和黛安娜起源于古意大利，阿波罗则是来源于希腊神话，且没有与之对应的罗马神灵。酒神巴克斯及其狂欢节都具有重要的宗教意义。罗马神灵逐渐被希腊化，并与在希腊神话中具有相同定义的神灵一一对应。

　　罗马人对于宗教持务实的态度。繁荣、成功、胜利或失败取决于是否严格遵守朝拜程序，以祈求神灵的庇佑。信奉的目的是为了获得美好的愿望或期待神灵将如何改变百姓的未来；因此用于供奉给神灵的祭品和用于预测未来的占卜仪式都是罗马人民生活中的十分重要的公共仪式。这些仪式由复杂的程序组成，并接受祭司的管理。在罗马帝国时期，君王会被授予最高神职或大祭司的头衔。这一皇权的基本头衔也被印刻在货币上。

　　当获得胜利的屋大维改名奥古斯都这一寓意尊贵的名字时，他已为自己死后的封号作好了准备，同时这也转变了罗马宗教的基础；他已被神化，他似乎已赋予罗马太多，足以让罗马视他为神。之后这也成了一种惯例，如果一位帝王在有生之年有杰出的贡献，那他死后便会被封作罗马神灵。这一惯例的后果发展成了帝国的一种迷信。它们团结为一股力量，信奉罗马本身。从此以后，帝王被认为是神圣不可侵犯的，并且是具有天赐神力的化身。

　　个人举办的宗教仪式关系到家庭生活、日常生活和商业生活的许多方面，由一家之长负责。宗教与其说是一种精神上的经历，倒不如说是人与神灵的契约关系，它保障着人们的生活幸福安康。

守护家园的神灵主要有两位，较重要的是守卫者，门神雅努斯（*Janus*）。精灵神的中心是灶台和灶上的火，而这些通常是由房屋的女主人来照看的，因此房屋的第二位正式守卫者就是女灶神维斯塔。吃饭时，会在一旁放置些食物，或将其投入灶火，以示供奉之意。

家神拉尔（*Lares*）是祖先的灵魂，对于罗马家庭是极其重要的。人们将家神的小雕像供奉在神龛之中。它是最重要的神灵，世代看守家族的命运。每天人们都会向其祈祷，供奉食物。在宗教日或特殊的日子，还会举行特别的仪式。另一位家神是吉尼斯（*genius*），通常以一条蛇或是阴茎状符号的形式出现。某种意义上说，它意味着赋予丈夫，即孩子的生父"男子气概"，它也可用于特定的私人仪式，以祈求繁衍子嗣。

礼拜仪式也用来拜祭神灵以祈求幸福安康。在农村，人们拜祭农业神对农作物的庇佑，城市中的商人拜祭墨丘利神和其他与保佑财运相关的神灵。那些代表抽象意义的神灵也为人们所拜祭，例如和平之神康考迪亚娅（*Concordia*）、健康和繁荣之神萨卢斯（*Salus*）、命运之神福耳图那和丰收之神阿班丹提亚（*Abundantia*）。

罗马人对来世没有过多的奢望；传统的罗马宗教也很少提及来世。一个人死后，他的灵魂会与其他逝者的灵魂一起成为家神之一。葬礼仍然是人生的重要部分，特别是作为财富或权利的表现形式。根据法律，坟墓必须建于城墙之外；富人通常在城市主要通路边上建造一座陵墓，而穷人则竖立一块刻有碑文的石柱（又叫墓碑）。

直到公元1世纪，火化成为了人们首选的埋葬方式，各种骨灰坛用于存放骨灰。随后，土葬更为常见，尸体被存放于石棺之中。如果逝者是富人，石棺由昂贵的大理石制造并刻有装饰性的图案。如果逝者仅为小康，则采用简单的木棺。其后，基督教徒也采用了这一埋葬方式。

Like the Greeks before them, the early Romans worshipped of a few "high gods" and rites were closely tied to their environment and agrarian cycles. Vaguely personified, these gods had no myths, did not form married pairs, had no offspring, but possessed superhuman powers that could be called upon to intervene for the benefit of the worshipper. Important divinities were Mars, the god of war, and Quirinus, Mars' equivalent in time of peace. Chief among the Roman gods, however was Jupiter, a sky god like his Greek equivalent, Zeus. He was the god of weather, the sender of rain in drought and was worshipped on hilltops throughout Italy. All places struck by lightening were made his property. Jupiter was also the god who embodied moral concepts, who led the hero down the path of duty.

Gods and goddesses of Imperial times were a blend of religious influences; in fact, religious tolerance and assimilation was characteristic of the Roman civilization. Many were introduced via the Greek colonies of southern Italy. Others had their roots in the religious beliefs of the ancient Etruscans or Latin tribes. From Greek influence in Etruria, Jupiter was given as partners the goddesses Juno and Minerva, (identified with Hera and Athena). The temple dedicated to the three divinities dominated the Roman Forum. Such a temple was present in every settlement throughout the empire. Venus, Fortuna and Diana emerged from native Italian sources. Imported from Greece was the cult of Apollo that had no Roman equivalent. Bacchus, the god of wine, and bacchanalian festivities were also of religious importance. Gradually, a process of Hellenization took place and the Roman gods assumed the features associated with the Greek mythology of their equivalents.

The Romans had a practical attitude to state religion. Prosperity, success, victory or defeat depended on the strict performance of rituals intended to guarantee the favour of the Gods. The purpose of worship was to obtain their good will or to discover how the gods might influence the future; hence sacrifice, intended to please the gods, and divination rites, used to foretell the future, were very important public ceremonies in Roman life. Composed of complicated rituals, these ceremonies were regulated by an elaborate priesthood. In Imperial Rome, the Emperor was given the title of supreme priest or *pontifex maximus*. A fundamental definition of Imperial power, the title was often inscribed on coinage.

When the victorious Octavian assumed the name of Augustus, a term implying reverence, he prepared the way for his own posthumous deification and a transformation of the Roman religious foundation; he was deified because he seemed to have given Rome gifts worthy of a god. It then became customary for emperors, if they were worthy in their lifetimes, to be elevated to divinity upon their deaths. The ramification of this was the Imperial cult that developed throughout the empire. Encouraged as a unifying force, the cult included worship of Rome herself. Overtime, the emperors were treated as divine and seen as the selected representation of divine powers.

Private religious rituals, overseen by the head of the family, the *pater familias*, related to various aspects of family life, daily life and work or business life. Religion was less a spiritual experience than a contractual relationship between man and the gods that were believed to control one's existence and well-being.

Two main gods protected the home. Chief guardian was Janus, the god of doorways and beginnings. The spiritual center however was the hearth and the fire of the hearth was an element tended to by the woman of the house, so the second official deity of the home was Vesta, the goddess of the hearth. During meals, food might be set aside and passed into the fire as an offering.

The spirits of the ancestors, the *Lares*, were extremely important to Roman families. They were represented by small figurines that were kept in their own shrine, the *lararium*. The *Lar familiaris*, the benevolent god that watched over the family's fortunes from generation to generation was the most important. On a everyday basis, short prayers and small offerings were made to the Lares. On sacred days or on special occasions, more elaborate rituals were held in their honour. Another household spirit was the *genius*, often represented in the form of a snake or phallic symbol. This was in a sense the 'manhood' of the family, which empowered the husband to father children and an important function of certain private rituals was to insure fertility.

Devotional rites were also rendered to deities that affected the individual's livelihood and well-being. In rural villages, great care was taken to honour the agrarian deities that watched over the crops just as merchants in the city honoured Mercury and other gods associated with trade. The divine personifications of abstract concepts such as *Concordia* (peace), *Salus* (health and prosperity), *Fortuna* (fortune) and *Abundantia* (abundance) were also honoured.

The Romans had an uncomplicated view of the afterlife; traditional Roman religion offered little hope of eternal life. The spirit of the deceased joined all the other spirits of the dead and became one of the family *lares*. Still, funeral rites were an important part of life, especially as a social affirmation of wealth or power. By law, tombs had to be built outside city walls; the wealthy often built mausoleums along the main access roads of the city while the less fortunate erected an inscribed *stele* (tombstone) to mark the grave site.

Until the I century CE, cremation was the preferred burial practice and a variety of urns were used to hold the ashes. Subsequently, when internment became the more common practice, the body would be placed in a sarcophagus. If the deceased was wealthly, the sarcophagus would be made of expensive marble and incised with decorative motifs. Simple wood coffins were used for the less well-to-do, and this type of burial was later adopted by the Christians.

大祭司奥古斯都石像
Head of Augustus as Pontifex Maximus

公元前 27世纪~公元14世纪
大理石
高21厘米
佛罗伦萨国家考古博物馆

27 BCE - 14 CE
Marble
H. 21 cm
National Archeological Museum, Florence

奥古斯都皇帝在这尊雕像里蒙头（*apite velato*），全然一幅大祭司的模样（*Pontifex Maximus*）。这个未来的皇帝以年轻男子的形象示人，卷曲的短发衬托出他瘦削的脸。事实上，奥古斯都在很年轻的时候就已经加入了最高祭司团。

Here the Emperor Augustus is depicted *capite velato* (the head is veiled) that is to say as Pontifex Maximus. The future emperor is portrayed in this statue as a young man, whose oval face is framed by wavy locks. Indeed, Augustus became a member of the Pontifical College when he was very young.

密特拉杀牛救赎石雕
Relief with Mithras Killing a Bull

帝国时期
大理石
高70厘米
佛罗伦萨国家考古博物馆

Imperial Age
Marble
H. 70 cm
National Archeological Museum, Florence

东方诸神及异教传播至发源地之外常常被赋予了其他的特质，比如早期的异教和仪式通常与农业相关，但之后就作为个人救赎的方式。异教的神或女神的崇拜者借助入门式得以与神分享克服逆境的胜利。被冠以"神秘宗教"之名的"入门式"（initiation）是源自希腊术语奥秘（mysteria）。密特拉教是其中最受欢迎的一种。

密特拉是波斯神，其信仰在1~2世纪传播至整个帝国，在3世纪尤为强盛。密特拉教排斥女性，在罗马军队中非常流行，被认为具有非常高的灵性。密特拉教的入门式通常在洞穴或仿照洞穴建造的地下室进行。仪式中杀牛的象征意义还不为人知，或许代表着密特拉教的崇拜者以参与祭祀活动实现自我救赎。

As oriental gods and cults spread beyond their lands of origin, they often took on a different character-cults and rituals that earlier might have had to do with agriculture, for example, came to be understood as paths to personal salvation. By means of initiation rituals, worshippers identified with the god or goddess of the cult, and thereby shared in the god's victory over adversities. These are called "Mystery Cults" after the Greek term for "initiation" (mysteria). One very popular mystery cult was Mithrism. Mithrus was Persian god whose cult spread throughout the empire during the 1st and 2nd centuries CE, and was especially strong during the 3rd century. It was for men only, very popular among Roman soldiers, and characterized by a high level of spirituality. Mithraic initiation rituals were celebrated in caves or in underground chambers constructed to resemble caves. The symbolism of slaying of a bull is unclear, but somehow it was understood to be an act of salvation in which the worshippers participated directly with the sacrificial act.

主神朱庇特石头像 上[…]

主神朱庇特石头像
Head of Jupiter

帝国时期
大理石
高39厘米
佛罗伦萨国家考古博物馆

Imperial Age
Marble
H. 39 cm
National Archeological Museum, Florence

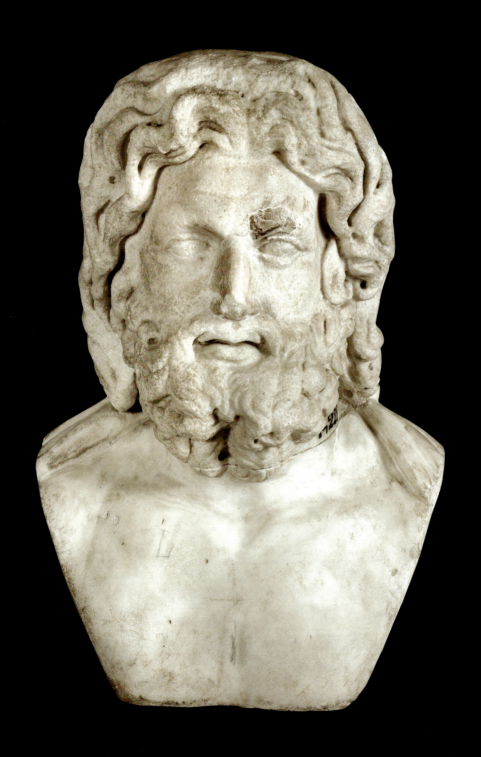

罗马的朱庇特与希腊的宙斯一样被认为是众神的父亲，所以他们的形象也相似，留着胡子，脸上垂着卷曲的长发。

Roman Jupiter was identified with Greek Zeus, the father of many gods, and he is depicted accordingly—bearded, with his face framed by long, wavy hair.

罗马帝国的诸神
THE MANY GODS AND GODESSES OF THE ROMAN EMPIRE

　　随着帝国的扩张，罗马人接触了外国的神灵和女神，罗马的宗教变得日益国际化。

　　罗马人经常将他们自己的神灵与外国的神灵等同化，特别是希腊的神灵，认为他们有相似的性格和作用，罗马宗教由此融合了"奥林匹亚"的神话。罗马的朱庇特相当于希腊的宙斯，罗马的朱诺相当于希腊的赫拉，罗马的维纳斯相当于希腊的阿佛洛狄特等等。

　　罗马的神灵也对应于东方的神灵。朱庇特-塞拉皮斯，是罗马朱比特、希腊宙斯-哈得斯和埃及的奥西里斯、阿比斯的结合体。福耳图那-伊希斯是罗马的福耳图那和埃及的伊希斯的结合体。

As the Empire expanded and Romans encountered foreign gods and goddesses, Roman religion became increasingly international.

The Romans often equated their own gods with foreign gods that had similar characteristics and functions. This was especially true of Greek gods, and in this way Roman religion incorporated the stories of "Olympian" mythology. Roman Jupiter came to be equated with Greek Zeus, Roman Juno with Greek Hera, Roman Venus with Greek Aphrodite, and so on.

Roman gods were equated with oriental gods as well. Jupiter Serapis was a combination of Roman Jupiter, Greek Zeus-Hades, and Egyptian Osiris Apis. Fortuna-Isis combined Roman Fortuna with Egyptian Isis.

朱庇特·塞拉皮斯石胸像
Small Bust of Jupiter Serapis

帝国时期
雪花石膏
高35厘米
佛罗伦萨国家考古博物馆

Imperial Age
Alabaster
H. 35 cm
National Archeological Museum, Florence

塞拉皮斯由埃及国王托勒密一世（公元前305~282年）引入，用来吸引希腊和埃及的国民。它结合了希腊的宙斯-哈得斯和埃及的奥西里斯神-阿比斯神，塞拉皮斯从亚历山大港传播至地中海东部和意大利南部，最后传遍整个罗马世界。

Serapis was introduced by Ptolemy I of Egypt (305-282 BCE) and intended to appeal to both his Greek and Egyptian subjects. A combination of Greek Zeus-Hades and Egyptian Osiris-Apis, Serapis spread from Alexandria to the eastern Mediterranean, southern Italy and eventually throughout the Roman world.

智慧女神密涅瓦石头像
Head of Minerva

公元2世纪
大理石
高27厘米
佛罗伦萨国家考古博物馆

2nd century CE
Marble
H. 27 cm
National Archeological Museum, Florence

密涅瓦女神头像戴有头盔，头
发从大护颈下垂落。雕像的一
大特色是有帽沿的头盔衬托了
女神的面庞。

The head portrays Minerva wearing a
helmet while her hair falls down from
the large neck shield. The visor of her
helmet, replicating the face of the
goddess, is an extraordinary feature
of this statue.

智慧女神密涅瓦石头像
Head of Minerva

小型诸神铜像 Small bronze figurines of gods and goddesses

小型铜质神和女神雕像均作为愿望实现后供奉给神灵的祭司品，也可作为家中的宗教供奉神像。

Small bronze figurines of gods and goddesses used both as votive offerings—gifts to the gods in fulfillment of vows—and as cult figurines in household shrines.

智慧女神密涅瓦铜像
Small Statue of Minerva

帝国时期
铜
高10.5厘米
佛罗伦萨国家考古博物馆

Imperial Age
Bronze
H. 10.5 cm
National Archeological Museum, Florence

祭祀铜像
Small Statue of Veiled Sacrific

帝国时期
铜
高10.1厘米
佛罗伦萨国家考古博物馆

Imperial Age
Bronze
H. 10.1 cm
National Archeological Museum, Florence

辛运女神福耳图那-伊希斯石像
Statue of a Woman Portrayed as the Goddess Fortuna-Isis

图拉真时期（公元98~117年）
大理石
高130厘米，宽45厘米，重130千克
佛罗伦萨国家考古博物馆

Reign of Trajan (98-117 CE)
Marble
L. 130 cm, W. 45 cm, D. 130 kg
National Archeological Museum, Florence

幸运女神福耳图那-伊希斯的右臂低垂，左臂弯曲，手里端着以棕榈叶图案为装饰的聚宝盆（象征丰饶的羊角）。她的头上盘着发辫并在脑后连接。这样的发型说明雕像是在图拉真统治时代（公元98~117年）制造的。雕像的头上还佩戴镶有两条蛇盘踞于中央的长方形发卡。

幸运女神是早期很受欢迎的罗马女神，她能带来繁衍和财富。伊西斯则是埃及女神，奥西里斯的妻子。公元2世纪中期，伊西斯的异教影响传遍了罗马世界。福耳图那和伊西斯合二为一成为福耳图那-伊西斯，被认为是能够掌管命运，并给人们带来财富的女神。聚宝盆是其象征。

The goddess Fortuna-Isis' right arm is lowered and the left is bent, holding a cornucopia decorated with palm leaves. Her hairstyle, with a series of braids around the head and joined at the back, suggests that the statue was made during the reign of Trajan (98-117 CE). She also wears a hair band decorated with two snakes converging at a central, rectangular ornament.

Fortuna was a Roman goddess popular from earliest times, bringer of fertility and increase. Isis was an Egyptian goddess, consort of Osiris, whose cult had spread throughout the Roman world by the middle of the 2nd century CE. The two were fused as Fortuna-Isis, believed to determine fate and provide wealth, as symbolized by the cornucopia.

命运女神福耳图那铜像
Small Statue Representing the Goddess Fortuna

帝国时期
铜
高15.3厘米
佛罗伦萨国家考古博物馆

Imperial Age
Bronze
H. 15.3 cm
National Archeological Museum, Florence

命运女神福耳图那左手拿着象
征着财富的聚宝盆坐立。福耳
图那也称作福斯·福耳图那，
与希腊女神堤喀一样是掌管命
运、机遇和幸运的女神。

Fortuna sits with a cornucopia in her
left hand, the symbol of abundance.
Also known as Fors Fortuna, and
identified with the Greek goddess
Tyche, she was the goddess of fate,
chance, and luck.

Hecateion (Stand with the Goddess Hecate)/ Hecateion

公元前1世纪
大理石
高53厘米，宽30厘米
佛罗伦萨国家考古博物馆

1ˢᵗ century BCE
Marble
H. 53 cm, W. 30 cm
National Archeological Museum, Florence

赫卡忒是色雷斯人的月亮女
神，通常为三位身着长衣手拿
火把的女人。赫卡忒原有的信
奉区集中在小亚细亚，但是之
后常常与相似的神灵阿耳特弥
斯和珀尔塞福涅相混淆。

Hecate was a Thracian moon goddess
often shown as three women dressed
in long tunics and with torches in
their hands. She originally had her
own cult, concentrated especially
in Asia Minor, but later was often
confused with similar deities such as
Artemis and Persephone.

月亮女神戴安娜铜像
Small Statue of Diana

帝国时期
铜
高12.4厘米
佛罗伦萨国家考古博物馆

Imperial Age
Bronze
H. 12.4 cm
National Archeological Museum, Florence

爱神厄洛斯铜像
Small Statue of the Eros

帝国时期
铜
高6.4厘米
佛罗伦萨国家考古博物馆

Imperial Age
Bronze
H. 6.4 cm
National Archeological Museum, Florence

大力神赫拉克勒斯铜像
Small Statue Representing Hercules

帝国时期
铜
通高12.4厘米
佛罗伦萨国家考古博物馆

Imperial Age
Bronze
H. 12.4 cm (with the base)
National Archeological Museum, Florence

持霍恩角的裸体英雄石像
Small Statue of "Naked Hero with the Horne on the Right Hand"

帝国时期
大理石
高72厘米
佛罗伦萨国家考古博物馆

Imperial Age
Marble
H. 72 cm
National Archaeological Museum. Florence

这件波利克利特斯风格的雕塑表现了一个年轻的裸体男子。事实上，它是波利克利特斯的战神赫拉克勒斯系列复制品中的一件，与其传统有关联。此高仿雕像证明了这类小雕像在罗马悠久的艺术传统中广受欢迎。

The sculpture represents a young naked man in the style of Policleto; as a matter of fact, it has been included in the series of replicas of Policleto's Hercules, and it still remains associated to that tradition. However, the high quality of the modelling of the bust proves that the series of small statues such this one had an important success and long time tradition in the Roman art.

爱神爱摩尔石像
Small Statue of Amor

公元2世纪早期
红色细粒大理石，部分为白色细粒大理石重塑作品
高102厘米
佛罗伦萨国家考古博物馆

Early 2nd century CE
Red-grained marble; some reconstruction with fine-grained. white
marble
H. 102 cm
National Archeological Museum, Florence

雕像中的爱摩尔（Amor是古罗
马爱神丘比特的别名，相当于
希腊的厄洛斯）长着翅膀，头
偏向左肩，右手高拿斗篷，斗
篷上有插入多层褶皱中的圆形
搭扣。此作品由同类大理石的
碎片塑成，很难判断是原作品
和复制品，但躯干和头部确为
原作。

This statue represents a winged
Amor with his head bent on the
left shoulder and the right arm
raised. The arm holds a cloak with
a circular *fibula* (buckle) inserted
into the heavy folds. Because this
piece has been reconstructed from
numerous fragments of similar types
of marble, it is difficult to distinguish
between the original sculpture and
the reconstruction. The torso and
the head are certainly original to the
piece.

爱神厄洛斯石像
Statue of Sleeping Eros

公元2世纪中期
大理石
高23厘米，长48厘米，宽45厘米
佛罗伦萨国家考古博物馆

Mid-2nd century CE
Fine-grained. white marble
H. 23 cm. L. 48 cm . W. 45 cm
National Archeological Museum, Florence

年轻的带着翅膀的厄洛斯睡在椭圆形基座上，基座明显覆盖着狮皮。狮头的下方可见箭袋的下部。厄洛斯的左边是一个火把。厄洛斯沉睡的姿势有其他例子的记载，通常基于希腊化晚期的原型。除了厄洛斯右脚大脚趾外，此雕像完好无损。

A young winged Eros sleeps on an oval base, apparently a rock covered by a lion skin. The lower part of a quiver is visible under the lion's head, and there is a torch near Eros' left. The sleeping Eros in this position is documented by other examples, all probably based on a late Hellenistic prototype. The statue is intact except for a part of the big toe on the right foot.

牧神潘石像
Herm of the God Pan

帝国时期
大理石
高153厘米
佛罗伦萨国家考古博物馆

Imperial Age
Marble
H. 153 cm
National Archeological Museum, Florence

自然田园之神潘与酒神巴克斯
（希腊狄俄尼索斯）关系密
切。他通常为半人半羊的形
象，但这尊雕像几乎完全为人
形。他身穿鹿皮，头戴尖帽，
是典型的牧羊人形象。他的右
肩扛着一只小山羊，左手拿着
一个桶状容器。

Pan was a god of pastoral life and
nature, closely associated with
Bacchus (Greek Dionysus), and often
depicted as half-man and half-goat.
Yet this statue depicts him as almost
completely human. He is wearing a
deerskin and pointed hat typical of
shepherds. He carries a small goat
on his right shoulder and has a *situla*
(bucket) in his left hand.

森林神萨梯石头像
Head of Satyr

公元1～2世纪
大理石
高27厘米
佛罗伦萨国家考古博物馆

1ˢᵗ – 2ⁿᵈ century CE
Marble
H. 27 cm
National Archeological Museum, Florence

萨梯是与酒神巴克斯、自然之
神潘有关的森林之神，代表着
大自然孕育的力量。通常为半
人半羊形象。

Satyrs were gods of the woods tied
to Bacchus and Pan and symbolized
the fertility forces of nature; they are
represented by half-man, half-goat
figures

森林神西勒努斯石像
Silenus

帝国时期
大理石
高95厘米
佛罗伦萨国家考古博物馆

Imperial Age
Marble
H. 95 cm
National Archeological Museum, Florence

留着胡子的西勒努斯（森林神萨蒂的别称）像头戴常春藤和藤叶编制的冠冕，身穿兽皮衣服。这种类型的人物肖像雕塑最初起源于古罗马晚期，直到帝国时期中期才广为流行。此后，人们常用此类雕塑装点花园和喷泉。

The statue represents a *silenus* with beard, crowned with ivy or vine leaves and dressed with an animal-skin. The origin of this type of representation can be dated to the Late Hellenistic period, and it had a great success until the Mid Imperial Age, as it was used to decorate gardens and fountains.

农神西尔瓦诺斯铜像
Small Statue Representing the God Silvanus

帝国时期
铜
高13.4厘米
佛罗伦萨国家考古博物馆

Imperial Age
Bronze
H. 13.4 cm
National Archeological Museum, Florence

西尔瓦诺斯是森林和放羊人之
神。他也供奉于民间神龛，尤
其流行于社会地位低下的奴隶
阶层。

Silvanus was the god of the woods
and of shepherds. He was also
honored in domestic shrines, and
was especially popular with slaves of
low social standing.

商业神墨丘利铜像
Small Statue Representing the God Mercury

帝国时期
铜
高12厘米
佛罗伦萨国家考古博物馆

Imperial Age
Bronze
H. 12 cm
National Archeological Museum, Florence

墨丘利与希腊的赫耳墨斯一样
是商业贸易之神。

Mercury, identified with Greek
Hermes, was a god of trade and
commercial success.

医神埃斯库拉庇俄斯石像
Small Statue of Aesculapius

帝国时期
大理石
高30厘米
佛罗伦萨国家考古博物馆

Imperial Age
Marble
H. 30 cm
National Archeological Museum, Florence

埃斯库拉庇俄斯是医神，在所信奉的地区要举行该神崇拜的治疗仪式。他的形象与朱庇特类似。他站立着，手拿缠蛇的棍棒紧靠右腿边。

Asclepius was the patron god of medicine and the god of cult places where healing rites were practiced. He is depicted similarly to Jupiter. Here he stands with a club, around which coils a snake, held next to his right thigh.

健康女神海吉娅石像
Small Statue of Hygeia

帝国时期
大理石
高50厘米
佛罗伦萨国家考古博物馆

Imperial Age
Marble
H. 50 cm
National Archeological Museum, Florence

海吉娅源自希腊的健康女神，与之等同的罗马女神有萨卢斯。海吉娅通常与医术之神阿斯库勒庇俄斯相联系，共同代表着均衡健康的概念。

Hygeia was a healing goddess of Greek origin whom the Romans equated with their goddess Salus. Often associated with Asclepius, Hygeia represented the abstract ideas of health and the equilibrium of physical well-being.

家神拉尔铜像
Small Statue of a Lar God

公元1世纪
铜
高10厘米
佛罗伦萨国家考古博物馆

1st century CE
Bronze
H. 10 cm
National Archeological Museum, Florence

拉尔是起源意大利的乡村神灵，供奉于旷地，之后作为家庭的守护神。拉尔神龛通常树立在旷地或交叉路口。每家都可用小神龛供奉拉尔神、佩纳特斯和祖先神灵。

The *Lares* were divinities of Italic origins originally related to rural properties and venerated in open spaces. Later they came to be understood as protectors of home and family. Shrines for Lares stood in open spaces and at crossroads. Also each family would have a small household shrine for its Lares, Penates (other domestic deities) and ancestral spirits.

家神拉尔铜像
Small Statue of a Lar God

公元1世纪
铜
高8厘米
佛罗伦萨国家考古博物馆

1st century CE
Bronze
H. 8 cm
National Archeological Museum, Florenc

生育之神普里阿普斯铜像
Small Statue Representing the God Priapus

帝国时期
铜
高6.7厘米
佛罗伦萨国家考古博物馆

Imperial Age
Bronze
H. 6.7 cm
National Archeological Museum, Florence

普里阿普斯是自然界繁殖力之神，他的形象特点是一个大型的生殖器，象征着繁衍兴旺。他也代表着人们对于酒神狄俄尼索斯－巴克斯的崇拜。普里阿普斯的雕像可作为花园的装饰或家庭神龛。

Priapus was a god of the regenerative forces of nature and his image, characterized by a large sexual organ, symbolized fertility and prosperity. He also figured in the worship of Dionysus-Bacchus. Statues of Priapus decorated gardens and were included in the household shrines.

智慧之神赫耳墨斯铜像
Small Statue Representing Anherm with Erect

帝帝国时期
铜
高5.6厘米
佛罗伦萨国家考古博物馆

Imperial Age
Bronze
H. 5.6 cm
National Archeological Museum, Florence

此微型赫耳墨斯代表的是男性生殖神普里阿普斯。典型的赫耳墨斯像为顶部有人头像的立石，下方镶嵌着男性生殖器，有时石碑两边会有小的残臂。赫耳墨斯通常放置于街边、十字路口、门前等交通要道。这种小像也在家中供奉。

This miniature Herm apparently represents Priapus, the phallic divinity. Herms typically consisted of a vertical pillar of stone with a human head on top, a phallus below, and sometimes small stumps of arms on either side. Herms were placed along streets, at crossroads, in front of doors and anywhere there was a place of transition. A small one such as this may have stood in a household shrine.

铜阴茎护身符
Pendant Amulet in the form of a Phallus

帝国时期
铜
器长9.5厘米，链长16.5厘米
锡耶纳国家考古博物馆

Imperial Age
Bronze
L. (body) 9.5 cm, L. (chain)
16.5 cm
National Archeological
Museum, Siena

考古学家在罗马地区发现了许多形状、大小不同的阴茎护身符，佩戴这些护生符可以驱赶邪恶，增强男子气概，提升战斗力。

Many phallus amulets of different shapes and sizes have been discovered by archaeologists at Roman sites. They were worn to ward off evil, enhance virility, and increase strength in battle.

铜阴茎护身符
Amulet in the form of a Phallus

帝国时期
铜
长4 厘米，宽3.6厘米
锡耶纳国家考古博物馆

Imperial Age
Bronze
L. 4 cm , W.3.6 m
National Archeological Museum, Siena

铜阴茎护身符
Amulet in the form of a Phallus

帝国时期
铜
长5.2厘米
锡耶纳国家考古博物馆

Imperial Age
Bronze
L. 5.2 cm
National Archeological Museum, Siena

铜阴茎护身符
Amulet in the form of a Phallus

帝国时期
铜
长4厘米
锡耶纳国家考古博物馆

Imperial Age
Bronze
H. 4 cm
National Archeological Museum, Siena

铜神谕
Oracle

帝国时期
铜
长14.8厘米，宽2厘米
佛罗伦萨国家考古博物馆

Imperial Age
Bronze
L. 14.8 cm, W. 2 cm
National Archeological Museum, Florence

Sorti Oracolari 是铜或石制的小器物，通常在命运女神的庙宇中可以找到。膜拜者从刻有女巫预言的几个神谕中挑选一个，神父则从中解读膜拜者的命运。该神谕上的刻文难以辨认，大意是："遵守女巫的指示就能成功。"

Sorti Oracolari were small bronze or stone objects usually found in temples dedicated to Fortuna. Worshippers would choose from several such oracles, each inscribed with a prophecy of the Sibyl, and a priest would then interpret the prophecy as it related to the worshipper's future. The inscription on this oracle is illegible, but the meaning seems to be: "if you will follow the Sibyl's indications, you will be successful".

向死者致敬
HONORING
THE DEAD

　　罗马宗教不支持永生的理论。人死后进入黑暗的地狱不能转生，但是丧葬仪式和对祖先的崇拜是生活中非常重要的部分。

　　帝国初期火葬很流行，死者被放置在柴堆上燃烧，骨灰被放进一个火葬瓮里（骨灰罐），骨灰盒放在公墓或者家族墓地里。帝国时代后期也有不施行火葬（土葬）的，而且越来越盛行，富有的罗马人把死者放置在有精美雕刻的石棺里。

　　公墓通常在城外，沿着大路，路过的人就可以看到墓碑和精美的坟墓。

Roman religion offered little hope for eternal life, just the dark underworld from which there was no return. Yet funerary rites and the veneration of ancestors were very important parts of life.

Cremation was favored during the early Imperial Period—the dead burned on a pyre, the ashes and bones placed in a cremation urn (*cinerarium*), and the container buried in a cemetery or family tomb. Burial without cremation (inhumation) was practiced also and became increasingly popular during the later Imperial Period, with the bodies of wealthy Romans placed in elaborately carved stone sarcophagi.

Cemeteries were outside the cities, often along a main road, where tombstones and more elaborate funerary monuments could be seen by passers-by.

石棺残件
Sarcophagus Side with Scene of Mourners

公元2世纪
大理石
长80厘米，宽70 厘米，厚12厘米
佛罗伦萨国家考古博物馆

2ⁿᵈ century CE
Marble
L. 80 cm, W. 70 cm, Th. 12 cm
National Archeological Museum, Florence

此石棺残件上装饰的是墨勒阿格神话的一幕，其中墨勒阿格的母亲爱菲娅和妻子克利奥帕特拉在它的墓前哭泣。

This fragment belongs to a sarcophagus decorated with scenes from the myth of Meleager. Meleager's mother Althaea and his wife Cleopatra weep at his tomb.

石棺残件
Sarcophagus Side with Mithologic Scene

公元2世纪
大理石
长80厘米，宽70 厘米，厚12厘米
佛罗伦萨国家考古博物馆

2nd century CE
Marble
L. 80 cm, W. 70 cm, Th. 12 cm
National Archeological Museum, Florence

骨灰盒瓮
Urn with Raised Stripes on Body

奥古斯都时期（公元前27~公元14年）
大理石
高35厘米，宽30厘米
佛罗伦萨国家考古博物馆

Reign of Augustus (27 BCE — 14 CE)
Marble
H. 35 cm, W. 30 cm
National Archeological Museum, Florence

此骨灰瓮代表方形建筑物，瓮盖
呈屋顶形状，边缘上扬。正面
铭文上方是卡皮托林母狼正在
喂养罗慕洛和罗穆斯的图案。

This cinerarium represents a square
building, the lid in the shape of a
roof with raised edges. The front
has an inscription under which the
Capitoline wolf nurses Romulus and
Remus.

圆柱形石骨灰瓮
Cylindrical Urn

奥古斯都时期（公元前27~公元14年）
大理石
高42厘米，宽34厘米
佛罗伦萨国家考古博物馆

Reign of Augustus (27 BCE – 14 CE)
Marble
H. 42 cm, W. 34 cm
National Archeological Museum, Florence

骨灰瓮通常是用贵重的材质制
成，比如大理石、雪花石膏、
玻璃和陶。瓮身由小爱神厄洛
斯手举着花环，瓮盖的纽作成
叼蛇的鹰。

Funerary urns often were made of
valuable materials such as marble,
alabaster, glass and ceramic. The
body of this one is decorated with
garlands held up by small Eros
figures. The handle of the lid is in the
shape of a hawk that holds a snake in
its beak.

石骨灰瓮
Urn with Raised Stripes on Body

奥古斯都时期（公元前27~公元14年）
大理石
高41厘米，宽31.5厘米
佛罗伦萨国家考古博物馆

Reign of Augustus (27 BCE —14 CE)
Marble
H. 41 cm, W. 31.5 cm
National Archeological Museum, Florence

石骨灰瓮
Urn

公元1世纪
雪花石膏
高39厘米
佛罗伦萨国家考古博物馆

1st century CE
Alabaster
H. 39 cm
National Archeological Museum, Florence

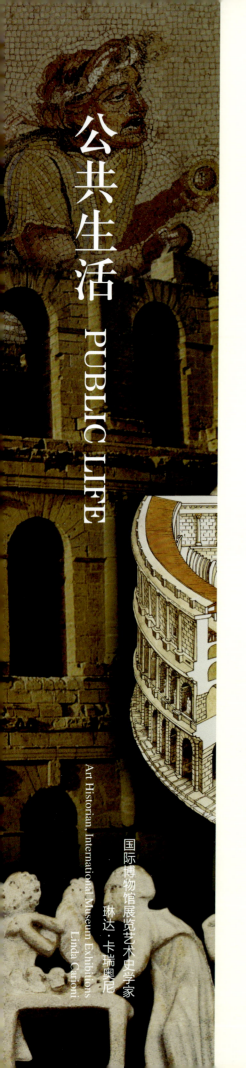

公共生活 PUBLIC LIFE

国际博物馆展览艺术史学家
琳达·卡瑞奥尼
Art Historian, International Museum Exhibitions
Linda Carioni

在罗马社会中，市民生活是多元化的。罗马人不论其身份地位大都乐于参与各式各样的娱乐活动。

罗马浴场的考古遗址是最能体现罗马市井生活的美好和复杂的代表之一。只有罗马人才能把一种洗浴行为提升成一门建筑艺术，也只有帝王浴场最能体现其细致和奢华。

每天会有各种阶层的人出入浴场，洗浴俨然成为了社会生活中十分重要的一部分。浴场除了提供满足个人卫生和护理的需求设备外，也是交友、谈生意、辩论、交流信息，以及得到友谊和社区感的场所。

人们通常会在午后去浴场。在更衣室更衣后就可踏入一个有温水浴池（*tepidarium*）的暖房，再去热水浴池（*caldarium*）。在热水浴池隔壁有桑拿间和蒸汽室。通常旁边还有与露天游泳池相连的冷水浴池（*frigidarium*）。去浴场还意味着可以去健身房从事些体育活动。选择如跑步、拳击、摔跤、掷铁饼还有各式球类游戏。最后人们会选择用丰富的橄榄油和芳香油来一把细致按摩从而结束一场洗浴。在浴场几个小时的放松过后，罗马人接着会去马戏团，圆形露天竞技场或戏院玩个尽兴。

娱乐活动充满了活力，是罗马公共生活不可分割的一部分。在宗教节日或政治军事庆典中，经常安排的庆祝活动有：战车比赛，角斗士竞赛，剧院演出和音乐会。

在整个罗马帝国，战车比赛非常流行。竞技场的赛道是长800米，宽80米，沿其长轴划分而成的椭圆形。每一场比赛需要4辆战车参赛（有双马式战车或四马战车式），且每位参赛者必须对抗其余所有参赛者。参赛者按照亢奋的拥护者（他们通常会赌结果）分类。罗马的马克西姆竞技场一次可容纳25万观众，全天可以观摩多达24场比赛。然而，作为一名战车参赛者。这是一项非常冒险的赌博，只有他们中最杰出的人可以得到大量金钱和巨大声望。

在露天剧场举办的角斗士格斗和斗兽表演是整个罗马帝国最流行，也是最臭名昭著的一种娱乐模式。公元80年，从韦帕芗皇帝到他儿子提图斯统治时期，罗马斗兽场成为了家喻户晓的露天剧场。椭圆形的斗兽场结构复杂，由实木和沙土混凝构成，周围的座位严格按照观众的不同社会阶级地位而被分成不同片区。斗兽场下面连接着一个庞大复杂的地下室，活板门里关押着角斗士，斗兽和战俘，也存放着一些武器和装备。

罗马帝国的一些节日庆祝可长达百天，成千上万的角斗士和野兽面临着生死角逐。比赛中，既可让人（或兽）直接攻击对方直到死亡，也可等对抗到某种程度让游戏的赞助人，或是皇帝或其代表决定生死。

观众可以通过挥动衣物，同时举起右手大拇指朝上为技巧高超的角斗士请求活命。如果败者表现的过于懦弱或不讨人喜爱，观众会把拇指朝下以示谴责。

众多角斗士都是有技巧的格斗者，他们之中有战俘、奴隶和死刑犯。角斗士也有许多类别，他们用出生地的地名，或者用过的武器来命名。按照现代标准，这些竞技场面极其残忍。有时判刑的罪犯被直接扔进斗兽场被猛兽撕成碎片。此外，成千上万的基督徒也因这种方式丧命。

在白天，剧场提供多样化的悲剧、喜剧、默剧和哑剧，观众可以大声呼喊、发泄或开开玩笑。表演却不是一个受人尊重的职业，男演员一般都是无公民权和社会地位的男性奴隶或是已被解放的男性奴隶，他们被称为默剧表演者。他们头顶假发，脸戴张着大嘴的悲喜假面，连接假面的是个金属漏斗以用作演员扩声。情色哑剧是最炙手可热的风格。不戴假面的男演员嘲讽着爱情、婚姻和通奸。大多数剧院有骑楼，外观呈半圆形，且都配备了舞台机械设备，一般可以容纳一万五千名，甚至更多的观众。

到公元1世纪，罗马俨然成为了一座拥有一百万人口的大型城市，并且许多商业行为融入了市民生活。日常生活中，市民们经常光临工匠作坊、烘烤面包或买卖蔬菜瓜果鲜肉这样的零售摊位。在街道上摆摊的生意可以让家人和他们的奴隶一起经营。这些市民生活中最重要的鸡毛店遍布罗马的大街小巷，许多壁画和大理石浮雕上均有呈现。

一些早期的小店逐渐演变成了一些专业销售葡萄酒和食物的酒馆。它们通常由一个或多个房间组成，有一个底部为烤箱的石器台面，及用来存放食物和饮料的几个瓶罐。家具仅限于最基本的需求：一张桌子，或一些椅子，但更多地是一条长凳。罗马人在这里能买到便宜的食物和葡萄酒，它也为顾客提供赌博和卖淫这类常见活动。

In Roman cities, public life was multi-faceted and most Romans, regardless of status, interacted with a variety of its manifestations.

Archaeological ruins of Roman baths represent one of the most common, beautiful and sophisticated expressions of Roman public life. It was the Romans who elevated the act of bathing to a form of art in architecture, and it is the baths of the emperors that best represent the luxurious refinement attained.

Attended daily by people from all classes, the baths were a fundamental part of social life. Besides providing all the facilities needed for personal care and hygiene, they were considered as a place to meet friends, do business, debate, exchange news and receive a sense of companionship and community.

A visit to the baths usually occurred in the afternoon. After undressing in the changing room (*apodyterium*), one would enter the warm room (*tepidarium*) and from there, the *calidarium* where pools of hot water were located. In the *calidarium*, or in adjacent rooms, there were the *laconicum* (sauna) and the *sudatorium* (steam room). Next was a plunge into the cold water of the *frigidarium*, followed by a swim in the pool (*natatio*), usually located in the open air.

A visit to the baths included sporting activities in the gymnasium. Among the choices were running, boxing, wrestling, the discus throw and ball games. Delicate massage, with abundant use of olive oil and perfumed oils, completed the visit. Rejuvenated by a few hours at the baths, Romans were then ready to enjoy themselves at the circus, at the amphitheatre or at the theatre.

Entertainment was a vibrant and integral part of Roman public life. Chariot races, gladiator contests, theatre presentations and musical concerts were often organized in connection with religious festivals or celebrations of political and military events.

Throughout the empire, chariot races were very popular events. The track of a hippodrome (*circus*) was 800 meters long, 80 meters wide, divided along its major axis to form an oval shape. Four chariots (either a *biga*, a two-horse chariot, or *quadriga*, four-horse chariot) participated in each race; each against all others. Contestants were divided into factions supported by excited fans who would usually bet on the outcome. The hippodrome in Rome, the Circus Maximus, could hold 250,000 spectators who watched as many as 24 races per day. To be a charioteer was a dangerous trade, but the best of them earned a great deal of money and enjoyed enormous popularity.

Gladiator combat and pitting men against wild beasts were the most popular and ultimately, infamous forms of entertainment held at amphitheatres throughout the Empire. The most famous amphitheatre was the *Colosseum* in Rome, begun by the Emperor Vespasian and inaugurated by his son Titus in 80 CE. Complicated in structure, an oval arena, constructed of wooden planks covered with sand, was surrounded by seats grouped into sections that strictly corresponded to the social ranking of the spectators. Underneath, there was a vast complex of underground chambers connected to the arena by trapdoors where gladiators, beasts, captives, arms and machinery were kept.

During some festivals that could last for one hundred days, thousands of gladiators and beasts met their deaths. Men (or beasts) fought against each other until death or defeat at which point the decision of life or death was given to the patron of the games, either the emperor or one who represented him.

For bravery or skill, the crowd could ask for a life to be spared by waving pieces of cloth in the air while holding their right thumbs in the air. But if the defeated had acted cowardly or was disliked, the crowd could condemn him by pointing their thumbs to the ground.

Most gladiators were skilled combatants who were prisoners of war, slaves or those condemned to death. There were many categories of gladiators; some took their names from their place of birth, others from the types of weapons they used. By modern standards, these spectacles were extremely cruel. At times, criminals condemned to execution were thrown into the arena where they were torn apart by vicious animals. Thousands of Christians also died this way.

During the daytime, theatres offered a varied program of tragedies, comedies, mimes and pantomimes to which the audience reacted loudly with yells, outbursts and jokes. Acting was not an esteemed profession; actors called *histriones or cantares* were generally male slaves or freed slaves, without civil rights or social status. They wore wigs and tragic or comic masks with a large mouth opening and metal funnel attached that amplified the actor's voice. Mime with erotic themes, however was the most popular genre; love, marriage and adultery were ridiculed by unmasked actors. Most theatres were semicircular in shape with arcaded facades and equipped with theatrical machinery. Capacity could be 15,000 spectators or more.

By the 1st Century CE, Rome had become a very large city with a population of about one million and there were many commercial activities woven into the fabric of public life. Citizens interacted daily with artisan workshops and retail stalls dedicated to the baking of bread or the sale of vegetables, fruit or meat. Opening onto the streets, these businesses were run families and their slaves. These were the original *tabernae*, small shops lining the streets of Rome, whose importance in daily life is represented in many frescoes and marble reliefs.

The early *tabernae* evolved into taverns (*vinaria*) specialized in the sale of wine and food. They usually consisted of one or more rooms; in the first was a stone countertop, with an oven underneath, and many large vases for storing food and beverages. Furnishings were limited to the barest essentials; a table, perhaps some chairs, but more often, a bench. Here, Romans could find inexpensive food and even cheaper wine. Both gambling and prostitution were among the common activities available for patrons.

石棺残件
Fragment of Sarcophagus

公元3世纪上半叶
大理石
长75厘米
佛罗伦萨国家考古博物馆

First half of the 3rd century CE
Marble
L. 75 cm
National Archeological Museum, Florence

这块残件是石棺盖的一部分，采用的是自公元2世纪最后几十年到公元3世纪上半叶颇为常见的样式。石棺盖的四角应该刻有表现舞台面具的装饰图案，前方的正中间刻有提及死者名字的铭文。若死者为女性，在碑文左边会镶有该女子的半身像。

This fragment belongs to the cover of a sarcophagus, of a type that was common from the last decades of the 2nd century CE through the first half of the 3rd century. It would have had decorative motifs engraved at the corners of its lid depicting stage masks, and in the middle of its front the sarcophagus might have borne an inscription with the name of the deceased. The female bust engraved to the left of the tablet suggests this sarcophagus contained the remains of a woman.

剧场石面具
Theater Mask

公元2世纪
大理石
高29厘米
佛罗伦萨国家考古博物馆

2ⁿᵈ century CE
Marble
H. 29 cm
National Archeological Museum, Florence

它可能用于装饰石棺盖的角落。

This piece probably decorated the
corner of a lid to a sarcophagus.

剧场面具图陶灯
Lamp with Theater Mask

帝国时期
红陶
通长9.5厘米，直径6.4厘米
锡耶纳国家考古博物馆

Imperial Age
Terracotta
L. (max) 9.5 cm, D. 6.4 cm
National Archeological Museum, Siena

弹琴人物图陶灯
Theater Mask

公元1~2世纪
红陶
长11厘米 直径8.5厘米
佛罗伦萨国家考古博物馆

1st– 2nd century CE
Terracotta
D. 1. 11 cm diam. 8.5 cm
National Archeological Museum, Florence

个人肖像
PRIVATE PORTRAITURE

肖像是罗马艺术门类中高度发达的一类，个人肖像尤其反映出现实主义的意味。

很多流传下来的个人肖像的对象是男性老者——他们无疑是杰出和富有的公民，但也有端庄的女子甚至儿童。人物极微小的细节也刻画了出来，毫不避讳地反映其真实面貌。雕塑家也竭力去表达对象诸如聪明、智慧、坚定、甚至无情的人格特质。

罗马肖像的现实主义风格可能与其葬俗紧密相关，家庭神龛里也保存有祖先的面模和胸像。

Portraiture was a highly developed aspect of Roman art, and especially private portraits reflect a taste for realism.

Many of the private portraits that have survived are of older men—prominent and wealthy citizens no doubt—but there are stately women as well and even children. Subjects are depicted with attention to the smallest details, including unflattering features. The sculptors managed to convey personality traits as well—intelligence, wisdom, firmness, and even ruthlessness.

Roman portraiture seems to have been closely associated in its origins with funerary customs, which helps explain the taste for realism. Also masks and busts of ancestors were kept in household shrines.

哑剧演员铜像
Small Statue of a Mime

帝国时期
青铜
高9厘米
佛罗伦萨国家考古博物馆

Imperial Age
Bronze
H. 9 cm
National Archeological Museum, Florence

罗马人所见到的各种场面在他们的社会生活中发挥着重要的作用。因此，哑剧演员、杂技演员和戏剧演员通常作为青铜小雕像的主题。

The various types of spectacles viewed by the Romans played an important role in their social life. As a result, mimes, acrobats and actors were often the subject of small bronze figurines.

娱乐
ENTERTAINMENT

罗马剧院最大特别之处在于仅使用男演员。他们戴着不同角色的面具，以区分男女。哑剧和默剧也很流行。罗马社会生活的另一个方面，也是和我们当代社会紧密相关的，是体育赛事吸引了大量的公众。

战车竞赛非常流行。罗马的赛道，如能容纳25万观众的马克西姆斯马车竞技场，一天可以进行24场比赛。更加盛行的可能是角斗——男人对男人（有时是女人）、男人对野兽。绝大部分角斗士是奴隶、犯人或者死刑犯。其他的是自愿成为角斗士的人，这个职业在竞技场不一定都意味着最后走向死亡。

Roman theater featured only male actors, who wore masks to distinguish their roles, male or female. Pantomime and mime were popular as well. Another characteristic aspect of Roman social life, and one that finds a close parallel in our society today, was the large number of public spectator sporting events.

Chariot racing was very popular. Rome's race track, the *Circus Maximus*, could hold 250,000 spectators who might watch as many as 24 races in a day. Gladiatorial combat—men (and occasionally women) against each other, and men against wild beasts—was perhaps even more popular. Most gladiators were slaves, prisoners, or criminals condemned to execution. Others became gladiators voluntarily, and the profession did not necessarily lead to eventual death in the arena.

男演员铜像
Statuette of an Actor

帝国时期
青铜
高4.5厘米
佛罗伦萨国家考古博物馆

Imperial Age
Bronze
H. 4.5 cm
National Archeological Museum, Florence

该演员戴的喜剧面具是张大嘴巴、蓄着短胡子的样子。

The actor wears a comedy mask whose mouth is wide open and framed by a short beard.

角斗士铜像
Statuette of a Gladiator

帝国时期
青铜
高9.2厘米
佛罗伦萨国家考古博物馆

Imperial Age
Bronze
H. 9.2 cm
National Archeological Museum, Florence

这位角斗士戴着头盔，手持盾牌和刀剑，头盔顶部还高耸着羽冠。

The gladiator is fully armed with a helmet, shield and sword, and his helmet is topped with a high crest.

角斗士铜像
Small Statue of Gladiator

帝国时期
青铜
高16.7厘米
佛罗伦萨国家考古博物馆

Imperial Age
Bronze
H. 16.7 cm
National Archeological Museum, Florence

该像刻画了角斗士向后跌倒的瞬间，此时他不得不屈服于对手。

The gladiator is depicted here falling over backwards, apparently at the moment he succumbs to his adversary.

男子石像
Portrait of Unknown Person (Male)

提比略时期（公元14~37年）
意大利大理石
高39.4厘米
佛罗伦萨国家考古博物馆

Reign of Tiberius (14 – 37 CE)
Italian marble
H. 39.4 cm
National Archeological Museum, Florence

该像刻画的是一名体貌独特的
中年男子，带有浅浅皱纹的方
额头，鬓骨凹陷，颧骨高耸，
长长的鹰钩鼻，嘴唇肥厚，宽
圆的下颚。与其他肖像相比，
这尊肖像显然更为上乘，估计
是出自提比略统治后期。

This portrait shows a middle-aged
man with very individual physical
characteristics. He has a squared
forehead with some shallow lines and
his temples have deep grooves. His
cheekbones are very pronounced, his
nose is long and hooked, and he has
large lips and a wide, rounded chin.
This is undoubtedly a work of high
quality and, based on comparison
with other portraits, can be dated to
the late years of the reign of Tiberius.

斗兽场
Colosseum

奏乐者图陶板
Fragment of Slab with Figures Playing Musical

公元前1世纪
红陶
最高33厘米，长44厘米
佛罗伦萨国家考古博物馆

1ˢᵗ century BCE
Terracotta
H. (max) 33 cm, L. 44 cm
National Archeological Museum, Florence

左边的女人在弹奏里拉琴，右
边的男子在吹奏长笛。

A woman on the left plays a lyre
while a man on the right plays a flute.

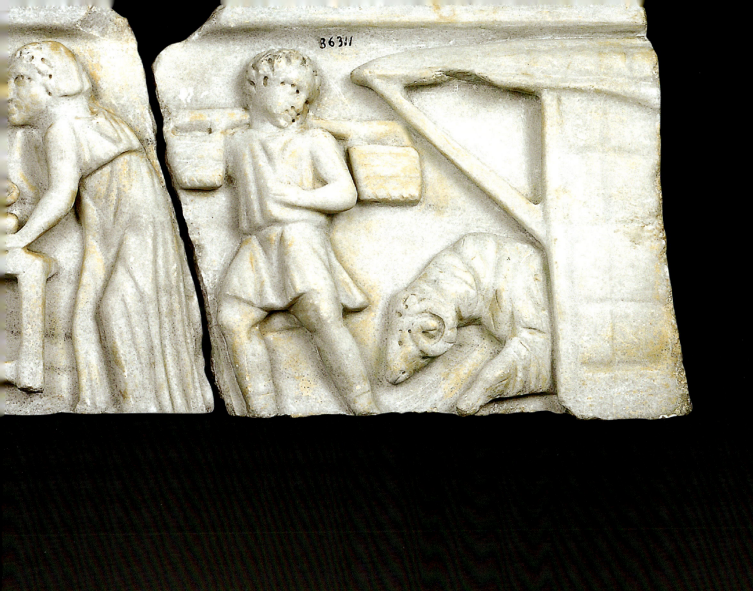

古罗马市场
Ancient Rome Market(FORO ROMANO)

罗马人的饮食 THE ROMAN DIET

罗马人的食物主要依赖于粮食，而下层人民的主食是一种叫"普尔"（puls）的稀饭。

普尔一般是小麦或大麦做成，用橄榄油和植物调料来调味，同各种蔬菜或山羊奶酪一起食用。富裕的罗马人享用各种食物：水果，鸡蛋，肉，鱼和甜糕点。富人吃的更加奢侈，有时宴飨各种令人难以置信的食物。

人们根据不同季节食用蔬菜和水果，肉类和鱼吃新鲜的，也吃烟熏的、盐渍的或者腌制品。葡萄酒必须经过稀释，通常再用蜂蜜增甜，用苦艾酒、玫瑰花瓣、肉桂或者藏红花来调味。一种很受欢迎的经过发酵及盐渍的鱼（一种伍斯特酱）出口到帝国的不同地区。

The Roman diet depended heavily on grains, and a mainstay for lower classes was a kind of porridge called *puls*.

Puls could be made from wheat or barley, flavored with olive oil and herbs, and served with vegetables or goat cheese. Affluent Romans could afford a variety of foods—fruit, eggs, meat, fish and sweet pastries. The wealthy ate lavishly, sometimes feasting on a staggering variety of foods.

Vegetables and fruits were eaten in season. Meat and fish had to be eaten fresh as well unless smoked, salted or pickled. Wine was always diluted, often sweetened with honey, and flavored with absinthe, rose petals, cinnamon or saffron. A popular condiment of fermented, salted fish (a type of Worchester sauce!) was exported throughout the empire.

球状玻璃油瓶
Spherical Oil Holder

帝国时期
玻璃
高3.8厘米
锡耶纳国家考古博物馆

Imperial Age
Glass
H. 3.8 cm
National Archeological Museum, Siena

玻璃油瓶
Elongated Oil Holder

帝国时期
玻璃
高6厘米
锡耶纳国家考古博物馆

Imperial Age
Glass
H. 6 cm
National Archeological Museum, Siena

管状玻璃油瓶
Tubular Oil Holder

帝国时期
玻璃
高13厘米
佛罗伦萨国家考古博物馆

Imperial Age
Glass
H. 13 cm
National Archeological Museum, Florence

拉长的梨状油瓶起源于公元1
世纪上半叶。

The elongated pyriform shape can
be dated to the first half of the 1st
century CE.

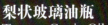

梨状玻璃油瓶
Tronco-Conic Oil Holder

公元1世纪上半叶
玻璃
高9.2厘米
锡耶纳国家考古博物馆

First half of the 1st century CE
Glass
H. 9.2 cm
National Archeological Museum, Siena

管状玻璃油瓶
Tubular Oil Holder

帝国时期
玻璃
高10.2厘米
佛罗伦萨国家考古博物馆

Imperial Age
Glass
H. 10.2 cm
National Archeological Museum, Florence

球形玻璃油膏瓶
Spherical Oil-Holder

公元1世纪上半叶
黄色玻璃
高4厘米
锡耶纳国家考古博物馆

First half of 1st century CE
Yellow glass
H. 4 cm
National Archeological Museum, Siena

这种药瓶特征是口缘有三个
瓣、短颈、几乎很难与圆形的
瓶身区分开来。这种药瓶十分
罕见，曾在意大利东北地区出
现过。

This unguentary is characterized
by a *trliobate* (three-mouthed) rim
and a short neck, hardly discernable
from the spherical belly. This kind
of unguentary is quite rare, but
similar examples have been found at
northeastern Italian sites.

陶油罐
Oil Jar

帝国时期
红陶
高7.5厘米，宽 5厘米
佛罗伦萨国家考古博物馆

Imperial Age
Terracotta
H. 7.5 cm , W. 5 cm
National Archeological Museum, Florence

陶油罐
Oil Jar

帝国时期
红陶
高12厘米，宽8厘米
佛罗伦萨国家考古博物馆

Imperial Age
Terracotta
H. 12 cm, W. 8 cm
National Archeological Museum, Florence

陶盘
Plate

公元前1世纪
红陶
直径18厘米
佛罗伦萨国家考古博物馆

1st century BCE
Terracotta
D. 18 cm
National Archeological Museum, Florence

陶盘
Plate

公元前1世纪
红陶
直径18厘米
佛罗伦萨国家考古博物馆

1st century BCE
Terracotta
D. 18 cm
National Archeological Museum, Florence

陶盘
Plate

公元前1世纪
红陶
直径18厘米
佛罗伦萨国家考古博物馆

1st century BCE
Terracotta
D. 18 cm
National Archeological Museum, Florence

陶杯
Cup

帝国时期
红陶
最大直径12厘米
佛罗伦萨国家考古博物馆

Imperal Age
Terracotta
D. (max) 12 cm
National Archeological Museum, Florence

薄胎陶罐
Thin Walled Vase

公元前世纪~公元1世纪
红陶
高8厘米
佛罗伦萨国家考古博物馆

1st century BCE −1st century CE
Terracotta
H. 8 cm
National Archeological Museum, Florence

公元前1世纪末，一种模仿玻璃厚度的薄胎陶器开始出现。这也许是该时期出土器皿中最具价值的陶器餐具。

Towards the end of the 1st century BCE, a type of thin walled pottery was produced that imitated the thickness of glass. It was perhaps among the most valuable ceramic tableware produced during this period.

薄胎双耳陶杯
Thin Walled Double-Handled Cup

公元前1世纪~公元1世纪
红陶
高9厘米
佛罗伦萨国家考古博物馆

1st century BCE − 1st century CE
Terracotta
H. 9 cm
National Archeological Museum, Florence

薄胎双耳陶瓶
Thin Walled Double-Handled Vase(Olla)

公元前1世纪~公元1世纪
红陶
高10厘米
佛罗伦萨国家考古博物馆

1st century BCE — 1st century CE
Terracotta
H. 10 cm
National Archeological Museum, Florence

珀库罗陶杯
Poculo

公元前1世纪~公元1世纪
红陶
高10厘米
佛罗伦萨国家考古博物馆

1st century BCE — 1st century CE
Terracotta
H. 10 cm
National Archeological Museum, Florence

陶罐
Pitcher

公元前1世纪～公元1世纪
红陶
高7厘米
佛罗伦萨国家考古博物馆

1st century BCE - 1st century CE
Terracotta
H. 7 cm
National Archeological Museum, Florence

这是典型的罗马粗劣器皿的形状，可能用于盛放酒类。

This piece is a typical Roman coarse ware shape, probably used as a container for wine.

铜刮肤板
Strigil

公元1世纪
青铜
长23厘米
佛罗伦萨国家考古博物馆

1st century CE
Bronze
L. 23 cm
National Archeological Museum, Florence

刮肤板用于运动后清除身上的油脂和汗水。

The strigil was used to clean oil and sweat from the body after exercise.

铜勺
Casserole

公元1世纪
青铜
通长25.3厘米
佛罗伦萨国家考古博物馆

1st century CE
Bronze
L. (max) 25.3 cm
National Archeological Museum, Florence

这种铜勺通常是在沐浴时与搔
肤器和香水一起使用。

Used at baths along with strigils and
perfume.

小商店
TABERNAE

罗马及整个帝国的街道遍布着各色小商店（*tabernae*）。

典型的小商店一般都是家庭经营的小酒馆，专门售卖葡萄酒和食物，店里只有很基本的陈设：石头台面上面放着烤箱和几个盛着食物和饮料的大罐子，一张桌子，几把椅子，但更多的是长条凳。在这里，你可以找到便宜的食物（奶酪、蔬菜、鸡蛋、鲜果）和更便宜的葡萄酒。这里通常也可能发生赌博和卖淫。

其他的专门店铺（面包房、肉铺、磨面坊）和技术性的手工作坊（纺织品、陶器、纸莎草甚至玻璃）会雇佣几个奴隶和学徒。生而自由的罗马人大部分认为从事这种职业不体面。

Small shops (*tabernae*) lined the streets of Rome and other cities throughout the empire.

Typical of these were small, family-run taverns that specialized in the sale of wine and food with very basic furnishings—a stone countertop with an oven and a few large vases for storing food and beverages, a table and perhaps some chairs, but more often a bench. Here one could find inexpensive food (cheese, vegetables, eggs, fresh fruits) and even cheaper wine. Often gambling and prostitution were available as well.

Other specialty businesses (bakers, butchers, grain millers) and workshops of more artisan character (textiles, pottery, tiles, papyrus and even glass) might employ a few slaves and apprentices. Freeborn Romans often considered it beneath their dignity to engage in such businesses.

铜量（塞克图斯）
Measure of Volume (*Sextus*)

帝国时期
青铜
高21.5厘米
佛罗伦萨国家考古博物馆

Imperial Age
Bronze
H. 21.5 cm
National Archeological Museum, Florence

铜量塞克图斯既是谷物的测量单位，也是铜量的名字。

The *sextus* was both a unit measure of volume for grain and the name for the container used to do the measuring.

铜天秤
Small Balance(Stadera)

帝国时期
青铜
最长20厘米
佛罗伦萨国家考古博物馆

Imperial Age
Bronze
L. (max) 20 cm
National Archeological Museum, Florence

这个小天平秤由托盘和砝码组合而成，可用于称药或妆粉。

This small balance scale, consisting of a plate and fixed weight, was probably used for measuring medicinal or cosmetic powders.

铜砝码
Set of Weights

帝国时期
青铜
最大直径4厘米，最小直径1.5厘米
锡耶纳国家考古博物馆

Imperial Age
Bronze
D. (max) 4 cm, D. (min) 1.5 cm
National Archeological Museum, Siena

这套碗状砝码与一个精确的天平秤配套使用。最大砝码有一个双搭扣的圆形盖子，并刻有小圆圈纹，整套砝码边沿均刻有该纹饰。这种砝码自帝国时期初出现，并一直延用至今。

This series of bowl-shaped weights was used with a precise balance. The largest weight, which holds the others, has a circular lid with a double clasp and is decorated with a series of small incised circles. This decoration is repeated on the upper border of the entire series. This type of weight set appeared at the beginning of the Imperial period and continued to be used until modern times.

铜砝码
Weight

帝国时期
青铜
高4.7厘米
佛罗伦萨国家考古博物馆

Imperial Age
Bronze
H. 4.7 cm
National Archeological Museum, Florence

"罗曼娜"铜秤
Balance Also Known as "Romana"

帝国时期
青铜
长21厘米
佛罗伦萨国家考古博物馆

Imperial Age
Bronze
L. 21 cm
National Archeological Museum, Florence

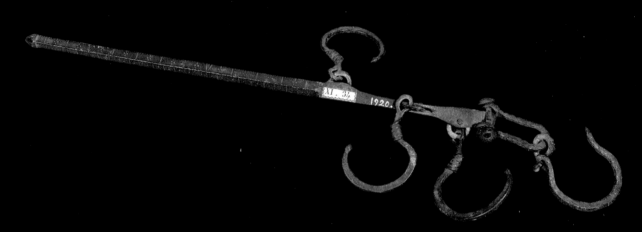

在帝国时期，人们普遍使用天平来称量货物。物品放在悬挂于短杆的容器里，砝码悬挂于长杠杆的挂钩上。拉丁语中有多种不同的称量词汇，不同的称重就使用不同的词汇。最常见的要数"提秤"，称重相对简单快捷，同时也不失精确。

The use of balance scales for weighing merchandise was common during the Imperial age. The item to be weighed was placed in a container suspended from the shorter arm while a counterweight was suspended from one of the hooks on the longer arm. Diverse words existing in Latin for balance scales indicate that different kinds of scales were used for different weighing operations. The most common was the *stadera*, which allowed for a relatively easy, quick, and nevertheless exact measurement of weight.

皇帝像铜砝码
Weight Figurine(Emperor)

帝国时期
青铜
高13厘米
佛罗伦萨国家考古博物馆

Imperial Age
Bronze
H. 13 cm
National Archeological Museum, Florence

战神像铜砝码
Weight Figurine(Mars)

公元1世纪
青铜
高13.5厘米
佛罗伦萨国家考古博物馆

1st century CE
Bronze
H. 13.5 cm
National Archeological Museum, Florence

双耳瓶状铅砝码
Weight in the Form of an Amphora

帝国时期
铅
高7.4厘米
锡耶纳国家考古博物馆

Imperial Age
Lead
H. 7.4 cm
National Archeological Museum, Siena

螺纹铅砝码
Lead Weight for Thread

帝国时期
青铜
通高2.3厘米，最大直径2.4厘米
佛罗伦萨国家考古博物馆

Imperial Age
Bronze
H. (max) 2.3 cm, D. (max) 2.4 cm
National Archeological Museum, Florence

石匠和木匠用铅锤来校准垂直面和水平面。铅锤同样也是罗马土地勘测员所使用的测量仪器格罗马（Groma）的要件。格罗马是一个由等长交叉的木制垂臂构成的木制十字架，铅锤悬挂于十字垂臂的末端。测量人员可以利用格罗马两边铅锤的视觉垂线画出垂直线。第五个铅锤位于十字架的中心，使格罗马能精确定位在已知点上。

Used by masons and carpenters to make true vertical and horizontal surfaces. Plumb-bobs served also as elements of a surveying instrument (*groma*) used by Roman surveyors (*gromatici*). [The groma consisted of a wooden cross with perpendicular arms of equal length attached to a long wooden rod. Plumb-bobs were attached to the ends of the perpendicular arms, and the surveyor would line up two plumb lines on opposite sides of the groma in order to create a straight line of sight. A fifth plumb-bob was attached to the center of the cross so that the groma could be placed precisely over a known point.

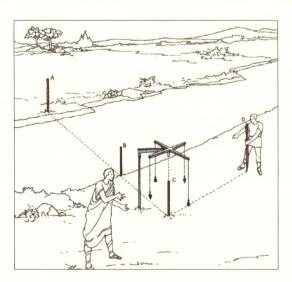

石砝码
Weight

帝国时期
玄武岩
高6厘米
佛罗伦萨国家考古博物馆

Imperial Age
Basalt
H. 6 cm
National Archeological Museum, Florence

石砝码
Small Weight

帝国时期
玄武岩
高2.6厘米，直径4.8厘米
锡耶纳国家考古博物馆

Imperial Age
Basalt
H. 2.6 cm, D. 4.8 cm
National Archeological Museum, Siena

石砝码
Weight

帝国时期
玄武岩
高7.5厘米
佛罗伦萨国家考古博物馆

Imperial Age
Basalt
H. 7.5 cm
National Archeological Museum, Florence

铜圆规
Compass

帝国时期
青铜
长13.9厘米
锡耶纳国家考古博物馆

Imperial Age
Bronze
L. 13.9 cm
National Archeological Museum, Siena

铜印章
Seal

帝国时期
青铜
长6.6厘米，宽2.7厘米，厚2.7厘米
佛罗伦萨国家考古博物馆

Imperial Age
Bronze
L. 6.6 cm, W. 2.7 cm, Th. 2.7 cm,
National Archeological Museum, Florence

这枚刻有卢修斯（*Lucius*）的
奴隶格洛特（*Gelote*）名字的
印章用于标记货物、粮食等
商品。

This stamp, bearing the name *Gelote*
a slave of *Lucius*,.was used to mark
merchandise, provisions or the like.

铜印章
Seal

帝国时期
青铜
高6.8厘米
佛罗伦萨国家考古博物馆

Imperial Age
Bronze
H. 6.8 cm
National Archeological Museum, Florence

这枚印章的印面文字显示它属于*l. Pisentius Polyclitus*。该印章在罗马时代十分普遍，用于陶瓷及青铜物件上。

This *"in planta pedis"* (on the sole of the foot) stamp belonged to *L. Pisentius Polyclitus*. This kind of stamp was common in Roman times and used for both ceramic and bronze objects.

铜印章
Seal

帝国时期
青铜
高8厘米
佛罗伦萨国家考古博物馆

Imperial Age
Bronze
H. 8 cm
National Archeological Museum, Florence

这枚印章印面被制以脚部的形状。

This *"in planta pedis"* (on the sole of the foot) stamp is shaped in the form of a foot.

铜印章
Stamp

帝国时期
青铜
长5厘米，宽2.5厘米，厚1.5厘米
佛罗伦萨国家考古博物馆

Imperial Age
Bronze
L. 5 cm. W. 2.5 cm. Th. 1.5 cm
National Archeological Museum, Florence

铜骨节
Pair of Knucklebones

帝国时期
青铜
通长2.5~3厘米
佛罗伦萨国家考古博物馆

Imperial Age
Bronze
L. (max) 2.5 – 3 cm
National Archeological Museum, Florence

铜骨节
Pair of Knucklebones

帝国时期
青铜
通长2.5厘米
佛罗伦萨国家考古博物馆

Imperial Age
Bronze
L. (max) 2.5 cm
National Archeological Museum, Florence

棋子
Gaming Pieces

帝国时期
玻璃和石
直径1.3~1.7厘米
佛罗伦萨国家考古博物馆

Imperial Age
Glass and stone
D. 1.3 – 1.7 cm
National Archeological Museum, Florence

个人生活
PRIVATE LIFE

Art Historian International Museum Exhibitions
琳达·卡瑞奥尼
Linda Carioni

罗马社会是以家庭为基础的。婚姻具有许多重要的社会意义，包括倚靠政治联姻创造或巩固社会地位等。相对来说，女孩十二、十三岁嫁人，男孩十四岁娶妻。在结婚前有个订婚仪式（依照婚约），双方父亲需在场，新郎需赠礼给新娘，双方互换戒指。举办婚礼那天会有一场动物祭祀仪式，此时将验看动物的内脏，以占卜这对夫妇的婚姻是否幸福美满。

婴儿出生时将被放在父亲的脚边，父亲可以接受或拒绝这个孩子。生理有缺陷的孩子，尤其是女孩通常会被拒绝抚养。当父亲从脚边抱起婴儿的那一刻，便代表他承认了这个孩子作为家庭成员。未被接受的孩子通常会被丢弃在公共场所，其他人会带回去领养。出生后九天，婴儿会随父姓（家族姓氏）。

男孩的教育传统上由父亲负责。到了罗马帝国时代，这个任务落到了公立学校身上，有钱人会请一位希腊奴隶作为家庭教师来教育孩子。男孩小的时候学习读、写和基本的算术。学生在覆有蜡、猪皮纸或草纸的木板上用木头、象牙或金属尖头笔书写。

文学和艺术品是了解帝国时代的公民私生活的基本来源。大理石的私人胸像和雕像比那些用来代表帝国或公众人物的典型雕像更为写实。

罗马人的日常服饰很简单，主要是无袖束腰的外衣。以白色宽厚的羊毛罩衫托加袍缠绕身体。罗马最为著名的服饰便是绕身穿的托加袍，长约18英尺、最宽处约5.5英尺。先把它垂在身前围绕身体，其余的布从右腋下经左肩披向身后。因此右臂是自由的。托加逐渐成为了仪式的礼服。在罗马帝国时代，只有罗马市民才能穿着托加。而女性会穿着稍长一点的短袖束腰裙斯托拉。她们在户外会穿一种可包裹头部的斗篷帕拉。至于鞋类，男女都会穿凉鞋和各种款式的靴子。

随着帝国的扩张，帝国容纳了不同风俗和不同气候地区的民族，服饰上的多样性越发明显，逐渐朝着色彩绚丽、装束奢华的风格发展。人们通过贸易获得了更加多样和考究的面料，例如来自印度的棉花和来自东方的丝绸。

罗马服饰也反映着社会阶层的划分，名流会使用特定的颜色、面料和款式。著名的染料泰尔紫是从软体动物紫螺（purpura）腺体中提取，由于提取源体积很小，该染料十分昂贵。因此，只有少数人才能穿紫色的衣服。紫色之名虽源于紫螺，紫螺却是紫红色的。

在奥古斯都统治期间（公元前27年~公元前14年），人们的发型和装饰都较为朴素。在罗马帝国富庶的刺激下，个人装饰风格和程度越来越精致和有艺术性。女人开始佩戴昂贵的首饰，例如金耳环、珠宝、项链以及镶宝石的手镯。

男女都会花大量的时间打扮自己，使用香水、化妆品。上流社会的女性使用粉饼、胭脂、眼影和眼线。所使用的油、香水和化妆品通常由专职奴隶制作，他们从植物中萃取香料，将液体与橄榄油混合，存放于由大理石、玻璃或陶制的容器中。

久之，女性的发型有了很大的变化，这成了雕塑断代的依据。在奥古斯都时代，精致的大波浪卷盛行一时。必要的梳妆工具有梳子、铁制的卷发棒和由铜、银或玻璃制成的镜子。假发、发卡和发带也常用。某些发色特别流行，因此许多人会染发和带假发。在高卢和日耳曼战役期间，戴战俘发色的金色假发风靡一时。

到奥古斯都末期，男人剪平头，后来也尝试用卷发棒卷成各种样式。到公元2世纪早期的哈德良时代，男人留胡须，甚至是络腮胡，留长发并且定期烫卷。

罗马人依靠法术、宗教和一些医疗方法预防疾病。许多在罗马定居的希腊人受过医学训练，能看病和能用草药治疗多种疾病。训练有素的外科医生能做诸如剖腹产、清除白内障、拔牙、切除扁桃体和疝气等手术。许多手术器械并非专用，都是一些日常家庭中使用的工具，如镊子。

Roman society was based on the family. Matrimony had a number of important social consequences, serving to create or solidify position and political alliances. Girls were married by the age of twelve or thirteen; boys could take a wife by the age of fourteen. The act of marriage was preceded by the engagement ceremony (*sponsalia*) involving the fathers of both parties, the groom offering gifts to his bride, and an exchange of rings. The day of the wedding was celebrated with a ritual animal sacrifice followed by the examination of the sacrificial entrails to ascertain how favourable the union might be.

When a baby was born, it was placed at the feet of the father, who could either accept or reject the child. Physically deformed children were often rejected, as were girls. If the father picked up the infant and held it in his hands, then it was legitimized and became a member of the family. A rejected child was often abandoned in a public place where someone might take and raise it. Nine days after birth, the infant was given the family name (*gens*) that was passed from father to child.

Traditionally, the education of boys was left to the father. By Imperial times, this task was often entrusted to public schools or for the wealthy, a slave who was generally a Greek teacher. Young boys learned how to read, write and do basic arithmetic. Students wrote on wooden tablets covered with a layer of wax or paper made of pigskin or papyrus. Using a *stilus* made of wood, ivory or metal.

A great deal of what is known about the private lives of Roman citizens during the Imperial age is based on literary and artistic sources. Private portraiture in the form of marble busts and statues reveals a realism that is in contrast to the classical models used to represent the Imperial dynasty or other public figures.

Basic Roman attire was quite simple; the main article was the tunic, usually with no sleeves and tied around the waist. The toga, a wide cloak of heavy wool, usually white, then wrapped around the body. A toga, the garment for which Rome is most famous, was a segment of a circle, measuring about 18 feet along the chord of the segment and about 5.5 feet at its widest point. To drape it, the straight edge of the fabric was placed against the front of the body. The rest of the material was then thrown over the left shoulder, passed around the back, under the right arm, and once again over the left shoulder and arm. The right arm was therefore left free; the reason why the toga gradually became a ceremonial garment. During the Imperial Age, the toga functioned as a note of rank; wearing a toga was restricted to Roman citizens. Over a longer tunic, women wore the *stola*, a short-sleeved dress, belted at the waist and elegantly draped. A cloak, the *palla*, was worn outdoors and could also cover the head. Footwear for both sexes consisted in sandals and several other styles of boots.

As the Empire expanded, incorporating peoples of different customs and climate, a greater complexity became apparent in costume. The trend was toward a more ornate, richly coloured and luxurious attire. Through trade, more varied and elegant fabrics were available; cotton from India and silks from the East.

Roman dress also reflected divisions of social class, with certain colours, fabrics, and styles reserved for important personages. The famous dye of the classical world was Tyrian purple. This was obtained from glands in the mollusc *purpura* and was costly owing to the small size of the source material. Thus, the wearing of purple was reserved for a few. Although the name purpura gave rise to the word purple, the colour was actually a crimson.

Throughout the reign of Augustus (27 to 14 BCE), coiffure and adornment remained rather simple, however, with the wealth and luxury fueled by the Empire, the style and degree of personal decoration became more elaborate and artificial. Women wore expensive jewellery such as gold earrings, cameos, necklaces and bracelets set with precious stones.

Both men and women devoted a great deal of time to their toilette and the use of perfumes and cosmetics. Face powder, rouge, eye shadow, and eyeliner were lavishly applied by upper-class women. The preparation of oils, perfumes and cosmetics was frequently the job of a specialized slave who separated fragrances from plants, mixed liquids with olive oil and stored the scents and oils in containers of alabaster, glass or terracotta.

Feminine hairstyles changed so much over time, that it is considered an indication by which to date statues. In the Augustan Age, huge, elaborate constructions of curls became fashionable. Necessary tools were the comb, the *calamistrum*, an iron rod heated on fire to make the curls, and the mirror, made of bronze, silver or glass. Wigs and hair pieces, combs and ribbons were also commonly worn. Certain colours of hair were more fashionable than others and the tinting of hair and hairpieces was also widely practiced. During the Gallic and Teutonic campaigns, blonde wigs made from the hair of captured slaves were in vogue.

Until the end of the Augustan period, men wore their hair short and simple, but in later times, they also began to arrange their hair in more elaborate styles and used the *calamistrum* to add curls. By the reign of Hadrian in the early II century CE, men were growing beards, moustaches, wearing their hair long and having it regularly curled.

Romans relied on a mixture of magic, religion and method to prevent disease. Many Greeks residing in Rome were trained in medicine and capable of both diagnosing and treating a variety of illnesses, generally with herbal remedies. There were also trained surgeons capable of performing a number of effective treatments, such as C-sections, the removal of cataracts, teeth and tonsils, as well as hernia operations. Many of the surgical instruments, such as tweezers, were not very specialized and could be put to other uses within the household.

弗拉维式妇女石像
Bust of a Flavian Woman

公元70~80年
大理石
高52厘米
佛罗伦萨国家考古博物馆

70-80 CE
Marble
H. 52 cm
National Archeological Museum, Florence

这是一尊成年女子的胸像，用钻头雕出小卷发的发冠遮盖住了女子前额和鬓骨。这款发型在弗拉维皇帝统治时期风靡一时，提图斯皇帝的妻子和女儿朱丽娅·蒂塔尤其喜欢。

This is a mature woman whose forehead and temples are covered by a high crown of small curls made with a drill. This type of hairstyle was popular during the reign of the Flavian emperors, in particular with the wife of the emperor Titus and his daughter Julia Tita.

石女子胸像
Female Bust

帝国初期
大理石
高42厘米，宽30厘米
佛罗伦萨国家考古博物馆

First Imperial Age
Marble
H. 42 cm, W. 30 cm
National Archeological Museum, Florence

石女子头像
Portrait of Unknown Person (Female)

奥古斯都时期（公元前27年~公元14年）
意大利大理石
高22厘米
佛罗伦萨国家考古博物馆

Reign of Augustus (27 BCE-14 CE)
Italian Marble
H. 22 cm
National Archeological Museum, Florence

这是一名老妇人的肖像。她额头布满皱纹，小而略微凹陷的眼睛下方有许多褶皱的眼纹。发型盘成屋大维娅和利维娅之类的皇室成员较为流行的圆锥形。该肖像可能出自制作过一系列老妇人胸像的城市作坊。

The portrait represents an elderly woman. She has a high forehead with large furrows, small and slightly inset eyes with numerous wrinkles underneath. The hair was placed in a conic shape according to the style that was popular among members of the imperial family, made popular by Octavia and then Livia. The portrait, perhaps produced in an urban workshop, forms part of a series of portraits of elderly women.

无名女子石肖像
Portrait of an Unknown

奥古斯都时期（公元前27年~公元14年）
意大利大理石
高30.2厘米
佛罗伦萨国家考古博物馆

Reign of Augustus (27 BCE–14 CE)
Italian marble
H. 30.2 cm
National Archeological Museum, Florence

这尊老妇人像低额，略凹的
杏仁眼稍显灰暗，丰满的脸
颊，圆圆的下颚，小嘴唇略
微下垂。她的发型、前额、
鬓骨的许多部位已看不清
楚。她用发卡将辫子盘绕
在头上，几缕卷发紧贴着脸
颊。由于该妇女的前额处已
损坏，无法辨认这究竟是什
么发型，有可能是奥古斯都
时期丧葬浮雕上常见的中分
发型。雕像背面雕刻粗糙，
脖子处的形状和这些特点暗
示出这座雕像可能是放在壁
龛中的。

The statue portrays an old woman:
her forehead is low, her almond-
shaped eyes are slightly sunken and
shadowed, the cheeks are chubby
and the chin is round while the lips
of her small mouth are bent down.
Many parts of the hair framing her
forehead and temples are missing.
The woman wears her hair in plaits
pinned up around the head, while
small curls lie on her cheeks. Because
of damage to the forehead of the
woman, it is not possible to suggest
what the hairstyle looked like. It is
possible she wore her hair parted in
the middle, a style that is extremely
common in the funerary reliefs of
Augustan age. The back of the statue
is only roughly carved. This feature,
together with the shape of the neck,
suggests that the portrait would have
been placed inside a niche.

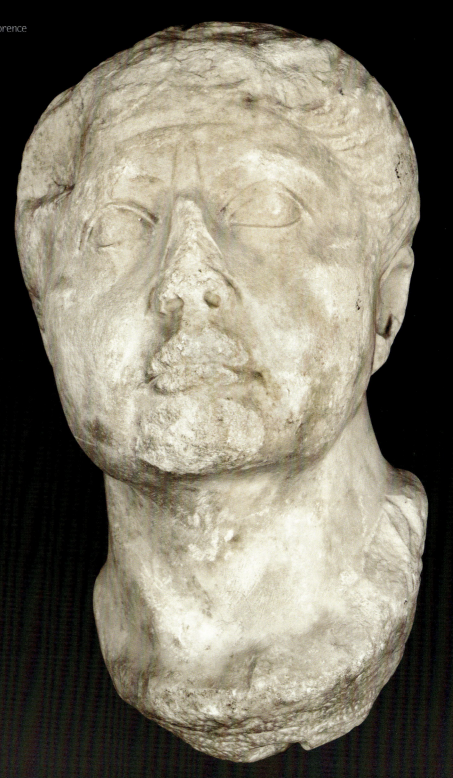

孩童石像
Small Statue of a Child

图拉真时期（公元98~117年）
大理石
高115厘米，宽35厘米
佛罗伦萨国家考古博物馆

Reign of Trajan (98–117 CE)
Marble
L. 115 cm, W. 35 cm
National Archeological Museum, Florence

梨形玻璃药瓶
Pyriform Unguentary

公元41~117年
玻璃
高6厘米
锡耶纳国家考古博物馆

41-117 CE
Glass
H. 6 cm
National Archeological Museum, Siena

梨形玻璃药瓶
Pyriform Unguentary

公元41~117年
玻璃
高5.4厘米
锡耶纳国家考古博物馆

41-117 CE
Glass
H. 5.4 cm
National Archeological Museum, Siena

梨状药瓶出现于奥古斯都统
治时期，克劳迪乌斯至图拉
真统治时期尤为盛行。

The pyriform shape (bulbous, like a
pear) unguentary began to appear
during the reign of Augustus, but
became especially popular during
the reigns of Claudius through Trajan.

梨形玻璃药瓶
Pyriform Unguentary

公元41~117年
玻璃
高7厘米
锡耶纳国家考古博物馆

41-117 CE
Glass
H. 7 cm
National Archeological Museum, Siena

梨形玻璃药瓶
Pyriform Unguentary

公元1世纪上半叶
玻璃
高4.9厘米
锡耶纳国家考古博物馆

1st half of 1st century CE
Glass
H. 4.9 cm
National Archeological Museum, Siena

这种长梨形状瓶可追溯到公
元1世纪上半叶。

This elongated pyriform shape can
be dated to the first half of the 1st
century CE.

梳洗图釉陶灯
Lamp with "Toilette" Scene

公元2世纪
粘土和红釉
长15厘米，宽11.3厘米
锡耶纳国家考古博物馆

2nd century CE
Clay and reddish glaze
L. 15 cm, W. 11.3 cm
National Archeological Museum, Siena

这盏盘状油灯有一个圆口和圆环状把手。背部以葡萄藤和常春藤作装饰，主体有一个裸体女子梳洗的场景，场景底部圆孔用来添加油。

This oil lamp is disc-shaped with a small circular mouth and a ring-shaped handle. Its back is decorated with vines and ivy, the main body with a nude female figure grooming herself. The hole near the bottom of the scene is for filling the lamp with oil.

仪表
APPEARANCES

个人饰品在奥古斯都统治期一直简单，但在帝国后期越来越精致和巧夺天工。

上层阶级的妇女在脸庞上涂粉、胭脂，画眼影和眼线，浓妆艳抹。她们佩戴昂贵的耳环、项链、手镯和宝石。香水则保存在精美贵重的由雪花石膏、玻璃或赤陶制作的盒子里。

妇女的发型变化很快，这为断定雕塑和肖像的年代提供了重要线索。男人的仪表风格也有变化。在奥古斯都时代，男人还是短发和简朴的形象，但在公元2世纪的末期，男人留起了带有卷曲的长发长胡和长须。有时男女也染发和戴假发。

Personal adornment remained simple through the reign of Augustus, but became increasingly elaborate and artificial during the later years of the empire.

Upper class women lavishly applied face Powder rouge, eye shadow and eyeliner. They wore expensive earrings, necklaces, bracelets and cameos. Perfumes were stored in delicate and expensive containers of alabaster, glass or terracotta.

Women's hairstyles changed rapidly, and provide important clues for dating statues and portraits. Men's styles changed as well. In the age of Augustus, men still wore their hair short and simple. By the end of the second century CE men were wearing their hair long, having it curled, and growing beards and moustaches. Both men and women sometimes died their hair or wore wigs.

齿状铜镜
Toothed Mirror

公元1世纪
青铜
直径14.5厘米
佛罗伦萨国家考古博物馆

1st century CE
Bronze
D. 14.5 cm
National Archeological Museum, Florence

这面圆形铜镜有一个雕刻细齿的边框。

This big round mirror has a fret-worked frame.

宝石金发簪
Hair Pin

帝国时期
黄金和绿宝石
长6.6厘米
锡耶纳国家考古博物馆

Imperial Age
Gold and emerald
L. 6.6 cm
National Archeological Museum, Siena

珍珠金戒指
Statuette of an Actor

帝国时期
黄金和珍珠
直径2.5厘米
佛罗伦萨国家考古博物馆

Ring with pearl
Imperial Age
Gold and pearl
D. 2.5 cm
National Archeological Museum, Florence

金手镯
Arm Ring

帝国时期
黄金
直径7.7厘米
佛罗伦萨国家考古博物馆

Imperial Age
Gold
D. 7.7 cm
National Archeological Museum, Florence

这个手镯端部印有蛇头图案，令人想起在罗马帝国依然流行希腊化的风格。

The ends of this arm band represent snakes heads---a feature reminiscent of Hellenistic style that was still very common in Imperial Rome.

金戒指
Ring

奥古斯都时期（公元前27年~公元14年）
黄金和玛瑙
直径2.1厘米
佛罗伦萨国家考古博物馆

Reign of Augustus (27 BCE – 14 CE)
Gold and cornelian
D. 2.1 cm
National Archeological Museum, Florence

戒指上雕刻了一个坐着的狮身人面像。

The engraving forming the setting of this ring shows a seated Sphinx.

金戒指
Ring

公元前1世纪~公元1世纪
黄金和绿宝石
直径1.75厘米
佛罗伦萨国家考古博物馆

1st century BCE – 1st century CE
Gold and emerald
D. 1.75 cm
National Archeological Museum, Florence

金戒指
Ring

公元1世纪
黄金和玛瑙
直径1.8厘米
佛罗伦萨国家考古博物馆

1st century CE
Gold, chalcedony and agate
D. 1.8 cm
National Archeological Museum, Florence

这枚戒指的宝石上刻有山羊的图案。

An engraved goat decorates the gemstone of this ring.

金戒指
Ring

公元1世纪
黄金
直径1.6厘米
佛罗伦萨国家考古博物馆

1st century CE
Gold
D. 1.6 cm
National Archeological Museum, Florence

这枚严重磨损的戒指以伊希斯神半身像浮雕作装饰。这种风格流行于公元1世纪。

This ring, badly worn, is decorated with a bust of Isis worked in relief. The style was common during the first 1st century CE.

金戒指
Ring

帝国时期
黄金和玛瑙
直径1.8厘米
佛罗伦萨国家考古博物馆

Imperial Age
Gold. chalcedony and agate
D. 1.8 cm
National Archeological Museum. Florence

宝石上刻有一条鱼。

A fish is engraved on the gemstone.

金戒指
Ring

公元1~2世纪
黄金和翡翠
直径1.2厘米
佛罗伦萨国家考古博物馆

1st – 2nd century CE
Gold and emerald
L. 1.2 cm
National Archeological Museum. Florence

金戒指
Ring

公元1~2世纪
黄金和绿宝石
直径1.2厘米
佛罗伦萨国家考古博物馆

1st – 2nd century CE
Gold and emerald
D. 1.2 cm
National Archeological Museum. Florence

金戒指
Ring

公元1~2世纪
黄金和玉髓
直径1.4厘米
佛罗伦萨国家考古博物馆

1st – 2nd century CE
Gold and chalcedony
D. 1.4 cm
National Archeological Museum. Florence

宝石上雕刻了一个站立着的
女性形象。

A standing female figure is engraved
on the gemstone.

金戒指
Ring

公元1~2世纪
黄金
直径1.4厘米
佛罗伦萨国家考古博物馆

1st – 2nd century CE
Gold
D. 1.4 cm
National Archeological Museum, Florence

这枚戒指以浮雕的花瓣为装饰。
This ring is decorated with a flower whose petals are in relief.

金戒指
Ring

公元1~2世纪
黄金和紫晶
直径2厘米
佛罗伦萨国家考古博物馆

1st – 2nd century CE
Gold and amethyst
D. 2 cm
National Archeological Museum, Florence

紫晶上雕刻着一只鸟。
A bird is engraved on the amethyst.

金戒指
Ring

公元1~2世纪
黄金和石榴石
直径1.6厘米
佛罗伦萨国家考古博物馆

1st – 2nd century CE
Gold and garnet
D. 1.6 cm
National Archeological Museum, Florence

金戒指
Ring

公元2世纪
黄金和红玛瑙
直径2.44厘米
佛罗伦萨国家考古博物馆

2nd century CE
Gold and onyx
D. 2.44 cm
National Archeological Museum, Florence

金戒指
Ring

公元2世纪下半叶
黄金
直径1.9厘米
佛罗伦萨国家考古博物馆

Second half of the 2nd century CE
Gold
D. 1.9 cm
National Archeological Museum, Florence

这枚戒指镶有两名男子面对面站立的浮雕肖像，一个是马可·奥里略，另一个可能是卢修斯·维鲁斯。

This ring is decorated with portraits, worked in relief and standing face to face, of two male personalities. One is Marcus Aurelius, the other possibly Lucius Verus.

金戒指
Ring

帝国时期
黄金和碧玉石
直径2.5厘米
佛罗伦萨国家考古博物馆

Imperial Age
Gold and jasper
D. 2.5 cm
National Archeological Museum, Florence

金戒指
Ring

帝国时期
黄金
直径1.8厘米
佛罗伦萨国家考古博物馆

Imperial Age
Gold
D. 1.8 cm
National Archeological Museum, Florence

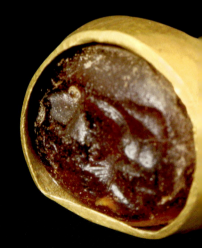

金戒指
Ring

公元3~4世纪
黄金
直径2.5厘米
佛罗伦萨国家考古博物馆

3rd – 4th century CE
Gold
D. 2.5 cm
National Archeological Museum, Florence

这枚戒指上有两只面对面小鸟的装饰。

The ring is decorated with two birds face to face.

金戒指
Ring

公元3~4世纪
黄金和蓝宝石
直径1.4厘米
佛罗伦萨国家考古博物馆

3rd – 4th century CE
Gold and sapphire
D. 1.4 cm
National Archeological Museum, Florence

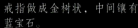

戒指做成金树状，中间镶有蓝宝石。

The ring was from gold leaf and provided with a sapphire setting.

雅典娜像金戒指
Ring with Head of Athena

帝国时期
黄金
直径2.5厘米
佛罗伦萨国家考古博物馆

Imperial Age
Gold
D. 2.5 cm
National Archeological Museum, Florence

金耳环
Pair of Earrings

帝国时期
黄金
直径1.9厘米
佛罗伦萨国家考古博物馆

Imperial Age
Gold
D. 1.9 cm
National Archeological Museum, Florence

金耳环
Earring

公元1~2世纪
黄金
长3.5厘米
佛罗伦萨国家考古博物馆

1st – 2nd century CE
Gold
L. 3.5 cm
National Archeological Museum, Florence

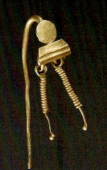

这副耳环的坠子可能是由亚宝石装饰制成。

The pendants dangling from this earring would have been embellished with semi-precious stones.

金耳环
Pair of Earrings

公元1~2世纪
黄金
长2.5厘米
佛罗伦萨国家考古博物馆

1st – 2nd century CE
Gold
L. 2.5 cm
National Archeological Museum, Florence

宝石金耳环
Earring

公元2世纪
黄金和绿宝石
直径2厘米
佛罗伦萨国家考古博物馆

2nd century CE
Gold and emerald
D. 2 cm
National Archeological Museum, Florence

金耳环
Earring with Agate Pendant

公元2~3世纪
黄金和玛瑙
长4.6厘米
佛罗伦萨国家考古博物馆

2nd – 3rd century CE
Gold and agate
L. 4.6 cm
National Archeological Museum, Florence

金耳环
Pair of Earrings

帝国时期
黄金
直径1.1厘米
佛罗伦萨国家考古博物馆

Imperial Age
Gold
D. 1.1 cm
National Archeological Museum, Florence

黄金融化入模具中，然后打
造成耳环。

The gold was shaped in a mold and
then bent to form earrings.

金耳环
Earring with Pendant Form

帝国时期
黄金
长3厘米
佛罗伦萨国家考古博物馆

Imperial Age
Gold
L. 3 cm
National Archeological Museum, Florence

金项链
Necklace

帝国时期
黄金
长43.5 厘米
佛罗伦萨国家考古博物馆

Imperial Age
Gold
L. 43.5 cm
National Archeological Museum,
Florence

这串项链由37个 "8" 形的
双环扣组成。项链一端焊有
套管的钩子，另一端有焊有
钩子的一小环。项链扣呈轮
状。这种项链自公元前3世纪
就开始出现，并一直流行于
帝国时期。

Each of the thirty-seven double links
that form the chain of this necklace is
shaped like a figure eight. The chain
ends on one end with a hook welded
to a tube, and on the other with a
small ring on which a second hook is
welded. The clasp of the necklace is
in the shape of a wheel. This type of
necklace began to be manufactured
in the 3rd century BCE and remained
popular into the Imperial Age.

金项链
Necklace with a Pendant

公元3世纪
黄金
长21.4厘米
佛罗伦萨国家考古博物馆

3rd century CE
Gold
L. 21.4 cm
National Archeological Museum, Florence

项链的月牙形石头吊坠装饰
已遗失。

The stone that embellished the
crescent has been lost.

金项链
Necklace with a Pendant

公元3世纪
黄金
长21.4厘米
佛罗伦萨国家考古博物馆

3rd century CE
Gold
L. 21.4 cm
National Archeological Museum, Florence

金胸针
Brooch

公元1世纪
黄金和玉髓
直径4厘米
佛罗伦萨国家考古博物馆

1st century CE
Gold and chalcedony
D. 4 cm
National Archeological Museum, Florence

这枚轮状胸针精致地装饰有
八个小人头交替在八条放射
线两边，中间为玉石。

This brooch in the shape of a wheel
is elaborately decorated with eight
small heads alternating with rays.
The middle stone is chalcedony.

玻璃臂钏
Arm Ring

公元1世纪
玻璃
直径9.6厘米
基亚齐亚诺考古博物馆

1st century CE
Glass
D. 9.6 cm
Museo Civico Archeologico delle Aque, Chianciano Terme

这种玻璃臂钏出现于希腊化
时期，其风格延续到公元1
世纪。

This type of glass armlet began to
appear during the Hellenistic Period
and remained in style into the 1st
century CE.

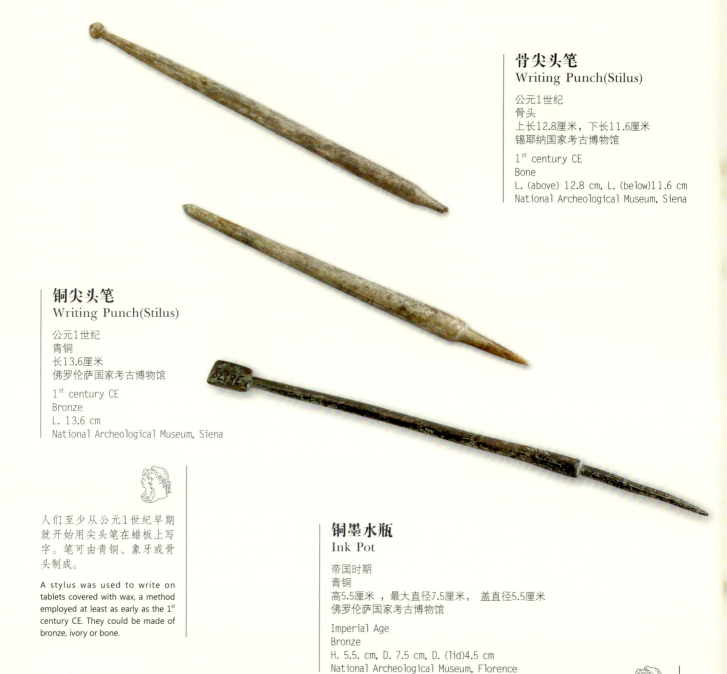

骨尖头笔
Writing Punch(Stilus)

公元1世纪
骨头
上长12.8厘米，下长11.6厘米
锡耶纳国家考古博物馆

1st century CE
Bone
L. (above) 12.8 cm, L. (below)11.6 cm
National Archeological Museum, Siena

铜尖头笔
Writing Punch(Stilus)

公元1世纪
青铜
长13.6厘米
佛罗伦萨国家考古博物馆

1st century CE
Bronze
L. 13.6 cm
National Archeological Museum, Siena

人们至少从公元1世纪早期就开始用尖头笔在蜡板上写字。笔可由青铜、象牙或骨头制成。

A stylus was used to write on tablets covered with wax, a method employed at least as early as the 1st century CE. They could be made of bronze, ivory or bone.

铜墨水瓶
Ink Pot

帝国时期
青铜
高5.5厘米，最大直径7.5厘米，盖直径5.5厘米
佛罗伦萨国家考古博物馆

Imperial Age
Bronze
H. 5.5. cm, D. 7.5 cm, D. (lid)4.5 cm
National Archeological Museum, Florence

墨水池需要搭配墨水和笔杆使用。通常笔杆是一支尖头簧片，一头磨尖，开一细孔。有时笔杆由金属制成。在艺术作品中，墨水池象征着贵族或受过高等教育的人士。

The essential complements to an inkwell were ink (atramentum) and a quill (calamus). Typically the quill was a fine-pointed reed, sharpened at one end, and incised with a tiny hole in the center of the point. Occasionally quills were made of metal. When depicted in artwork, an inkwell symbolized nobility and education.

石墓碑
Grave Stela

帝国时期
大理石
长101厘米，宽67厘米，厚4 厘米
佛罗伦萨国家考古博物馆

Imperial Age
Marble
L. 101 cm, W. 67 cm, Th. 4 cm
National Archeological Museum, Florence

这块大理石板曾覆盖于一块葬礼纪念碑之上，纪念碑是用来纪念一个名叫法拉修斯·赫尔墨斯的男子、他的两任妻子、儿子以及后代。碑文下方和左边刻有女子盥洗所需的物品和饰品。右边刻有男性工作所需的工具。女性的物件中有发卡、镜子、梳子、油瓶和卷发铁棍。男性的物品有尺、火把、铅笔和三角尺。

This marble slab once covered a funerary monument dedicated to man named Ferrarius Hermes, his two wives, his son, and all his descendants. Depicted below the inscription and to the left are items necessary for a woman's toilet and typical feminine ornaments. To the right are instruments typical of a man's work. Among the women's accessories are a hairpin, mirror, comb, oil holder, and iron for making curls. Among the man's, a drawing rule, torch, pencil and square.

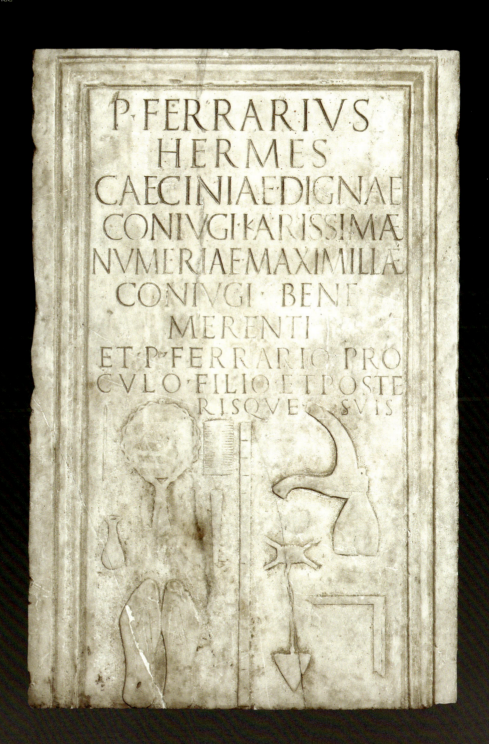

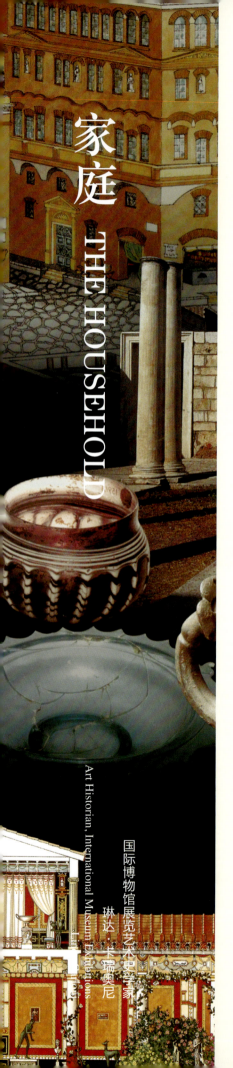

家庭

THE HOUSEHOLD

国际博物馆展览艺术史学家

琳达·卡瑞奥尼

Art Historian, International Museum Exhibitions

罗马帝国的私人住宅的奢华与否取决于设计概念是强调内部庭院和花园，还是外墙面。穿过朝向街面的入口和前庭，便可进入中庭。房屋的雨水被收集于方形天井水池内，水池与主水源地下蓄水池相连。餐厅在中庭，连着一个正对门厅的大客厅。穿过客厅，就进入到带有廊柱、装饰喷泉和水池的宽大花园。在与世隔绝的高墙内，花园常使用大理石雕像等装饰物。围绕柱廊边缘为私人生活区域，如卧室或靠墙可以放床的起居间。大多数房屋都设有小神龛（它是一个带画饰壁龛和雕像的小廊道）以表达对守护神和先祖的崇拜。

凡是重要的房间都会彩绘和粉刷，并在地板上铺设马赛克。大多数家庭只有少量的家具，毕竟上乘的家具价格昂贵且相对占用空间。所有的房间都有床，有些床用于睡觉也有的用于进餐。罗马人用油灯照明，有台座的陶灯或青铜灯放在壁龛里，或利用附件悬挂在天花板上。

厨房没有明确的位置。有时安置于一个还没衣橱大的房间里，有时就是房间的一处小角落，或楼梯的下方。厨房只配备一个水槽、一个烤炉和一个置于烹饪区上方的原始烟囱。至于陶或铜壶、煎锅等统统挂在墙上，而其他一些容器和罐子不是扔进柜子或放在架子上，就是放在靠近厨房的储藏室里。

罗马人的主食是谷物，比如大麦和小麦熬成的粥，用准备好的橄榄油和香草调味。普通市民都以此维生，罗马帝王和富裕的贵族却能享用惊人的丰盛美食。多数罗马人都是一日三餐。早餐包括浸过美酒的面包、奶酪、鸡蛋、水果和蜂蜜，这些快速简便的食物有时也会出现于午餐中。然后是一天中最为丰盛的晚餐。晚餐通常在黄昏后开始，由三道菜组成，遇到宴会场合可能持续至深夜。

罗马人的饭厅被称为躺卧餐桌，因摆设了三个用餐的躺椅，每个可坐三位宾客。因为罗马的宴请只接受九位宾客。罗马人沿用了希腊人躺卧吃饭的方式。装菜肴的盘子依据家庭的财富和地位由不同材料制作。普通的上菜盘由陶制和木制，而富人则会使用精致的陶瓷、玻璃和银制餐具。

第一道菜肴意在刺激食欲。紧接着是大量种类繁多的肉类和野味。饭后以甜点水果secundae mensae（其本意是第二桌，这样叫法原本就是第二桌抬上来）结束。然后开始酒会（Symposium），即希腊语"一起喝酒"的意思。古代酒由于酒精含量高且呈半流质状态，饮用前要加水进行稀释。

由于地中海气候的缘故，这里的建筑更注重光线和通风。即使皇宫也遵循这个基本原则，一系列的园林随意地散布在帕拉丁山，这里就是罗马最富裕的市民聚集区。这些概念被完好的保存下来，并迅速传遍整个罗马帝国，以至于欧洲北部的气候条件下，不得不修改建筑手法，增加了供热系统。

在大城市中，贫民可以租用廉价公寓。这些经济适用房设在城市人口密集的地段。这种房屋虽是砖瓦结构，尽管法律限制高度，但通常却有五层或更多。街道建筑的底层通常是工匠作坊和其他商铺。经严密设计以节省空间的公寓套房则建于楼上，可由一个设于室内中央庭院的公共楼梯达到。采光和通风需来自外墙和室内庭院。许多廉租公寓带有阳台。然而生活质量并不太高，条件拥挤，大多数人还得睡地板。由于水源只能送到低楼层的住户，因而楼层高的居民必须依靠公共供水。有限的水资源和廉价的建设频繁引起火灾和坍塌事故。

大多数人在农村生活，不是在小农场，就是在城市富人拥有的大庄园里干着农活。除了创造财富外，大庄园也让那些厌倦城市生活的非业主居住。在帝国时代，许多富有的家庭放弃了城市的住宅，而安身郊外的别墅里。农庄建筑有仓库、奴隶宿舍和富丽堂皇的别墅，别墅与城市住宅的建筑布局和装饰并无不同，往往更加奢华。

In Imperial Rome, private residences (*domus*) of modest to palatial proportions were constructed around architectural concepts that emphasized interior courtyards and gardens rather than the external facade, passing through a vestibule, open to the street, and an entranceway (*fauces*), one entered a covered courtyard (*atrium*). Rainwater was collected in a basin called the *impluvium* that was attached to a cistern buried beneath the floor that served as the primary source of water. A dining area was located just off the *atrium*, along with a large living room, the *tablinium*, that was positioned opposite the entrance hall. Through this *tablinium* one could also enter a wide, colonnaded garden, the *peristylium*, decorated with fountains and basins. Enclosed by high walls and hidden from the outside world, the garden often contained marble statues and other decorative elements. Around the edge of the peristyle were located the private living quarters such as bedrooms (*cubicula*) or niches along the walls where beds were placed. Most homes also included a *lararium*, a niche or gallery housing tablets and statuettes honouring the *Lares* or family gods and ancestors.

Important rooms were decorated with paintings and stucco; the floors covered with mosaics. Most homes had relatively little furniture; fine furniture could be expensive and rooms were frequently quite small. All homes contained beds, both those for sleeping (*cubiculares*) and those for dinning (*triclinares*). For illumination, Romans used oil lamps made of ceramic or bronze placed in wall niches, in candelabra stands or attached to fixtures hanging from the ceiling.

The kitchen did not have a standard location. Sometimes placed in rooms no larger than closets, small corners, or beneath stairwells, they were equipped with a water basin, an oven, and a primitive chimney in the wall above the cooking area. Ceramic and bronze pots and pans dangled on the walls, while other containers and vases were kept either in an armoire, on a set of shelves, or in a separate, small room adjacent to the kitchen known as the *apotheca*.

The basis of the Roman diet consisted of grains, such as barley and wheat from which a porridge, flavoured with olive oil and herbs, was prepared. Ordinary citizens subsisted on this mainstay while the Roman emperors and wealthy aristocrats feasted on a staggering variety of foods. Most Romans ate three meals a day. Breakfast in the morning consisted of bread soaked in wine along with cheese, eggs, fruit and honey followed by a quick and simple meal at midday. Then there was the *cena*, the largest meal of the day, consisting of three courses, which began in the late afternoon and on a banquet occasion could last well into the night.

The dining room was called the *triclinium* because of the presence of three dining couches, each seating three guests since nine was the accepted number of guests for a Roman banquet. Romans ate reclined in the manner of the Greeks. Serving dishes were made of different materials depending on the status and wealth of the household. Modest serving platters were made of terracotta and wood, while the rich owned fine ceramic, glass and silver serving dishes.

During the first course, (*gustatio*), specialties were served to stimulate the appetite. This was followed by large quantities and varieties of meat and game. The meal concluded with the sweets and fruit of the *secundae mensae* (second tables, so called because originally second tables were carried in). Then began the *symposium*, which in Greek means "drinking together". In antiquity, wine was always diluted with water, due to its high alcoholic content and its semi-liquid consistency.

Even the palaces of the emperors followed this essential order, consisting of a series of gardens sprawling casually over the Palatine Hill that was home to the wealthiest citizens of Rome. Due to the Mediterranean climate, construction was light and airy. These concepts were maintained and even exported as much as possible to Roman settlements throughout the Empire, even though in the northern climates of Europe, modifications had to be made to add heating.

In the large cities, the poor could rent small apartments in the *insulae*. These were tenement houses in an urban setting that provided economical housing where population was dense. Constructed of bricks, they often were of five or more stories, although by law, there were height limitations. The street level typically housed artisan workshops and other commercial establishments. The apartments, planned with strict economy of space, were located above and accessed by a common staircase located in an interior, central courtyard. Light and air were received from both the external facade and the interior courtyard. Many *insulae* were trimmed with balconies. The quality of life was not very good; conditions were crowded and most people would sleep on the floor. Water could only be pumped to the lower floors so tenants on higher floors had to depend on public water. Limited water and cheap construction caused frequent fires and collapses.

Most people lived in the countryside and worked the land, either on small farmsteads or on large estates owned by wealthy city people. In addition to generating wealth, a large estate might also serve its absentee owner as a retreat from city life. During the Imperial period, many wealthy families abandoned their urban homes, installing themselves in country villas. Along with farm buildings, storehouses and slave quarters, there would be a palatial villa, not unlike an urban *domus* in architectural lay-out and decoration, but often more luxurious.

宴会   THE BANQUET

罗马的富人在他们气派正式的餐厅里设豪宴、开派对。

传统上罗马人坐着进食，但是富裕贵族们逐渐学着希腊人的姿态斜倚在沙发上吃东西。正式的餐厅一般都在房间的三面放置沙发，因此进餐时会放置一种名为"三面有躺椅的餐桌"（*triclinium*），同时在中间放一个矮桌子或几个桌子。

Wealthy Romans gave lavish dinner parties in their formal dining rooms.

Traditionally Romans ate while seated, but gradually the wealthy aristocrats began to eat while reclined on couches in the manner of the Greeks. Formal dining rooms usually had couches arranged around three sides of the room, thus the name *triclinium*, and a low table or tables in the middle where the food was served.

宴飨图石碑
Stela with Banquet Scene

帝国时期
大理石
高48.5厘米，长65厘米，厚 15 厘米，重90千克
佛罗伦萨国家考古博物馆

Imperial Age
Marble
L. 65 cm, H. 48.5 cm, Th. 15 cm, W. 90 kg
National Archeological Museum, Florence

山形石墙饰
Pediment

公元1世纪
镶有优质水晶的白色大理石
长62 厘米，宽21厘米，厚3厘米，重40千克
佛罗伦萨国家考古博物馆

1st century CE
White marble with fine crystals
L. 62 cm, W. 21 cm, Th. 3 cm, W. 40 kg
National Archeological Museum, Florence

早在公元前7世纪地中海艺术
作品中就有宴会场景。该场景
在风格上是公元1世纪的。宴
会场景在丧葬艺术中尤为常
见，有时配偶、奴隶和动物也
会出现于死者丧宴的场景中。

Banquet scenes were common
features of Mediterranean art dating
back as early as the 7th century BCE.
This one can be dated on stylistic
grounds to the 1st century CE.
Banquet scenes were a particularly
common feature of funerary art, with
the deceased banqueter sometimes
accompanied by his spouse, his
slaves and animals.

收获葡萄图陶板
Slab with Scene of Satyrs Harvesting Grapes

公元前1世纪
红陶
高24.5厘米，长57厘米，宽13.5厘米
佛罗伦萨国家考古博物馆

1st century BCE
H. 24.5 cm, L. 57 cm, W. 13.5 cm
Terracotta
National Archeological Museum, Florence

有翅膀的爱神厄洛斯神和狮鹫
被莨苕藤包围着。

A winged Eros and a griffin among
acanthus vines.

孩子和水果石像
Child with Fruit

帝国时期
大理石
高88厘米
佛罗伦萨国家考古博物馆

Imperial Age
Marble
H. 88 cm
National Archeological Museum, Florence

孩子身披一种希腊和罗马式的
罩衫，里面还塞着一些水果。
这尊雕像可能代表了四季的馈
赠，其古老原型可追溯至公元
前3世纪。

The child has a *clamus*, a Greek and
Roman mantle, and holds in his
smock some fruit. The statue may
represent a Genius of Seasons and
its ancient prototype can be dated to
the 3rd century BCE.

儿童与狗石像
Child with a Dog

帝国时期
大理石
高68厘米
佛罗伦萨国家考古博物馆

Imperial Age
Marble
H. 68 cm
National Archeological Museum, Florence

有四个与该像密切相关的作品
显示出相似性。事实上，研究
者认为，包括在佛罗伦萨国家
博物馆保存的这类雕像在内，
都是委托一家作坊为花园装饰
而作。

The statue has a strong connection
with another four artworks which
show similarities in terms of
representation and style. As a matter
of fact, researchers believe that this
kind of statue, including the version
preserved in the Florentine museum,
were made by the same workshop
and were commissioned for the
decoration of gardens.

私人家庭居所：
住宅
PRIVATE FAMILY
RESIDENCIES:
THE DOMUS

私家住宅建筑的重点是内部的庭院和花园不是外墙。

典型的住宅在一个中轴线上铺开，前部围绕中厅建有一组房间，主人在中厅接待宾客。私人寝室位于住宅的后部，是一个带有开放柱廊的庭院，四周有更多的房间。

客厅通常位于后面的庭院和前面的中央大厅之间，是一个开放式的起居室，也可以用帘子隔出一个私密的空间。每个住宅都有一个正式的餐厅，有时候还会因季节变化另设餐厅。有的住宅还设有具备水上游乐设施、雕塑和喷泉的精美花园。

Private family residencies were constructed with an emphasis on interior courtyards and gardens rather than external façade.

The typical *domus* was laid out on an axis, with a suite of rooms grouped around a central hall (*atrium*) near the front. Here a homeowner could receive visitors. The family's private living quarters would be situated toward the rear of the *domus* and feature an open colonnaded courtyard (*peristylium*) surrounded by more rooms.

The *tablinum*, often situated between the *atrium* and *peristylium*, was an open living room that could be curtained off for privacy. Every *domus* had a formal dining room (*triclinium*), and sometimes additional ones for different seasons. Also there would be splendid gardens with water games, statues and fountains.

马赛克残件
Fragments of Mosaic

帝国时期
石
高40厘米，宽60厘米，重60千克
佛罗伦萨国家考古博物馆

Imperial Age
Stone
H. 40 cm, W. 60 cm, W. 60 kg
National Archeological Museum, Florence

这两块马赛克残件可能是罗马乡村别墅中壁画的一部分，反映出帝国时期人们常用马赛克来装饰别墅。

These two mosaic fragments are probably from a Roman country villa where they could have been inserted into the frescoed walls, and represent the mosaic decorations common to villas of the Imperial Age.

乡村别墅 RURAL VILLAS

农业在罗马世界是很重要的，特别是当帝国扩张到了高卢、北非和埃及这些富饶高产的地区。

大部分人住在乡下并耕作土地，有些住在小型的农舍，有些富裕的城市居民则住在自己的大型农庄中。除了生产财富，大型农庄也是主人一个偶尔远离城市生活的僻静休息之处。在其他的农庄建筑、仓库和奴隶居所周边一般都会有一个富丽堂皇的别墅，其建筑布局和装饰上有别于都市"住宅"。

Agriculture was important in the Roman world, especially as the empire expanded to include the rich and productive regions of Gaul, North Africa and Egypt.

Most people lived in the countryside and worked the land, either on small farmsteads or on large estates owned by wealthy city people. In addition to generating wealth, a large estate might also serve its absentee owner as an occasional retreat from city life. Along with other farm buildings, storehouses and slave quarters, there would be a palatial villa not unlike an urban domus in architectural lay-out and decoration.

建筑 ARCHITECTURE

　　罗马人是建筑大师。罗马帝国时期壮观的建筑遗迹，从帝国的一端至另一端散布整个疆土，至今仍安然矗立，供后人瞻仰。

　　罗马建筑深受希腊建筑的影响，但是它们之间还是有很重要的区别，比如对拱门、拱顶、圆顶的广泛应用。在建造拱门的时候，罗马时期的建筑建有粗壮的横梁和美轮美奂的水槽。有了拱顶和圆顶，他们创造了足以遮蔽宽宽的室内空间的大型结构。混凝土是罗马人的另一个重大发明。

　　罗马的建筑在公元2世纪达到了鼎盛时期，即所谓的"五贤帝时代"。那一时期两个壮观的例子是图拉真建的古罗马广场和哈德良建的万神殿。

The Romans were master builders. Spectacular architectural remains from Imperial Rome are seen still today scattered from one end of the former empire to the other.

Roman architecture was influenced by Greek architecture, but there are important differences, such as the extensive use of arches, vaults and domes. With arches, architects of the Roman Period built strong bridges and amazing aqueducts. With vaults and domes, they created large structures that covered expansive interior spaces. Concrete was another essentially Roman innovation.

Roman architecture reached its zenith during the second century CE, the so-called "Era of Good Emperors." Two spectacular examples from that era are Trajan's Forum in Rome and the Pantheon built by Hadrian.

"L"形马赛克残件
Mosaic Fragments

帝国时期
石
高115厘米，长149厘米，宽115厘米
佛罗伦萨国家考古博物馆

Imperial Age
Stone
H. 115 cm, L. 149 cm, W. 115 cm
National Archeological Museum, Florence

本件为发掘于意大利托斯卡纳地区格罗塞托附近Settefinestre别墅客厅的地板残件。

One of three floor mosaic fragments from the floor of the tablinum of theVilla di Settefinestre, excavated near Grosseto in the Tuscany region of Italy area.

罗马浴室
ROMAN BATHS

考古发现的罗马浴室遗址遍及整个帝国，它是罗马社会中最普遍、最美丽和最复杂的代表之一。

一些浴室极为精致，特色鲜明。所有的浴室都有一个更衣区（*apodyterium*）、一个内设热水澡盆（*calidarium*）的热水区、一个温水区（*tepidarium*）和一个内设冷水澡盆（*frigidarium*）的冷水区。这需要有充足的水供应和火炉。其他设施还包括花园、露天游泳池、健身器材、按摩房、会客室、餐厅和有阅读区域的图书馆。

最令人难忘和奢侈的浴室当属由罗马皇帝们兴建的浴室，如提图斯、图密善、图拉真、卡拉卡拉和戴克里先。

Archaeological remains of Roman baths, found throughout the empire, represent one of the most common, beautiful and sophisticated expressions of Roman society.

Some baths were more elaborate than others and included more features. All had a dressing area (*apodyterium*), a hot water area with hot plunge bath (*calidarium*), a warm water area (*tepidarium*), and a cold water area with cold plunge bath (*frigidarium*). This required an ample water supply and furnace. Additional features might include gardens, open-air swimming pools, athletic facilities, massage rooms, meeting places, restaurant, and library with reading spots.

The most impressive and luxurious baths were those built in Rome by the emperors Titus, Domitian, Trajan, Caracalla and Diocletian.

马赛克残件
One of Two Fragments of the Mosaic Decorating

帝国时期
石
高105厘米，宽89 厘米
佛罗伦萨国家考古博物馆

Imperial Age
Stone
H. 105 cm, W. 89 cm
National Archeological Museum, Florence

薄胎陶厄拉杯
"Thin-Wall" Mug(Olla)

公元前1世纪~公元1世纪
褐陶
高9.5厘米
佛罗伦萨国家考古博物馆

1st century BCE −1st century CE
Hazelnut clay
H. 9.5 cm
National Archeological Museum, Florence

陶杯
Cup in South Gallic Sigillata

帝国时期
红陶
高9.2厘米，直径18.2厘米
佛罗伦萨国家考古博物馆

Imperial Age
Terracotta
H. 9.2 cm ,D. 18.2 cm
National Archeological Museum, Florence

阿雷蒂内陶杯
Matrix of Arretine Cup

帝国时期
红陶
高11厘米，直径20厘米
佛罗伦萨国家考古博物馆

Imperial Age
Terracotta
H. 11 cm, D. 20 cm
National Archeological Museum, Florence

陶瓶
Carafes (Lagynos)

公元前1～公元1世纪
红陶
左高24.6厘米，右高14.6厘米
锡耶纳国家考古博物馆

1ˢᵗ century BCE – 1ˢᵗ century CE
Terracotta
H. (left) 24.6 cm, H. (right) 14.6 cm
National Archeological Museum, Siena

陶盘
Plate of "Terra Sigillata"

公元前1世纪
红陶
高4.4厘米，直径22.1厘米
锡耶纳国家考古博物馆

1ˢᵗ century BCE
Terracotta
H. 4.4 cm, D. 22.1 cm
National Archeological Museum, Siena

巴尔博汀陶杯
Mug with *Barbotine* Gecoration

公元前1世纪
釉陶
高9.5厘米，最大直径11.5厘米，口沿直径6.5厘米
佛罗伦萨国家考古博物馆

1ˢᵗ century BCE
Glazed terracotta
H. 9.5 cm, D. (max) 11.5 cm , D. (rim) 6.5 cm
National Archeological Museum, Florence

该杯采用巴尔博汀工艺装饰，
用刷子或刮刀把水和黏土混合
物在陶杯表面涂成凹凸不平的
层次、斑点和条纹。容器经过
烧制之后，便会出现表面隆起
或波纹的浮雕装饰效果。

This mug is decorated with the
"barbotine" technique, which
involved applying a slip (mixture of
water and clay) to the surface of a
clay vessel in uneven layers, patches
and trails with a brush or spatula.
When the vessel was fired, this
produced a relief decoration with
small bumps and ripples.

阿雷佐陶杯
Cup of "Terra Sigillata" from Arezzo

帝国时期
红陶
高11.5厘米，直径16.3厘米
佛罗伦萨国家考古博物馆

Imperial Age
Terracotta
H. 11.5 cm, D. (max) 16.3 cm
National Archeological Museum, Florence

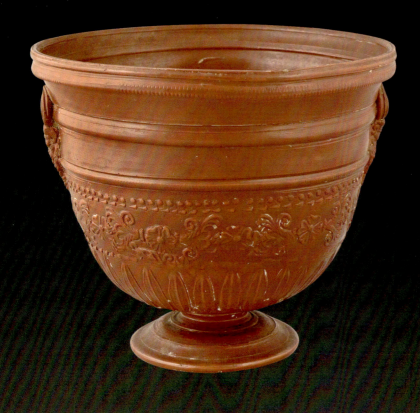

阿雷佐陶杯
Cup of "Terra Sigillata" from Arezzo

帝国时期
红陶
高16厘米 直径19.2厘米
佛罗伦萨国家考古博物馆

Imperial Age
Terracotta
H. 16 cm, D. 19.2 cm
National Archeological Museum, Florence

玻璃盘
Plate

公元2世纪
蓝、绿玻璃
高4厘米，直径19厘米
佛罗伦萨国家考古博物馆

2nd century CE
Blue and green blown glass
H. 4 cm, D. 19 cm
National Archeological Museum, Florence

玻璃盘
Plate

公元2世纪
蓝、绿玻璃
高3.9厘米，直径24.2厘米
佛罗伦萨国家考古博物馆

2nd century CE
blue and green blown glass
H. 3.9 cm, D. 24.2 cm
National Archeological Museum, Florence

这两个盘子或用作托盘。从造型和外观来看，大约产于公元2世纪。

These two plates were probably used as trays. By form and shape. they are dateable to the 2nd century.

有柄铜罐
Pitcher

帝国时期
青铜
通高16.3厘米
锡耶纳国家考古博物馆

Imperial Age
Bronze
H. (max) 16.3 cm
National Archeological Museum, Siena

双耳银杯
Cup with Two Handles

公元1世纪
银器
高6.5厘米，直径10.5厘米
佛罗伦萨国家考古博物馆

1st century CE
Silver
H. 6.5 cm, D. 10.5 cm
National Archeological Museum, Florence

这种盛酒用的银制器具在公元
1世纪的罗马较为常见。

This kind of drinking vessel was very
common in Roman silverware during
the 1st century CE.

罗纹玻璃杯
Steraked Cup

公元1世纪上半叶
紫色玻璃
高5.7厘米，直径13.5厘米
佛罗伦萨国家考古博物馆

First half of the 1st century CE
Violet colored glass
H. 5.7 cm, D. 13.5 cm
National Archeological Museum, Florence

这种杯子起源于希腊东部，可能是叙罗巴勒斯坦地区。它最早出现于公元前1世纪初，以丰富的装饰图案和出色的制作工艺而得名，在公元1世纪较为流行。

This kind of cup originated in the Hellenistic east, probably in the Syro-Palestinian region. The earliest known examples, distinguished by their rich decoration and superior craftsmanship, date from the beginning of the 1st century BCE. They were quite common during the 1st century CE.

千花玻璃杯
Millefiori(striped) Cup

奥古斯都时期（公元前27年~公元14年）
玻璃
高6.6厘米，最大直径10厘米
佛罗伦萨国家考古博物馆

Reign of Augustus (27 BCE – 14 CE)
Blue. red. yellow. green and uncolored glass
H. 6.6 cm, D. (max) 10 cm
National Archeological Museum, Florence

千花玻璃指的是将有色玻璃融化在容器表面的一种装饰工艺。有色玻璃可以化作如同这个杯子上的长形条纹状或其他图案。千花玻璃工艺可以追溯到公元前1世纪末期和公元1世纪初期，可能是在地中海东部地区流传开来的。

Millefiori refers to a decorative technique that involved melting colored glass on the surface of a vessel. The colored glass could be applied in long bands, as in the case of this cup, or in other patterns. The *millefiori* technique dates to the late1st century BCE and the early 1st century CE, and probably was developed in the eastern Mediterranean.

千花玻璃盘
Millefiori(striped) Plate

公元1世纪
玻璃
高4厘米，直径13.1厘米
佛罗伦萨国家考古博物馆

1st century CE
White. amber-yellow and uncolored glass
H. 4 cm, D. 13.1 cm
National Archeological Museum, Florence

方底玻璃瓶
Square Bottle

公元1世纪
玻璃
高17.8厘米
锡耶纳国家考古博物馆

1st century CE
Blue glass
H. 17.8 cm
National Archeological Museum, Siena

这款方形瓶在公元前1世纪中期的罗马被广泛用于盛酒。它采用直接将玻璃吹制入可拆卸的方形模具中，再去模取出的方法制成。

This type of jug—with a squared shape. used probably for wine was found throughout the Roman world by the middle of the 1st century BCE. They were produced by blowing glass directly into a square mold with removable walls.

双耳玻璃瓶
Small Amphora

帝国时期
玻璃
高14.1厘米
锡耶纳国家考古博物馆

Imperial Age
Glass
H. 14.1 cm
National Archeological Museum, Siena

双耳玻璃瓶
Small Amphora

公元1~2世纪
玻璃
高10.5厘米
锡耶纳国家考古博物馆

1st – 2nd century CE
Glass
H. 10.5 cm
National Archeological Museum, Siena

浮雕装饰玻璃瓶
Small Glass Amphora with Cameo Decoration

奥古斯都时期（公元前27年~公元14年）
玻璃
高13厘米
佛罗伦萨国家考古博物馆

Reign of Augustus (27 BCE - 14 CE)
Blue glass
H. 13 cm
National Archeological Museum, Florence

这款由浮雕玻璃制成的细颈瓶，配以酒神仪式场景做装饰，呈现出完美的玻璃生产工艺和罗马帝国初期流行的装饰风格。下方的蓝色和上方的白色这两层玻璃，均采用了用尖锐工具切割白色人形直到它浮现在深色背景上的技术。该技术也用于亚宝石的雕刻中。

This amphora, made of "cameo style" glass and decorated with scenes of a Dionysiac rite, represents an extremely refined technique of glass production and decoration that was in vogue during Early Imperial Age. The technique involved superimposing two layers of glass, blue underneath and white on top, and then incising with a sharp tool until white figures emerged against the darker background. This is the same technique used for producing cameos from semi-precious stones.

罗纹玻璃杯
Ribbed Cup

公元1世纪
玻璃
高6.9厘米，直径7.7厘米
佛罗伦萨国家考古博物馆

1st century CE
Glass
H. 6.9 cm, D. 7.7 cm
National Archeological Museum, Florence

柱形玻璃杯
Cylindrical Glass

帝国时期
玻璃
高7.9厘米，直径7.4厘米
佛罗伦萨国家考古博物馆

Cylindrical Glass
Imperial Rome
Glass
H. 7.9 cm, D. 7.4 cm
National Archeological Museum, Florence

这种带有吉语的杯子在公元
1世纪的希腊十分流行。这
个杯子上的铭文意为"振奋
和鼓舞"。

Vases of this sort with auspicious
inscriptions in Greek were quite
common in the 1ˢᵗ century. The
inscription on this one reads:
KATAXAIPE KAI EFPAINO ("Cheer up
and rejoice").

铜架、铜盆
Tripode with Movable Basin

公元1世纪
青铜
通高70厘米，直径44.5厘米
佛罗伦萨国家考古博物馆

1st century CE
Bronze
H (max). 70 cm, D. 44.5 cm
National Archeological Museum, Florence

双芯铜灯
Two-Wick Lamp

公元1世纪早期
青铜
高11厘米，长22.3厘米
佛罗伦萨国家考古博物馆

Early 1st century CE
Bronze
H. 11 cm, L. 22.3 cm
National Archeological Museum, Florence

这个雅致的双灯芯灯以链子悬挂于天花板上。铜灯的手柄呈葡萄叶形状。

This elegant two-wick lamp has an attached chain for suspending it from the ceiling. Its handle is in the shape of grape leaves.

铜烛台
Candelabra

公元前1世纪~公元1世纪
青铜
高90.3厘米
佛罗伦萨国家考古博物馆

1st century BCE - 1st century CE
Bronze
H. 90.3 cm
National Archeological Museum, Florence

铜烛台座
Candelabrum Base

公元1世纪
青铜
高38.5厘米
佛罗伦萨国家考古博物馆

1st century CE
Bronze
H. 38.5 cm
National Archeological Museum, Florence

铜三脚架
Tripod

公元前1世纪~公元1世纪
青铜
高16厘米，直径15厘米
佛罗伦萨国家考古博物馆

1st BCE – 1st century CE
Bronze
H. 16 cm, D. 15 cm
National Archeological Museum, Florence

铜盖壶
Pot with Lid

公元1世纪
镀银青铜器
高29厘米，盖直径17厘米
佛罗伦萨国家考古博物馆

Pot with lid
1st century CE
Silver plated bronze
H. 29 cm, D. (lid) 17 cm
National Archeological Museum, Florence

铜灯
Lamp

公元1世纪下半叶
青铜
高13 厘米，长26.5 厘米
佛罗伦萨国家考古博物馆

Second half of the 1st century CE
Bronze
H. 13 cm, L. 26.5 cm
National Archeological Museum, Florence

罗马人基本依靠油灯照明。罗马时期人们通常使用由红陶制灯，即一个封闭的壶体，顶部开有加油的小孔以及放灯芯的壶口，通常还有一个把手。贵重的油灯用青铜制造而成，有些油灯可放置多枚灯芯。加盐的橄榄油是较好的燃料，多半发黄光。也可以使用其他的油，如鱼油。灯芯可由多种材料所制，如亚麻、纸草或蓖麻纤维。

The Romans depended heavily on oil lamps for artificial light. Typically the lamps used during Roman times were made of terracotta (fired clay) and consisted of a closed bowl with a hole in the top for adding oil and a spout to hold the wick. Often there was a handle. More expensive lamps were made of bronze, and sometimes a lamp would be designed to accommodate more than one wick. A favored fuel was olive oil with salt added to give the light more of a yellow color. Other oils could be used, such as fish oil. Wicks could be made of various materials such as linen, papyrus or fibers of the castor plant.

铜灯
Lamp

帝国时期
青铜
高12.7厘米，长21厘米
佛罗伦萨国家考古博物馆

Imperial Age
Bronze
H. 12.7 cm, L. 21 cm
National Archaeological Museum, Florence

陶灯
Lamp

帝国时期
红陶
高10.7厘米，直径8厘米
锡耶纳国家考古博物馆

Imperial Age
Terracotta
H. 10.7 cm, D. 8 cm
National Archeological Museum, Siena

月亮神陶灯
Lamp with the Goddess Selene

公元1世纪下半叶
红陶
长9.6厘米，直径6.7厘米
锡耶纳国家考古博物馆

Second half of the 1st century CE
Terracotta
L. 9.6 cm, D. 6.7 cm
National Archeological Museum, Siena

这盏灯饰有月之女神塞勒涅半
身像的浮雕，其标识是她的头
部上方悬挂新月。

This lamp is decorated with a bust in
relief of Selene (the goddess of the
Moon), recognizable by the crescent
moon above her head.

铜调羹
Spoon

公元1世纪
青铜
上长14.9厘米，下长15厘米
锡耶纳国家考古博物馆

1st century CE
Bronze
L. (above) 14.9 cm, L. (below) 15 cm
National Archeological Museum, Siena

铜斗
Casserole

公元1~2世纪
青铜
长27.5厘米，直径15.3厘米
锡耶纳国家考古博物馆

1st – 2nd century CE
Bronze
L. 27.5 cm, D. 15.3 cm
National Archeological Museum, Siena

这种与浴盆配套使用的容器在意大利乡间和边境地区十分流行，许多作坊均有制作。它们在公元1~2世纪曾风靡一时，这种特征在公元1世纪尤为盛行，在当时庞贝城随处可见。

This type of vessel, associated with the bath was produced in many workshops and was popular in Italy, the provinces and along the *Limes* (frontier fortifications). These vessels were popular during both the 1st and 2nd centuries CE, but this particular variation was especially popular during the 1st century and was found in large numbers in Pompeii.

铜锅

Frying Pan

公元1世纪
青铜
长55厘米，直径26厘米
锡耶纳国家考古博物馆

1st century CE
Bronze
L. 55 cm, D. 26 cm
National Archeological Museum, Siena

铁刀

Knife

公元1世纪
铁
长29厘米
佛罗伦萨国家考古博物馆

1st century CE
Iron
L. 29 cm
National Archeological Museum, Florence

铜叉
Fork

公元1世纪
青铜
长13.1厘米
锡耶纳国家考古博物馆

1st century CE
Bronze
L. 13.1 cm
National Archeological Museum, Siena

铜锅
Frying Pan

公元1世纪
青铜
高3.5厘米，长56厘米
佛罗伦萨国家考古博物馆

1st century CE
Bronze
H. 3.5 cm, L. 56 cm
National Archeological Museum, Florence

奴隶的铜项圈
Slave's Collar(Torque)

帝国时期
青铜
直径13厘米
佛罗伦萨国家考古博物馆

Imperial Age
Bronze
D. 13 cm
National Archeological Museum, Florence

项圈用于"标识"那些曾经逃跑又被抓回主人身边的俘虏。这个项圈暗示佩戴它的俘虏不服管教。

Collars were used to "mark" fugitive slaves once they had been recaptured and returned to their masters. The collar signaled that the slave wearing it was rebellious.

磨石
Tronco-Conic Millstone

帝国时期
石灰华
通高38厘米
佛罗伦萨国家考古博物馆

Imperial Age
Travertine
H. (max) 38 cm
National Archeological Museum, Florence

磨石大小不一，小至一手就能拿起，大至放置在面包房中需要奴隶或骡子才能拖动。

Millstones existed in various sizes, from small ones like this that be turned by hand, to enormous ones in bakers' shops that were turned by slave or mule power.

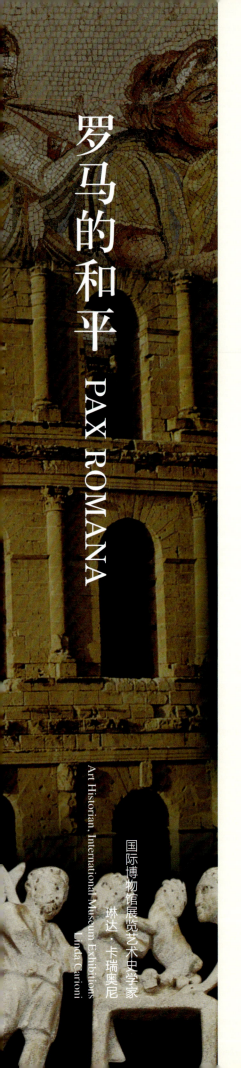

罗马的和平 PAX ROMANA

国际博物馆展览艺术史学家
琳达·卡瑞奥尼
Art Historian, International Museum Exhibitions
Linda Carrioni

罗马帝国在扩张巅峰期，横跨欧洲大陆，北及不列颠，西至莱茵河，南到多瑙河，并占有幼发拉底河域以西的亚洲大陆、北非的沿海和整个地中海地区。臣服于罗马统治意味着税收和奴役，但也意味着享受"罗马和平"带来的好处。罗马帝国提供了可靠的基础设施、军事安全，并开放了边贸促进当地经济的发展。

在古代文明里，罗马人建造的基础设施无人匹敌。杰出的例子是道路系统，使得帝国遥远的边境地区也能有效统治、管理和通商。罗马帝国之间的沟通，尤其是军队在尽可能短的时间里的沟通至关重要，因此道路尽可能的直。历史表明，罗马人共建了全长超过5万英里的快速路，至今仍有许多路以各种形式存在。当河山阻碍建设时，均被诸如桥梁、高架桥和连廊等宏伟工程所克服。渡槽也是罗马的一大特点。856个公共浴场，1352个罗马喷泉都由11个渡槽所联通，每天能提供100万立方的水量。

在曾为罗马帝国的今日世界里，随处可见的建筑都能找到罗马人别出心裁的证明。在罗马帝国时期，他们的建筑方式延伸到了帝国的各个角落且影响持久，其中包含了500座城市、90个露天罗马竞技场和150个戏院。罗马持续而无可争议的统治归功于其非凡的军事实力。罗马能够在几个世纪中处于不败之地的军事实力是多种因素的结果：人民的战斗意志、严密的组织、军队的广泛训练、战术和技术的优势。最初，要求每个自由公民据自身能力进行军事培训，在发生武装冲突时加入军队。罗马军团发明了灵活的梯形阵势（两翼部队位于中心主力前面）。在公元前1世纪，盖乌斯·马略组建了职业军团，所有入伍的士兵都是罗马公民，装备了头盔、胸甲、西班牙式短剑、盾和标枪。

在奥古斯丁的统治下，罗马军队改革，此后数百年间其形式只稍有调整。每个军团由10个大队组成，而每个大队分成6个分队，每分队80个人。指挥官是皇帝特使。17～25岁的军人在军团服役要满25年，由职业军官百夫长进行艰巨的军训任务。年轻士兵要学会使用各种武器、执行复杂的军事演习、组建营地和忍受长途跋涉。在战场上，军训赋予罗马军队的灵活和快速部署能力往往就是让敌人大为吃惊的秘密武器。另有一种值得一提的极为重要的战术，即罗马的龟甲阵。军团构成一个整体对外移动，每个甲兵只要简单地把盾牌向外竖起足以遮挡任何攻击。

罗马士兵都驻扎在边界军营，保卫国防是其永久的使命。士兵的职责还包括修建公路、桥梁、渡槽，甚至在新征服的领土开展建设。常驻营地通常建立在帝国边境沿线的战略要地，它会发展成一个具有浴场、医院及剧院的集市。因此在整个罗马帝国广袤的土地上，军队起到了传播罗马文化的根本性作用。服役结束后，许多士兵已深深融入当地的生活，一旦退役，他们可以选择服役附近的地方一块土地作为奖励。

罗马人还将他们压倒性兵力的策略用于海战，他们的军舰上都有一个铰链跳板和抓钩，可让大量士兵登敌船。罗马海军发展之迅猛，使罗马成为了整个地中海世界领先的海上力量。

在帝国统治期间，罗马城的人口已经超越了100万。供给大都市和其他罗马城市物资的巨大挑战都由海上运输完成。同时，帝国扩展的省份也在不断生产食物和供应手工艺品。事实上，创造当地财富的贸易是"罗马和平"的重要支柱，商船比起陆地上的大篷车的运载量更多，也更快捷。为了防海盗，罗马人建造了更小更轻便的快艇。罗马帝国时期广泛使用的大型陶罐中运输葡萄酒、橄榄油和其他食物。许多如精美的餐具的成品、香水、丝绸一类奢侈品和香料等被海运到各行省以满足罗马人民的需要。

罗马皇帝对海岸线的控制、港口和航线的制定给予高度重视，这也证明了海上供应系统的重要性。罗马人认为地中海是自己的私产。然而，众所周知拉丁文 Mare Nostrum意为"我们的海洋"。地中海流域里徜徉的不仅有罗马大军舰、商船和其护航舰，还有许多小艇和渔船。

At its maximum expansion, the Roman Empire encompassed Britain in the North, all of continental Europe west of the Rhine and south of the Danube, most of Asia west of the Euphrates River, the coastal areas of Northern Africa and all the Mediterranean islands. Domination and allegiance to Rome meant taxation and subjugation, but there were also benefits, signified by the expression *Pax Romana*, "the Roman peace." The Empire provided reliable infrastructure, military security and open borders that promoted commerce, trade and local wealth.

Among ancient civilizations, no one rivaled the infrastructure built by the Romans. One outstanding example of this is the system of roads that enabled conquest, administration and trade within its far-flung Empire. Communication between Rome, its Empire, and its armies in the shortest time possible was of paramount importance, so roads had to be as straight as possible. In all, the Romans built more than 50,000 miles of highways, many still existing in some form or another today. When rivers or hills obstructed construction, difficulties were overcome by engineering feats such as bridges, viaducts and galleries. Aqueducts were also a Roman speciality. The 856 public baths and 1,352 fountains of Rome were supplied by 11 aqueducts, capable of supplying 1,000,000 cubic meters of water per day.

Throughout the modern world in what was once the Roman Empire, testimony to the ingenuity and capability of the Romans in architecture can be found. During the Imperial age, their building program was monumental and extended to all corners of the empire, encompassing 500 cities, 90 amphitheatres, 150 theatres. The undisputed dominance that Rome exerted for such a long time was primarily due to the extraordinary military might of its armies. Invincible for centuries, Rome's military strength was the result of several factors: the warrior spirit of its people, solid organization, the extensive training of its troops, and tactical and technical superiority. In the beginning, every free citizen of Rome was called upon to arm themselves, according to their capabilities, and join their legion in times of conflict. The legion, a Roman invention, was a flexible formation of troops arranged in an echelon (two flanking units arranged ahead of a centre rear unit.) A permanent, professional army was created under the consul Gaius Marius in I BCE; all enlisted soldiers were Roman citizens, and were equally armed with the helmut, cuirass, sword (the *gladium* of Spanish origin), shield and javelin.

Under the reign of Augustus, the Roman army was reformed and the form it assumed would last, with only minor changes, for centuries: each legion consisted of 10 cohorts, each of which was further divided into six centuries of 80 men. The commander was called *Legatus*. Legionaries were enrolled at 17-25 years of age for a tour of duty lasting 25 years. Training was conducted by professional officers, the Centurions, and extremely arduous. Young soldiers learned how to handle different types of weapons, perform complex battlefield manoeuvres, build encampments and endure long marches. This training endowed Roman troops with an agility and capability of rapid deployment in the field that was often a secret weapon used to surprise the enemy. Also of utmost importance was another tactic, brilliantly employed: the *testudo*, a singular formation by which the legion could move forward as a single, armoured body, protected against any attack simply by turning their shields outwards both overhead and laterally.

The Roman soldier lived within the boundaries of his military camp whose maintenance and defence was his permanent duty. The soldiers' duties also included the construction of streets, bridges, aqueducts, even towns in newly conquered territories. Permanent camps, usually built in strategic location along the Empire's frontiers, evolved into larger settlements with local markets, baths, hospitals and even theatres. Thus the army itself played a fundamental role in the diffusion of Roman culture throughout the vast territories of the Empire. At the end of military service, many soldiers had developed so deep a bond with local life that once dismissed, they would choose as their reward a portion of land in the vicinity of where they had served their military duty.

The Romans applied their strategy of overwhelming force to battle at sea as well, equipping their warships with a hinged gangplank and grappling hook that permitted the boarding of the enemy ship by a superior number of men. As the Roman navy evolved so did its warships which were all quite large, enabling Rome to become the leading sea power throughout the Mediterranean world.

By the time of Imperial Rome, the city had reached a population of more than one million and the challenge to supply such a metropolis and other cities of the Empire was met through marine transport. Already much of the food supplies and artisan goods were being provided by and produced in the provinces of the extended Empire. In fact, trade which created local wealth was an important pillar of *Pax Romana* and merchantmen were faster and capable of carrying larger cargoes than overland caravans. To protect the merchantmen from piracy, the Romans built a smaller, lighter type of warship, the *liburnian*. Wine, olive oil and other foodstuffs were transported in large ceramic amphorae produced throughout the Empire. Manufactured goods such as fine tableware and luxury items such as perfume, silk and spices were also shipped from the provinces to meet the demands of Rome.

The care and attention paid by the emperors to the control of the coastline, harbours and sea routes demonstrated the importance of the maritime supply system. Romans considered the Mediterranean their own property; it was known as *Mare Nostrum*, our sea, and its waters constantly plied not only by large warships, merchantmen and their escorts, but also small skiffs and fishing boats as well.

军队
THE ROMAN ARMY

罗马的军事实力来自人民的勇武精神、严密的组织、频繁的军队训练以及在技术、战术方面的优势，因此几个世纪来战无不胜。

最早的罗马军队由罗马的自由民组成，他们自备武装，战时就参加他们自己的军团。公元前1世纪，奥古斯都重建了一支职业军队，之后的两个世纪其架构都相对保持不变。

除了战斗和戍边，军队也参与建设堡垒、修建道路及其他帝国基础建设。军队还在传播罗马文化方面担当了重要的角色。在25年服役的最后时期，许多战士在他们服役的遥远省份安顿了下来。

Invincible for centuries, Rome's military strength resulted from the warrior spirit of its people, solid organization, extensive training of its troops, and tactical and technical superiority.

At first Rome's armies consisted of free Roman citizens who armed themselves and joined their *legion* in times of conflict. A professional army was created during the first century BCE, reorganized under Augustus, and remained relatively unchanged in structure for the next two centuries.

In addition to fighting and guarding the frontiers, the army built forts, roads and other features of the empire's infrastructure. The military also played an important role in the diffusion of Roman culture. At the end of military service (25 years), many soldiers settled on land in distant provinces where they had served their military duty.

士兵像石墓碑
Small Stela of a Soldier

公元3世纪
大理石
高30 厘米，宽 20厘米
佛罗伦萨国家考古博物馆

3rd century CE
Marble
H. 30 cm, W. 20 cm
National Archeological Museum, Florence

碑上刻画持矛的士兵。

The soldier is armed with a spear.

铜头盔
Helmet

公元1世纪
青铜
通高20厘米
佛罗伦萨国家考古博物馆

1st century CE
Bronze
H. (max) 20 cm
National Archeological Museum, Florence

陶灯残件
Fragment of Lamp in the Form of a Disc

公元前1世纪~公元3世纪
红陶
长15厘米，宽10.5厘米
锡耶纳国家考古博物馆

1st century BCE − 3rd century CE
Terracotta
L. 15 cm, W. 10.5 cm
National Archeological Museum, Siena

灯上饰有一个罗马士兵的肖像。

Decoration on the lamp portrays a Roman soldier.

士兵像陶灯
Lamp with Soldier Decoration

公元1世纪下半期
红陶
长11厘米，直径8厘米
锡耶纳国家考古博物馆

Second half of the 1st century CE
Terracotta
L. 11 cm, D. 8 cm
National Archeological Museum, Siena

铜蒺藜
Tribulus (Weapon)

公元前1世纪~公元3世纪
青铜
高6.2厘米
佛罗伦萨国家考古博物馆

1st century BCE – 3rd century CE
Bronze
H. 6.2 cm
National Archeological Museum, Florence

带有尖倒钩的铜蒺藜散布于地面上以阻碍敌军尤其是骑兵的前进。

Pointed barbs like this one were scattered on the ground to hinder enemy advance, particularly enemy cavalry.

铜马具
Horse Harness

公元前1世纪~公元3世纪
青铜
长5.2厘米，宽 2.2厘米
佛罗伦萨国家考古博物馆

1st century BCE – 3rd century CE
Bronze
L. 5.2 cm, W. 2.2 cm
National Archeological Museum, Florence

本件源自马具饰件，由一个方形元件、两片不同的盾状片饰组成。顶端是一小片弯曲成钩形的金属舌状物。中间部分则饰有一个银圈或银环，银环的中心有一个纽扣装饰物。

This decorative pendant from a horse harness consists of a central, square element, with two distinct shield-shaped pieces. The upper parts of these pieces end in a small tongue of metal bent back into a hook. The central part is decorated with a silver circle or hoop, with a button in its center.

铜马具
Horse Harness

公元前1世纪~公元3世纪
青铜
长4 厘米，宽 2.6厘米
佛罗伦萨国家考古博物馆

1st century BCE – 3rd century CE
Bronze
L. 4 cm, W. 2.6 cm
National Archeological Museum, Florence

马具挂饰可以做多种款式，通常经裁剪或铸造可以打开。

Pendants for horse harnesses were modeled in many styles, often with open effects obtained through cutting or casting.

铜扣
Buckle

公元前1世纪~公元3世纪
青铜
长4.2厘米，宽3.7厘米
佛罗伦萨国家考古博物馆

1st century BCE – 3rd century CE
Bronze
L. 4.2 cm, W. 3.7 cm
National Archeological Museum, Florence

铜搭扣（马饰）
Fibula (Buckle)

公元1世纪
青铜
长5.2厘米
佛罗伦萨国家考古博物馆

1st century CE
Bronze
L. 5.2 cm
National Archeological Museum, Florence

铜搭扣
Hinged Fibula (Buckle)

公元1世纪
镀银青铜
长5厘米
佛罗伦萨国家考古博物馆

1st century CE
Silver plated bronze
L. 5 cm
National Archeological Museum, Florence

铜搭扣
Buckle

公元1世纪
镀银青铜
直径3.2厘米
佛罗伦萨国家考古博物馆

1st century CE
Silver plated bronze
D. 3.2 cm
National Archeological Museum, Florence

铜搭扣
Fibula (Buckle)

公元1世纪
青铜和珐琅
长4.8厘米
佛罗伦萨国家考古博物馆

1st century CE
Bronze and enamel
L. 4.8 cm
National Archeological Museum, Florence

铜搭扣
Fibula (Buckle)

公元1世纪
青铜和珐琅
长5.8厘米,直径4.3cm
佛罗伦萨国家考古博物馆

1st century CE
Bronze and enamel
L. 5.8 cm, D. 4.3 cm
National Archeological Museum, Florence

士兵石头像
Head of a Warrior

公元3世纪
红斑岩
高18厘米
佛罗伦萨国家考古博物馆

3rd century CE
Red porphyry
H. 18 cm
National Archeological Museum, Florence

这个士兵戴着一顶有浅顶和护颊、帽子状的头盔。

This soldier wears a cap-shaped helmet with a shallow crest and cheek guards.

士兵石头像
Head of a Soldier

公元前1世纪~公元3世纪
大理石
高16厘米
佛罗伦萨国家考古博物馆

1ˢᵗ century BCE — 3ʳᵈ century CE
Marble
H. 16 cm
National Archeological Museum, Florence

这个士兵戴着一顶出沿的球
形头盔。他的面部表情及头
朝左，表明这尊小头像是刻
画战争场面浮雕的一部分。

The soldier wears a spherical
helmet with a raised visor. His facial
expression and the position of his
head—bent leftward and turned
upward—suggest that this small
head was part of a relief portraying a
battle.

桌面石支架
Relief with Warrior and Knight

公元前1世纪
大理石
高39厘米，宽30厘米
佛罗伦萨国家考古博物馆

1st century BCE
Marble
H. 39 cm, W. 30 cm
National Archeological Museum, Florence

这个桌面支架饰有罗马人和蛮族之间的战争场景。

This table support is decorated with a scene of battle between Romans and barbarians.

非洲化身铜像
Personification of Africa

公元前1世纪~公元3世纪
青铜
高16.4厘米
佛罗伦萨国家考古博物馆

1ˢᵗ century BCE − 3ʳᵈ century CE
Bronze
H. 16.4 cm
National Archeological Museum, Florence

非洲化身为一位头戴大象
皮的女性。

Africa was typically personified
as a female with head covered by
elephant skin.

公民权铜册
Military Diploma

公元1世纪
青铜
长16.8厘米，宽13.7厘米
佛罗伦萨国家考古博物馆

1st century CE
Bronze
L. 16.8 cm, W. 13.7 cm
National Archeological Museum, Florence

这些青铜册上的文字记录了一名外国士兵在结束军旅生涯时被授予罗马公民权的判决。图密善皇帝在公元93年7月13日颁布了这一判决。这位名为Infante Veneto的士兵效力于达尔马希亚。

The text on these bronze tablets records an Imperial decree granting Roman citizenship to an auxiliary soldier at the end of his military career. The Emperor Domitian issued the decree on July 13, 93 CE. The soldier, whose name was Infante Veneto, had served in Dalmatia.

铜水阀
Water Valve

公元2世纪
青铜
通高28厘米
佛罗伦萨国家考古博物馆

2nd century CE
Bronze
H. (max) 28 cm
National Archeological Museum, Florence

铜锁具
Lock

帝国时期
青铜
长8厘米，宽8.5厘米
锡耶纳国家考古博物馆

Imperial Age
Bronze
L. 8 cm, W. 8.5 cm
National Archeological Museum, Siena

铜钥匙
Key

帝国时期
青铜
长4.9厘米
佛罗伦萨国家考古博物馆

Imperial Ag
Bronze
L. 4.9 cm
National Archeological Museum, Florence

狮头铜门环
Door-Knocker in the Shape of a Lion's Head

帝国时期
青铜
直径9.9厘米
佛罗伦萨国家考古博物馆

Imperial Age
Bronze
D. 9.9 cm
National Archeological Museum, Florence

铅排箫残件
Fragment of Pan

公元2世纪
铅
长29厘米
佛罗伦萨国家考古博物馆

2nd century CE
Lead
L. 29 cm
National Archeological Museum, Florence

贸易与商务　TRADE AND COMMERCE

罗马人在整个帝国发展了庞大的沟通和交通网络，以便于军事行动，同时也促进了商务活动。

由军队精心策划并修建（或者由国家付费）的道路，连接了主要的城市。而由地方社区出资修建的二级道路，则延伸向不同的方向。地中海海岸线上港口星罗棋布。"条条大路通罗马"，罗马人因此将地中海称作"我们的海"（*Mare Nostrum*）。

海上运输重货更快也更便宜。储存在大型陶制容器双耳细颈瓶(*amphorae*)中的葡萄酒、粮食、橄榄油和鱼酱（*garum*）是常见的商品。双耳细颈瓶通常有突出的底座，可以很容易地一层层的堆放起来。

The Romans developed a vast network of communications and transportation across the empire that facilitated military movement and encouraged commerce.

Carefully engineered roads built by the army (or at state expense) connected major cities, secondary roads financed by local communities branched off in various directions, and harbors dotted the shores of the Mediterranean Sea. "All roads led to Rome" and Romans referred to the Mediterranean as *Mare Nostrum* (our sea).

It was faster and less expensive to transport heavy goods by sea. Wine, grain, olive oil and fish sauce (*garum*) stored in large pottery vessels (*amphorae*) were common commodities. Amphorae often had pointed bases that made it easier to stack them in layers.

双耳细颈陶瓶
Amphora

公元3世纪初
红陶
高94厘米
佛罗伦萨国家考古博物馆

Beginning of the 3rd century CE
Terracotta
H. 94 cm
National Archeological Museum, Florence

这种被称作"大非洲"的双耳细颈瓶制作于非洲西北部。它们用作运送鱼酱汁或腌鱼。在整个帝国时代，尤其是塞普蒂米乌斯·塞维鲁（Septimius Severus）在位期间（公元193-211年），非洲是罗马和罗马帝国西部地区的主要食物和工业制成品的原产地。

Amphorae of this type, known as *africana grande*, were produced in northwest Africa. They were used especially for transporting fish sauce or preserved fish. Throughout the Imperial period, and particularly during the reign of Septimius Severus (193-211 CE), Africa was the main source of food and manufactured goods for Rome and the Western part of the Roman Empire.

双耳陶瓶
Amphora

公元2世纪
红陶
高84.5厘米，最大直径27厘米
佛罗伦萨国家考古博物馆

2nd century CE
Terracotta
H. 84.5 cm, D. (max) 27 cm
National Archeological Museum, Florence

双耳陶瓶
Wine Amphora with Flat Bottom

公元2世纪
红陶
高63厘米
佛罗伦萨国家考古博物馆

2nd century CE
Terracotta
H. 63 cm
National Archeological Museum, Florence

双耳陶瓶
Small Wine Amphora

公元1世纪
红陶
高43厘米
佛罗伦萨国家考古博物馆

1st century CE
Terracotta
H. 43 cm
National Archeological Museum, Florence

双耳陶瓶
Amphora

公元2世纪
红陶
高99厘米
佛罗伦萨国家考古博物馆

2nd century CE
Terracotta
H. 99 cm
National Archeological Museum, Florence

双耳陶瓶
Amphora

公元2世纪
红陶
高150厘米
佛罗伦萨国家考古博物馆

2nd century CE
Terracotta
H. 150 cm
National Archeological Museum, Florence

双耳细颈陶瓶
Amphora

公元2世纪
红陶
高100厘米
佛罗伦萨国家考古博物馆

2nd century CE
Terracotta
H. 100 cm
National Archeological Museum, Florence

"大非洲"双耳细颈陶瓶
"Africana Grande" Amphora

公元1~3世纪
红陶
高94厘米
佛罗伦萨国家考古博物馆

1st – 3rd century CE
Terracotta
H. 94 cm
National Archeological Museum, Florence

双耳细颈陶瓶
Amphora

公元2世纪
红陶
高120厘米
佛罗伦萨国家考古博物馆

2ⁿᵈ century CE
Terracotta
H. 120 cm
National Archeological Museum, Florence

双耳细颈陶瓶
Amphora

公元2世纪
红陶
高100厘米
佛罗伦萨国家考古博物馆

2ⁿᵈ century CE
Terracotta
H. 100 cm
National Archeological Museum, Florence

双耳细颈陶瓶
Wine Amphora

公元1世纪
红陶
高100厘米
佛罗伦萨国家考古博物馆

1st century CE
Terracotta
H. 100 cm
National Archeological Museum, Florence

双耳细颈陶瓶
Amphora

公元1世纪
红陶
高约90厘米
佛罗伦萨国家考古博物馆

1st century CE
Terracotta
H. (circa) 90 cm
National Archeological Museum, Florence

双耳细颈陶瓶
Amphora

公元1世纪
红陶
高约110厘米
佛罗伦萨国家考古博物馆

1st century CE
Terracotta
H. (circa) 110 cm
National Archeological Museum, Florence

双耳细颈陶瓶
Amphora

公元1世纪
红陶
高约90厘米
佛罗伦萨国家考古博物馆

1st century CE
Terracotta
H. (circa) 90 cm
National Archeological Museum, Florence

双耳细颈陶瓶
Amphora

公元1世纪
红陶
高约90厘米
佛罗伦萨国家考古博物馆

1st century CE
Terracotta
H. (circa) 90 cm
National Archeological Museum, Florence

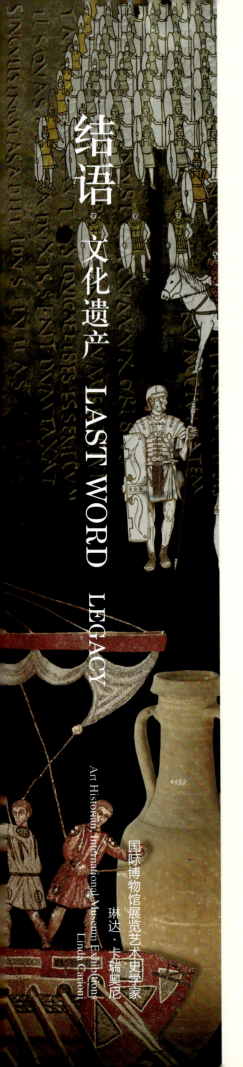

结语 文化遗产 LAST WORD LEGACY

Art Historian, International Museum Exhibitions
琳达·卡瑞奥尼
Linda Carioni
国际博物馆展览艺术史学家

　　在罗马帝国文化的大熔炉里，罗马统治者传统上对其他宗教的崇拜和信仰，包括占星术和巫术都相当宽容和开放，然而在怎样处理基督教上却犹豫不决。基督教因坚持只有一个上帝，近乎威胁到了帝国宗教宽容原则，此原则保证帝国人民享有永久的宗教和平。同时，基督徒拒绝膜拜凯撒大帝，这也与帝国官方宗教产生了冲突。如此一来，在罗马人的心中便判定了基督徒对罗马的不忠和背叛。然而从公元4世纪，也就是公元313年开始，新皇帝君士坦丁皈依了基督教，并且恢复了宗教宽容原则，基督教因此变得日益盛行。公元380年，狄奥多西（Teodosius）皇帝正式宣布基督教被为帝国的官方宗教。

　　随着后来神圣罗马帝国时期的宗教发展，罗马文明的遗产已深深根植于今天的西方文化。在罗马帝国的几个世纪中，博大精深的罗马文化广为传播，为当今曾属于这个昔日庞大帝国的社会和国家，或多或少的共性提供了依据。罗马人统治的持久影响几乎随处可见。它们体现在我们的司法、货币体系里，也体现在我们的艺术和建筑遗产中。许多人所说的现代罗曼语也是从拉丁语系（如意大利语、法语、葡萄牙语和西班牙语）演变而来，英语也和拉丁语有着密切的关联，我们今天仍在运用的26个字母表，以及一年365天分12个月的儒略历等，都进一步的说明它们曾是罗马帝国的遗产。

In the melting pot of cultures that was the Roman Empire, the Roman rulers were traditionally quite tolerant and open to other religious cults and beliefs, including astrology and magic, however, they hesitated over how to deal with Christianity. With its insistence on only one god, Christianity seemed to threaten the principle of religious toleration which had guaranteed religious peace for so long among the people of the Empire and clashed with the official state religion of the Empire, in that Christians refused to worship Caesar. This, in the Roman mindset, demonstrated their disloyalty and treason, however, by the beginning of the IV century CE, Christianity had grown so widespread that in 313 CE, the new emperor Constantine converted to Christianity and restored religious tolerance. In 380 CE, Christianity was declared the official religion of the Empire by Emperor Teodosius.

Beyond religious ramifications of the subsequent Holy Roman Empire, the legacy of Roman civilization is deeply embedded in the western culture of today. The profound and pervasive heritage of Roman culture, so widely diffused during the centuries of Imperial Rome, has provided the basis for the many or few common denominators shared today by the societies and nations of its once vast Empire. The lasting effects of Roman rule can be found almost everywhere. They can be seen in our judiciary and monetary systems, in our art and architectural patrimony. Many populations speak in the modern Romance languages evolved from Latin (Italian, French, Portuguese and Spanish) and English as well has ties to Latin. The alphabet of 26 letters, as well as the calendar of Julius Caesar comprised of 365 days, grouped into 12 months, that we use today, are further testimony to the legacy of what was once Imperial Rome.

附 录
APPENDIX

罗马年表
Chronology of Rome

	开始年代	结束年代	国王姓名
罗马王政时代 Roman Kingdom	753 BCE	716 BCE	罗慕洛 Romulus
	715 BCE	674 BCE	努玛·庞皮留斯 Numa Pompilius
	673 BCE	642 BCE	托里斯·奥斯蒂吕斯 Tullus Hostilius
	641 BCE	617 BCE	安库斯·玛尔提乌斯 Ancus Marcius
	616 BCE	579 BCE	卢修斯·塔克文·布里斯库 Lucius Tarquinius Priscus
	578 BCE	535 BCE	塞尔维乌斯·图利乌斯 Servius Tullius
	534 BCE	509BCE	卢修斯·塔克文·苏佩布 Lucius Tarquinius Superbus

	开始年代	结束年代	主要阶段
罗马共和制 Roman Republic	509 BCE	367 BCE	贵族时代 Patrician Era
	367 BCE	287 BCE	阶级冲突 Conflict of the Orders
	287 BCE	133 BCE	新贵族兴起 Supremacy of the New Nobility
	133 BCE	49 BCE	从格拉古兄弟到凯撒 From the Gracchi to Caesar
			平民和贵族 The populares and the optimates
			庞培、克拉苏和卡提林纳的阴谋 Pompey, Crassus and the Catilinarian Conspiracy
			三巨头 First Triumvirate
			前三巨头 The end of the First Triumvirate
	49 BCE - 27 BCE		过渡期 period of transition
			凯撒被暗杀和后三巨头 Caesar's assassination and the SecondTriumvirate

在 位	英文名	中文名	皇 号	备 注
27 BC - 14 CE	Augustus（Octavius）	奥古斯都（屋大维）	Imperator Caesar Divi Filivs Avgvstvs	第一位罗马皇帝
14 CE - 37 CE	Tiberius	提比略	Tiberivs Caesar Avgvstvs	
37 CE - 41 CE	Caligula	卡里古拉	Gaivs Caesar Avgvstvs Germanicvs	原名盖乌斯，卡里古拉为绰号，意为小靴子。开始罗马皇帝自封为神的习惯。被刺杀
41 CE - 54 CE	Claudius	克劳迪乌斯	Tiberivs Clavdlvs Caesar Avgvstvs Germanicvs Pontifex Maximvs	被皇后小阿格里皮娜毒死
54 CE - 68 CE	Nero	尼禄	Nero Clavdivs Caesar Avgvstvs Germanicvs	自杀
68 CE - 69 CE	Galba	加尔巴	Servivs Galba Imperator Caesar Avgvstvs	被奥索谋杀
69 CE	Otho	奥索	Imperator Marcvs Otho Caesar Avgvstvs	战败自杀
69 CE	Vitellius	维特里乌斯	Avlvs Vitellivs Germanicvs Imperator Avgvstvs	战败被处死
69 CE - 79 CE	Vespasian	韦帕芗	Imperator Veapasianvs Caesar Avgvstvs	
79 CE - 81 CE	Titus	提图斯	Imperator Titvs Caesar Vespasianvs Avgvstvs	
81 CE - 96 CE	Domitian	图密善	Imperator Caesar Domitianvs Avgvstvs	被法院人员暗杀

元首制 Principate

朱里亚·克劳狄王朝 Julio-Claudian Dynasty

四帝内乱期 Year of the Four Emperors

弗拉维王朝 Flavian Dynasty

		在 位	英文名	中文名	皇 号	备 注
元首制 Principate	五贤帝时代（安敦尼王朝） Nervan-Antonian Dynasty	96 CE - 98 CE	Nerva	涅尔瓦	Imperator Nerva Caesar Avgvatvs	
		98 CE - 117 CE	Trajan	图拉真	Imperator Caesar Divi Nervae Filivs Nerva Traianvs Germanicvs Avgvstvs	
		117 CE - 138 CE	Hadrian	哈德良	Imperator Caesar Traianvs Hadrianvs Avgvstvs	
		138 CE - 161 CE	Antoninus Pius	安敦尼	Imperator Caesar Titvs Aelivs Hadrianvs Antoninvs Avgvstvs	
		143年				二任皇帝
		161 CE - 180 CE	Marcus Aurelius	马可·奥里略	Imperator Caesar Marcvs Avrelivs Aatoninvs Avgvstvs	与维鲁斯为共治皇帝
		161 CE - 169 CE	Lucius Verus	维鲁斯	Imperator Caesar Lvcivs Avrelivs Vervs Avgvstvs	与马可·奥里略为共治皇帝
		175 CE	Avidius Cassius	卡修斯		篡位者，统治埃及和叙利亚，被一位百夫长所杀
		177 CE - 192 CE	Commodus	康茂德	Imperator Caesar Lvcivs Avrelivs Commodvs Avgvstvs	与马可·奥里略为共治皇帝
		从180年起			Imperator Caesar Lvcivs Avrelivs Commodvs Antoninvs Avgvstvs	在宫殿被暗杀

		在 位	英文名	中文名	皇 号	备 注
元首制 Principate	193年内乱期 Chaotic Period of 193 year	193 CE	Pertinax	佩蒂纳克斯	Imperator Caesar Pvblivs Helvivs Peptinax Avgvstvs	被士兵杀害
		193 CE	Didius Julianus	尤利安努斯	Imperator Caesar Marcvs Didivs Servervs Ivlianvs Avgvstvs	被元老院判死刑
	塞维鲁王朝 Severan Dynasty	193 CE - 211 CE	Septimius Severus	塞维鲁	Imperator Caesar Lvcivs Septimvs Severvs Pertinax Avgvstvsproconsvl	
		193 CE - 195 CE	Pescennius Niger	奈哲尔		叙利亚的争位者
		193 CE/195 CE - 197 CE	Clodius Albinus	阿尔拜努斯		不列颠的争位者
		198 CE - 217 CE	Caracalla	卡拉卡拉	Imperator Caesar Marcvs Avrelivs Severvs Antoninvs Pivs Avgvstvs / Imperator Caesar MarcvsAvrelivs Antoninvs Avgvstvspater Patrlae Britannicvs Maximvs Proconsvl	与盖塔为共治皇帝
		209 CE - 211 CE	Geta	盖塔	Imperator Caesar Pvblivs Septimvs Geta Avgvstvs	与卡拉卡拉为共治皇帝，被卡拉卡拉杀害
		217 CE - 218 CE	Macrinus	马克里努斯	Imperator Marcvs Opellivs Severvs Macrinvs Avgvstvs Pivs Felix Proconsvl	与迪亚杜门尼安为共治皇帝，被处死
		217 CE - 218 CE	Diadumenian	迪亚杜门尼安	Imperator Marcvs Opellivs Antoninvs DiadvMenianvs Caesar Severvs	与马克里努斯为共治皇帝，被处死
		218 CE - 222 CE	Elagabalus	埃拉伽巴路斯	Imperator Marcvs Avrelivs Antoninvs Pivs Felix Avgvstvs Proconsvl	被暗杀
		222 CE - 235 CE	Alexander Severus	亚历山大·塞维鲁	Imperaor Caesar Marcvs Avrelivs Severvs Alexander Pivs Felix Avgvstvs	被叛乱士兵杀死

在 位	英文名	中文名	皇 号	备 注
235 CE - 238 CE	Maximinus Thrax	马克西米努斯·色雷克斯	Imperator Caesar Gaivs Jvlivs Vervs Maximinvs Pivs Felix Invictvs Avgvstvs	被军队杀害
238 CE	Gordian I	戈尔迪安一世	Imperator Caesar Marcvs Antonivs Gordianvs Sempronianvs Africanvs	与戈尔迪安二世为共治皇帝，自杀
238 CE	Gordian II	戈尔迪安二世	Imperator Caesar Marcvs Antonivs Gordianvs Sempronlanvs Africanvs	与戈尔迪安一世为共治皇帝，阵亡
238 CE	Pupienus Maximus	普皮恩努斯	Imperator Caesar Marcvs Clodivs Pvpienvs Maximvs Avgvstvs	与巴尔比努斯为共治皇帝，被近卫军杀害
238 CE	Balbinus	巴尔比努斯		与普皮努斯为共治皇帝，被近卫军杀害
238 CE - 244 CE	Gordian III	戈尔迪安三世	Imperator Caesar Marcvs Antonivs Gordianvs Pivs Felix Avgvstvs	
240 CE	Sabinianus	萨宾尼亚努斯		自立为帝，战败
244 CE - 249 CE	Philip the Arab	阿拉伯人菲利普	Imperator Caesar Marcvs Ivlivs Phillipvs Pivs Felix Invictvs Avgvstvs	被德西乌斯杀死

三世纪危机
Crisis of the Third Century

危机高潮时的皇帝
Emperors During the Crisis of the Third Century

在 位	英文名	中文名	皇 号	备 注
248 CE	Pacatianus	帕卡提亚努斯		自立为帝，被士兵杀死
248 CE	Iotapianus	伊奥塔皮亚努斯		争位者
248 CE	Silbannacus	希尔班纳库斯		篡位者
249 CE - 251 CE	Decius	德西乌斯	Imperator Caesar Gaivs Messivs Qvintvs Traianvs Decivs Pivs Felix Invictvs Avgvstvs	阵亡
249 CE - 252 CE	Priscus	普里斯库斯		在东部自立为帝
250 CE	Licinianus	李锡尼亚努斯		争位者
251 CE	Herennius Etruscus	（伊特鲁利亚的）赫伦尼乌斯	Imperator Caesar Qvintvs Herennivs Etrvscvs Messivs Decivs Avgvstvv	阵亡
251 CE	Hostilian	霍斯蒂利安	Imperator Caesar Caivs Valens Hostilianvs Messivs Qvintvs Avgvstvs	与加卢斯为共治皇帝，死于瘟疫
251 CE - 253 CE	Gallus	加卢斯	Imperator Caesar Gaivs Vibivs Trebonianvs Gallvs Pivs Felix Invictvs Avgvstvs	被士兵杀死
251 CE - 253 CE	Volusianus	沃鲁西安努斯	Imperator Caesar Gaivs Vibivs Afinivs Gallvs Veldvmnianvs Volvsianvs Avgvstvs	与加卢斯为共治皇帝，被士兵杀死

在 位	英文名	中文名	皇 号	备 注
253 CE	Aemilianus	埃米利安努斯	Imperator Caesar Marcvs Aemilivs Aemilianvs Pivs Felix Invictvs Avgvstvs	被士兵杀死
253 CE - 260 CE	Valerian	瓦莱里安	Imperator Caesar Pvblivs Licinivs Valerianvs Pivs Felix Invictvs Avgvstvs	与加里恩努斯为共治皇帝，被波斯俘虏
253 CE - 268 CE	Gallienus	加里恩努斯	Imperator Caesar Pvblivs Licinivs Ecnativs Gallienvs Pivs Felix Invictvs Avgvstvs	与瓦勒良为共治皇帝至260年被暗杀
260 CE	Saloninus	萨洛尼努斯	Imperator Caesar Cornelivs Licinivs Saloninvs Valerlanvs Pivs Felix Invictvs Avgvstvs	与加里恩努斯为共治皇帝，被杀
258 CE - 260 CE	Ingenuus	因格努乌斯		自立者
260 CE	Regalianus	雷加里安努斯		自立者
260 CE - 261 CE	Macrianus Major	大马克里亚努斯		自立者，阵亡
260 CE - 261 CE	Macrianus Minor	小马克里亚努斯		自立者，阵亡
260 CE - 261 CE	Quietus	奎伊图斯		争位者
261 CE	Mussius Aemilianus	穆斯乌斯·埃米利安努斯		自立者
268 CE	Aureolus	奥雷奥路斯		自立者，向克劳狄二世投降

危机高潮时的皇帝 Emperors During the Crisis of the Third Century

三世纪危机 Crisis of the Third Century

在 位	英文名	中文名	皇 号	备 注
260 CE - 269 CE	Postumus	波斯杜穆斯	Imperator Caesar Marcvs Cassianvs Latinivs Postvmvs Pivs Felix Invictvs Avgvstvs	建立高卢帝国，从罗马帝国中分裂出去
269 CE	Laelianus	莱利亚努斯	Imperator Caesar Gaivs Vlpivs Cornelivs Laelianvs Pivs Felix Avgvstvs	自立为高卢帝国皇帝
269 CE	Marius	马里乌斯	Imperator Caesar Marcvs Avrelivs Marivs Pivs Felix Avgvstvs	
269 CE - 271 CE	Victorinus	维克托利努斯	Imperator Caesar Marcvs Piavonivs Victorinvs Pivs Felix Invictvs Avgvstvs	
270 CE - 271 CE	Domitianus	多米提安努斯		自立为高卢帝国皇帝
271 CE - 273 CE	Tetricus I	泰特里库斯一世	Imperator Caesar Gaivs Pivs Esvvivs Tetricvs Felix Invictvs Avgvstvs	被奥勒良击败，高卢帝国灭亡
271 CE - 273 CE	Tetricus II	泰特里库斯二世		与泰特里库斯一世为共治皇帝

高卢帝国 Imperium Galliarum

三世纪危机
Crisis of the Third Century

		在 位	英文名	中文名	皇 号	备 注
三世纪危机 Crisis of the Third Century	伊利里亚诸帝 Illyrian Emperors	268 CE - 270 CE	Claudius II	克劳狄二世	Imperator Caesar Marcvs Avrelivs Clivdivs Pivs Felix Invictvs Avgvstvs	死于瘟疫
		270 CE - 270 CE	Quintillus	昆提卢斯	Imperator Caesar Marcvs Avrelivs Clavdivs Qvintillvs Invictvs Pivs Felix Avgvstvs	暂时与奥勒良为共治皇帝，自杀
		270 CE - 275 CE	Aurelian	奥勒良	Imperator Caesar Lvcivs Domitivs Avrelianvs Pivs Felix Invictvs Avgvstvs	被近卫军杀害
		271 CE	Septimius	塞普蒂米乌斯		在达尔马提亚自立为帝，被士兵杀死
		275 CE - 276 CE	Claudius Tacitus	克劳狄·塔西佗	Imperator Caesar Marcvs Clavdivs Tacitvs Pivs Felix Avgvstvs	被杀
		276 CE - 276 CE	Florianus	弗洛里安努斯	Imperator Caesar Marcvs Annivs Florianvs Pivs Felix Avgvstvs	被杀
		276 CE - 282 CE	Probus	普罗布斯	Imperator Caesar Marcvs Avrelivs Probvs Pivs Felix Invictvs Avgvstvs	被士兵杀害
		280年	Saturninus	萨图尼努斯		自立为帝，被士兵所杀
		280年	Proculus	普罗库鲁斯		争位者，被普罗布斯所杀

在 位	英文名	中文名	皇 号	备 注
280年	Bonosus	博诺苏斯		自立为帝,被普罗布斯击败,自杀
282 CE - 283 CE	Carus	卡鲁斯	Imperator Caesar Marcvs Avrelivs Carvs Pivs Felix Invictvs Avgvstvs	死因不明
283 CE - 285 CE	Carinus	卡里努斯	Imperator Caesar Marcvs Avrelivs Carinvs Pivs Felix Invictvs Avgvstvs	与纽莫里安为共治皇帝,被杀
283 CE - 284 CE	Numerian	努梅里安	Imperator Caesar Marcvs Avrelivs Nvmerianvs Pivs Felix Avgvstvs	与卡里努斯为共治皇帝
284 CE - 305 CE	Diocletian	戴克里先	Imperator Caesar Gaivs Avrelivs Valerivs Diocletianvs Pivs Felix Invictis Avgvstvs Pontifex Maximvs Pater Patriae Proconsvl	与马克.西米安同为奥古斯都,掌管东部,黑色的十字,唯一一位含笑而终的罗马皇帝
286 CE - 305 CE	Maximian	马克西米安	Imperator Caesar Gaivs Avrelivs Valerivs Maximianvs Pivs Felix Invictvs Avgvstvs	与戴克里先同为奥古斯都,掌管西部,被迫自杀

三世纪危机 Crisis of the Third Century

伊利里亚诸帝 Illyrian Emperors

君主制 Crisis of the Third Century

四帝共治 The Four Tetrarchs

东西部各有两帝,一为正职,称奥古斯都,一为副职,称凯撒。正职退位后由副职补上,但这种承继制度在戴克里先死后无人执行

在　位	英文名	中文名	皇　号	备　注
305 CE - 311 CE	Galerius	伽列里乌斯	Imperator Caesar Galerivs Valerivs Maximianvs Pivs Felix Invictvs Avgvstvs	与君士坦提乌斯一世同为凯撒，305年成为东部奥古斯都，与塞维鲁二世为共治皇帝
305 CE - 306 CE	Constantius I Chlorus	君士坦提乌斯一世	Imperator Caesar Gaivs Flavivs Valerivs Constantivs Avgvstvs	与伽列里乌斯同为凯撒，305年成为西部奥古斯都，与伽列里乌斯为共治皇帝
306 CE - 307 CE	Severus II	塞维鲁二世	Imperator Severvs Pivs Felix Avgvstvs	305年成为凯撒，306年成为西部奥古斯都，与伽列里乌斯为共治皇帝
306CE - 312 CE	Maxentius	马克森提乌斯	Marcvs Avrelivs Valerivs Maxentivs Pivs Felix Invictvs Avgvstvs	306年起自称皇帝，被君士坦丁一世打败，被废黜
308 CE - 324 CE	Licinius	李锡尼	Imperator Caesar Gaivs Valerivs Licinivs Pivs Felix Invictvs Avgvstvs	308年起为奥古斯都，被迫退位
308年	Domitius Alexander	多米提乌斯·亚历山大		自立为帝
310 CE - 313 CE	Maximinus Daia	马克西米努斯	Imperator Caesar Galerivs Valerivs Maximinvs Pivs Felix Avgvstvs	305年起为东部凯撒，311年起自称奥古斯都，与李锡尼瓜东部，自杀

四帝共治 The Four Tetrarchs

东西部各有两帝，一为正职，称奥古斯都，一为副职，称凯撒。正职退位后由副职补上，但这种承继制度在戴克里先死后无人执行。

君主制
Crisis of the Third Century

在　位	英文名	中文名	皇号	备注
316年 - 317年	Valerius Valens	瓦莱里乌斯·瓦伦斯	Imperator Caesar Avrelivs Valerivs Valena Pivs Felix Invictvs Avgvstvs	与李锡尼为共治皇帝，被君士坦丁一世处死
324年	Martinianus	马提尼安努斯	Imperator Caesar Sextvs Marcivs Martinianvs Pivs Felix Invictvs Avgvstvs	324年起为西部奥古斯都，与李锡尼为共治皇帝，被杀
306 CE - 337 CE	Constantine I The Great	君士坦丁一世	Imperator Caesar Flavivs Constantinvs Pivs Felix Invictvs Avgvstvs Pontifex Maximvs Pater Patriae Proconsvl	原为四帝共治中的西帝，后击败其他诸帝，成为罗马帝国唯一统治者。第一位信基督教的皇帝
337 CE - 340 CE	Constantine II	君士坦丁二世	Imperator Caesar Flavivs Valerivs Constantinvs Avgvstvs	君士坦丁一世死后，国分为三，君士坦丁二世得一份，阵亡
337 CE - 361 CE	Constantius II	君士坦提乌斯二世	Imperator Caesar Flavivs Ivlivs Constantivs Avgvstvs	君士坦丁一世死后，国分为三，君士坦提乌斯二世得一份
337 CE - 350 CE	Constans	君士坦斯一世	Imperator Caesar Flavivs Ivlivs Ivlivs Constans Avgvstvs	君士坦丁一世死后，国分为三，君士坦斯得一份，被马格嫩提乌斯所杀

君主制

Crisis of the Third Century

君士坦丁王朝 Constantine Dynasty

		在 位	英文名	中文名	皇 号	备 注
君主制 Crisis of the Third Century	君士坦丁王朝 Constantine Dynasty	350 CE - 353 CE	Magnentius	马格嫩提乌斯	Imperator Caesar Flavivs Magnvs Magentivs Avgvstvs	篡位者，自杀
		350 CE	Vetriano	维特里亚诺		自立为帝
		350 CE	Nepotianus	尼波提亚努斯		自立为帝
		360 CE - 363 CE	Julian the Apostate	尤利安（背教者）	Imperator Caesar Flavivs Clavdivs Ivlianvs Avgvstvs	阵亡
		363 CE - 364 CE	Jovian	约维安	Imperator Caesar Flavivs Iovianvs Avgvstvs	暴死
	不列颠帝国 British Empire	286 CE - 293 CE	Carausius	卡劳修斯	Imperator Caesar Caravsivs Pivs Felix Avgvstvs	建立不列颠帝国，从罗马帝国中分裂出去，被阿勒克图斯所杀
		293 CE - 297 CE	Allectus	阿勒克图斯	Imperator Caesar Allectvs Pivs Felix Avgvstvs	被君士坦提乌斯一世所败

		在 位	英文名	中文名	皇 号	备 注
君主制 Crisis of the Third Century	瓦伦蒂尼安王朝 Valentinian Dynasty	364 CE - 375 CE	Valentinian I	瓦伦丁尼安一世	Imperator Caesar Flavivs Valentinianvs Pivs Felix Avgvstvs	西帝
		364 CE - 378 CE	Valens	瓦伦斯	Imperator Caesar Flavivs Ivlivs Valeens Pivs Felix Avgvstvs	东帝，阵亡
		365 CE - 366 CE	Procopius	普罗科皮乌斯		篡位者，被瓦伦斯处死
		367 CE - 383 CE	Gratian	格拉提安	Imperator Caesar Flavivs Gratianvs Pivs Felix Avgvstvs	被叛军所杀
		375 CE - 392 CE	Valentinian II	瓦伦丁尼安二世	Imperator Caesar Flavivs Valentinianvs Pivs FelixAvgvstvs	
		383 CE - 388 CE	Magnus Maximus	马格努斯·马克西穆斯		西部的篡位者，被狄奥多西一世处死
		386 CE - 388 CE	Flavius Victor	弗拉维乌斯·维克托		马格努斯·马克西穆斯之子，被狄奥多西一世所杀
		392 CE - 394 CE	Eugenius	欧根尼乌斯		西部的篡位者，阵亡
末期帝国 Theodosian Dynasty	狄奥多西王朝 Theodosius Dynasty	379 CE - 395CE	Theodosius I	狄奥多西一世	Imperator Caesar Flavivs Theodosivs Pivs Felix Avgvstvs	重新统一帝国

在 位	英文名	中文名	皇 号	备 注
393 CE - 423 CE	Honorius	霍诺里乌斯	Imperator Caesar Flavivs Honorivs Pivs Felix Avgvstvs	与君士坦提乌斯三世为共治皇帝
409 CE - 415 CE	Priscus Attalus	普里斯库斯·阿塔卢斯	Imperator Caesar Priscvs Attalvs Pivs Felix Avgvstvs	自立为帝
407 CE - 411 CE	Constantine III	君士坦丁三世		争位者
409 CE - 411 CE	Constans II	君士坦斯二世		争位者
411 CE - 413 CE	Jovinus	约维努斯		争位者
412 CE - 413 CE	Sebastianus	塞巴斯蒂安努斯		争位者
421 CE	Constantius III	君士坦提乌斯三世		与霍诺里乌斯为共治皇帝
423年 - 425年	Joannes	约翰尼斯		争位者
424 CE - 455 CE	Valentinian III	瓦伦丁尼安三世		
455 CE	Petronius Maximus	佩特罗尼乌斯·马克西穆斯		
455 CE - 456 CE	Avitus	阿维图斯		
457 CE - 461 CE	Majorian	墨乔里安		退位
461 CE - 465 CE	Libius Severus	利比乌斯·塞维鲁		

末期帝国
Theodosian Dynasty

西罗马帝国　Western Roman Empire

狄奥多西一世临终前，把罗马帝国分给他的两个儿子至此，罗马帝国正式分裂为西罗马帝国（首都罗马）和东罗马帝国（首都君士坦丁堡）

		在　位	英文名	中文名	皇　号	备　注
末期帝国 Theodosian Dynasty	狄奥多西一世临终前，把罗马帝国分给他的两个儿子至此，罗马帝国正式分裂为西罗马帝国（首都罗马）和东罗马帝国（首都君士坦丁堡）　西罗马帝国　Western Roman Empire	467 CE － 472 CE	Anthemius	安特米乌斯		被处死
		472 CE - 472 CE	Olybrius	奥利布里乌斯		
		473 CE － 474 CE	Glycerius	格利塞里乌斯		退位
		474 CE - 475CE (inItaly) 480 CE (in Gaul and Dalmatia)	Julius Nepos	尼波斯		退位
		475 CE － 476 CE (in Italy)	Romulus Augustulus	罗慕路斯·奥古斯都		最后的皇帝，被废

后　记
Postscript

　　"辉煌时代——罗马帝国文物特展"是本馆首次组织的境外文物展。自博物馆免费对公众开放以来，本馆已引进了国内外博物馆多项高水平的文物展览，但都是作为参展方。此次"辉煌时代——罗马帝国文物特展"巡回展是由佛罗伦萨国家考古博物馆（Museo Archeologico Nazionale di Firenze）策划，由意中桥（上海）会议展览有限公司Triumph Asia Co., Limited (TA)、意大利CP公司Contemporanea Progetti, Florence, Italy (CP)引进的介绍罗马帝国文物的大型文物展览。该展览部分内容曾在美国芝加哥博物馆、上海博物馆等地展出，受到好评。本次该展来中国巡展，经上海对外文化交流协会推荐，希望由本馆负责组织在中国的巡展工作。在湖北省文化厅、文物局的支持下，由本馆牵头，联合吉林省博物院和秦始皇帝陵博物院举办这次罗马帝国文物特展，这在本馆还是首次。特别要指出的是，本次罗马帝国文物巡展还得到了台湾文博界的支持，在台湾《联合报》的努力下，该展览计划将于吉林博物院展出完毕后前往台北展出。两岸共同举办文物巡展这也是历史上的首次。因缺乏组织巡展的经验和水平，展览当有不足之处，希望大家不吝批评。

　　本次展览资料是经第三方提供，存在若干问题无法一一解决。一是图版质量不理想，原先对方只提供五十几幅图版。经过协商后，才临时补齐全部电子档，但是事情仓促，图片质量受到影响。二是器物名称规范和文物参数无法统一。比如器物"时代"，有的写明了具体时间，有的阙如，有的就只写"帝国时代"。我们知道，罗马帝国完整的年代应该算到东罗马灭亡的1453年，就是到西罗马为止，也是475年，这些文物大多都是公元1~3世纪左右，个别的可能更晚，所以无法一一明确。三是器名的翻译没有按原文直译，如vase的本意是瓶，但是器物形制却与中文的瓶相差太远；又如"珀库罗杯"，原名为Glass(Poculo)，质地却是陶（Terracotta），显然其中有误，这类问题还相当普遍。为了方便读者和观众，我们适当对个别器物名称做了调整。

　　本次特展筹备过程中，我们得到各方面的大力支持，首先得到了各级领导的支持和鼓励，如国家文物局，湖北省文化厅和文物局、财政厅、教育厅及武汉海关、上海海关等一如既往地在项目审批、经费支持和教育推广等方面予以大力支持。其次展览的教育推广得到了学界的鼓励和肯定，如武汉大学、中南民族大学、华中师范大学、湖北美术学院、华中科技大学等高校教授、专家的大力支持。特别值得一提的是知名罗马史和秦汉史专家、台湾中研院史语所邢义田院士为展览图录提供专文使之生色不少。此外，台湾《联合报》的李威、赖素玲为展览在台北的举办做出了极大的努力。在展览筹备中，华中师范大学历史文化学院的实习生白娟、王超、顾玲，北京大学考古系的孔中华，英国莱斯特大学（University of Leicester）的李樱子等同学都先后参与了工作，在此一并表示感谢。

编者

2012年8月于东湖

责任印制：陈　杰

责任编辑：张征雁

图书在版编目（ＣＩＰ）数据

　　辉煌时代 ：罗马帝国文物 ／ 湖北省博物馆编. ——
北京 ：文物出版社，2012.9
　　ISBN 978-7-5010-3538-0

　　Ⅰ．①辉… Ⅱ．①湖… Ⅲ．①历史文物－罗马帝国－
图集 Ⅳ．①K885.46-64

　　中国版本图书馆CIP数据核字(2012)第207896号

辉煌时代——罗马帝国文物

编　者　湖北省博物馆

出版发行　文物出版社
社　　址　北京市东直门内北小街2号楼
网　　址　www.wenwu.com
邮　　箱　web@wenwu.com
制　　版　北京图文天地制版印刷有限公司
印　　刷　北京图文天地制版印刷有限公司
经　　销　新华书店
开　　本　889×1194　1/16
印　　张　18
版　　次　2012年9月第1版
印　　次　2012年9月第1次印刷
书　　号　ISBN 978-7-5010-3538-0
定　　价　300.00元